Beyond
the
Down
Low

Sex, Lies, and Denial in Black America

Beyond the Down Low

Sex, Lies, and Denial in Black America

KEITH BOYKIN

Foreword by E. Lynn Harris

CARROLL & GRAF PUBLISHERS

NEW YORK

BEYOND THE DOWN LOW
SEX, LIES, AND DENIAL IN BLACK AMERICA

Carroll & Graf Publishers
An Imprint of Avalon Publishing Group Inc.
245 West 17th Street
New York, NY 10011

AVALON
publishing group incorporated

Library of Congress Cataloging-in-Publication Data is available.

ISBN: 0-7867-1434-4

Book design by Maria E. Torres
Printed in the United States of America
Distributed by Publishers Group West

Contents

Foreword

When I self-published my first novel, *Invisible Life,* in 1991, the subject of bisexuality in the black community was rarely discussed in the mainstream media. Eight bestselling novels later, it is now clear that many of us were starving for these stories all along. Not only black women, but men and women of all races have begun to pay attention. Then a few years ago, I started getting phone calls from reporters asking about men on the down low who were in relationships with women but secretly having sex with men. Some of these men were becoming infected with HIV and passing the virus to their wives and girlfriends. Ever since then, the down low story has made front-page headlines in the *New York Times* and other newspapers across the country.

I first met Keith Boykin more than ten years ago when he was working in the White House for President Clinton. Since that time, I have seen him become an author, then an activist, and even a reality TV star. Now I'm pleased to see him writing a new book about an important topic once again.

As the AIDS epidemic grows in the black community, *Beyond the Down Low: Sex, Lies, and Denial in Black America* is timely and necessary. Over the years, I have met far too many black women and men whose lives have been dramatically affected by HIV, and I have seen how the down low discussion has drawn some of them apart. Indeed, the most visible public discussions about the down low lately have been more about finger-pointing and dividing the community than about establishing honest and open dialogue. Rather than blaming black men or black women, Keith offers a smart, thoughtful approach that suggests we try to move beyond fear to find ways to love ourselves and love one another.

Perhaps just as importantly, Keith reminds us that the down low is not a new phenomenon. In fact, his is the first book to identify the long history of the DL. He takes us back to the Harlem Renaissance and walks us through the popular culture and music of the twentieth century. From there, we continue on the journey through contemporary America. He takes us into the modern world of big-time professional sports, backstage in the hip-hop music industry, and behind the pulpit in the powerful black church.

Keith's purpose is to challenge us to think beyond the down low and to get us to re-think what we *think* we know. I have no doubt that this provocative book will spark controversy in some quarters, but it is time for us to have a healthy and informed discussion about these issues. Fortunately, Keith is not content to critique the problems without solutions, and he provides specific answers to what we can do. In fact, he gives us lists of concrete steps that any of us can take. All told, *Beyond the Down Low* is healing medicine for all of us.

E. Lynn Harris
November 2004

CHAPTER 1

A Thousand Different Meanings

I STARTED WORKING at Sears in the fall semester of my last year in high school. It was the best job I had ever had. That was not a great achievement because my other jobs had been pretty lousy. Well, actually, they were great jobs for a teenager. My first job was stuffing bags as a courtesy clerk at a local grocery store called Family Mart. I did that for six months and then moved up to fast food. In my next job, I cooked Big Macs and Quarter Pounders at McDonald's. Then I got my first big break.

I had just gotten back from a weeklong junior congressional internship in Washington, D.C., when my father offered me a job working for him in the summer before my senior year of high school. It was a desk job as a clerk/typist for my dad's beauty supply store in Clearwater, Florida. Working for family can be stressful, but it can be even more complicated when your boss doesn't pay you on time. My father felt I needed to have a more professional job if I was soon going to college, but I quickly realized that my father's business was not nearly as successful as McDonald's. By the beginning of the fall, I was still broke and eager to find a new job that could pay me consistently and where I didn't have to flip burgers. I found my salvation at Sears.

I started selling shoes at Sears in November of my last year in high school. I knew nothing about shoes or sales, but I knew how to count, and that was really the most important qualification I needed for the job. I could count the money that came into the register, and I could count the code numbers on the bottom of the shoes to match them with the code numbers in the stockroom. It was an easy job and a great way to meet people. It paid the bills and kept gas in the motorcycle that I drove to work. I did not ask for much more because I was too busy to know what I wanted. By the time I was seventeen, I was on the school's varsity track team and the debate team, president of the student government, writing a monthly column for the local newspaper, and serving a term on the city's parks and recreation board. In many ways, I was a model citizen and a model employee.

I loved working at Sears. It gave me a sense of pride to know they trusted me, and I stayed there for seven months, the longest period I had ever worked for anyone at that time. My career at Sears started to draw to a close after I graduated from high school. I had just been accepted at Dartmouth College, and I was spending the summer preparing myself for my first year away from home. A few weeks after graduation, I came into work one evening and was told to report to the manager's office before I punched in on the clock. I took the escalator upstairs to the manager's office, where I found my supervisor and the manager waiting for me in an office. "Sit down," they told me, "We have some questions we'd like to ask you." I sat down apprehensively. The tone of their voices was solemn, and immediately my mind started thinking about what I might have done wrong. Had I shown up late? No. I was still on time. Did I forget to put the shoes back on the rack the last time I closed? No.

It wasn't that. Was I dressed inappropriately? No again. I was wearing slacks, a dress shirt, and a tie. What had I done wrong? I could not think of what it might be.

My supervisor did most of the talking during the conversation, while the manager looked on from behind his desk. The supervisor told me that my drawer came up short the last time I worked. I did not remember any discrepancy the night I closed, but I knew I was not the only one who worked that night. "Do you know what happened to the money?" my supervisor asked. "No," I replied honestly. "I didn't know there was any money missing." My answer did little to convince either of them. Apparently, they had already decided what had happened to the money and they had already decided what to do about it. "Keith, we're gonna have to let you go," the manager told me. I listened to what he said, but I was so young and unaccustomed to the language of the work world that I did not understand what it meant to "let you go." I sat and stared for a moment until my supervisor told me himself. "You're being fired," he said. "I'm sorry we have to do it, but we won't report it to the police." And with those ignoble words, my career at Sears came to an abrupt and involuntary end.

The news left me in a daze. I slowly walked out of the office, down the escalator, past the shoe department, and out to my motorcycle. As I fastened the helmet, I could feel the fresh moisture of sorrow on my cheek. I would have to face my family and tell them what happened. I had just been fired from my job for stealing. But the worst part was even harder to accept and understand. The worst part was that I was not guilty.

There is nothing worse than being blamed for something you did not do. I know. The more I thought about being fired, the more frustrated I became. I had been accused, tried, and convicted without any real chance to explain my side of the story. In fact, I was never even told how much money was missing. I guess that was not important. For seven months, I had been a loyal and honest employee without a blemish on my record, and then suddenly I was dismissed for an incident I knew nothing about. In the end, I realized that I was guilty after all. I was guilty of an offense that I had forgotten was a crime. My crime was simple. I was a young black man in America.

I discovered early in life that black men make easy targets to blame for many of the problems in America. I had never thought of myself as a problem before, but from that day forward I realized that I was. Over the following years, I would be blamed for many more crimes that I had not committed. I made white women nervous and white men anxious. They created an image of me that even black people started to believe. I was responsible for murder, rape, drugs, guns, poverty, homelessness, welfare, illiteracy, teen pregnancy, and AIDS. And all because I am a black man.

As I said, there is nothing worse than being blamed for something you have not done. And that is exactly why the public discussion about black men on the down low is so dangerously wrong. Almost every time I hear talk about the down low, I remember the feeling of being blamed for something I did not do. Facts are not important in this environment. Perception is reality. I live in a world that has already been trained to fear and despise me. It is not because of what I have done. I have never murdered anyone. I have never smoked crack. I have never been in prison. And I have never passed a deadly disease to anyone. But none of that matters. I am still guilty, and I will be held accountable for the rest of my life.

Perhaps I should have learned my lesson in high school. I should have realized that perception is more important than truth. I should have known that I would be judged by the preconceived perception of me instead of the truth about me. But somehow I never learned that lesson. For some reason, I held fast to the belief that truth would always prevail eventually. Against all evidence to the contrary, I remained convinced that no lie, no matter how widely repeated, could stand forever. Maybe I was wrong, but deep in my heart I still believe the truth will always emerge.

In the meantime, I am forced to face the lies.

This is a story about lies. Actually, these days, anytime you read anything about the down low, you probably know it is about lies. But this is a different story. It's not just about the lies that men on the down low tell. It is a story about the lies that men *and women* tell themselves about their relationships. It is a story about the lies that we tell the media, which the media in turn tell back to us about who we are. Yes, it is a story about lies in black America, but it is also a story about lies in white America. It is a story about men lying, but it is also a story about women lying. It is a story about the way in which lies become mistaken for truth when repeated often enough, and how we use those lies to deny our personal responsibility to find the truth.

America's recent obsession with the down low is not about the truth. It is about avoiding the truth. The truth is, more than a generation after the so-called sexual revolution and decades after the beginning of the AIDS epidemic, we are still a nation in deep denial about sex, race, and relationships. In black America, with the all-too-willing assistance of white America, we are still afraid to hear, understand, and process the truth. And as a nation, we would rather talk about the down low than talk candidly about racism, homophobia, and AIDS, and about our collective responsibility to find solutions for these problems. Of course, it is easier to believe the hype than to engage in a sensible dialogue based on real information, but we cannot find solutions in a sensationalistic conversation based on fear and blame. The solutions lie in a conversation about love and personal responsibility. So it's time to get past the fear and the blame. It's time to go beyond the down low.

We begin in February 2001. George W. Bush has just been inaugurated as president after a controversial election in which he lost the popular vote yet won a disputed contest for the electoral ballot in Florida. Former President Bill Clinton has moved to New York with his wife, who has just been elected a U.S. senator from that state. Clinton has been hounded by a "vast right-wing conspiracy" throughout his tenure in office and impeached by a Republican Congress because he lied about a sexual relationship with an intern. I feel the president's pain. After eight years of living in Washington, I am ready to leave. I had moved to Washington to work in the Clinton White House as a special assistant to the president, and the city suddenly feels unwelcoming to an exiled Democrat. Then one day in 2001, I'm invited to dinner with three friends who were in town for an AIDS conference, and that's where I first heard about "the down low," a term I vaguely understood to mean men who have sex with men but do not identify as gay. As a black gay man, I had known about such men for a decade. Since I came out in 1991, I had been working on issues of race and sexuality during most of that time, and I had met or interviewed dozens of men who would qualify as down low. What could possibly be new about such an old occurrence, I wondered. Was it just a new word for an old behavior?

Over the years, I had heard a number of terms to describe these men and their behavior. Some were dismissed as "closeted." Many called themselves "bisexual." Some said they were only "messin' around" while others accused them of "creeping." Most of the supposedly straight men I had met had always seemed resistant to labels. Their interest in me was usually physical, not intellectual, so they were seldom willing to answer probing questions about their lives. Nevertheless, I had interacted with these men for years. There was the police officer I met in Los Angeles, the postal worker in Chicago, the corporate executive in Maryland, the Web designer in North Carolina, and the government official in Washington, D.C. All of them were black, several of them were married, and a few of them had young children. Then, there were dozens of men I had met at an infamous gym on L Street in Washington. Many of these guys seemed to be making hookups on a regular basis. It didn't seem very underground to me, but that was because I saw it happen so often. A few of the guys would talk to me on the sly, while others— who had seen me talking about gay issues on television or in the newspaper—would walk a country mile to steer clear of me. In fact, I could almost identify who was in the closet based on how much effort they put into avoiding me.

By 2001, the down low was old news to me, but for the mass media it was the beginning of a profitable period of exploitation of black grief. To some in the media, the down low seemed the missing link to explain the AIDS epidemic in the black community. HIV seemed to be spreading more rapidly among black women than in almost any other demographic group, and if these women were unknowingly having sex with black men on the down low, then that could explain the problem. The overwhelming majority of black women with HIV contracted the virus from heterosexual sex, and some black men who call themselves heterosexual also had sex with men. So these black men could have been responsible for spreading the virus to unsuspecting women. It all seemed to make sense.

Others were a bit more skeptical. There was no research to prove the down low was responsible for the spread of AIDS in the black community, and no one knew how to study a population that was unwilling to be identified. These skeptics feared that focusing on the down low would distract public attention and public resources from what they perceived were the real needs of the community. Focusing on the down low would mislead people into thinking that AIDS was spread by men on the DL rather than by HIV. And instead of encouraging individuals to focus on their own safe sex behavior, we would encourage them to focus on the behavior of their partners. Even worse, public policy decisions would have to rely on anecdotal evidence from those men who had once been on the down low, a group that was admittedly notorious for its untruthfulness. In other words, we would have to trust the liars to tell the truth about their lies.

Despite the uncertainty about the issue, just mention the words "down low" to someone in the media, and you're likely to hear remarkable tales of sex, lies, and deception—all supposedly brought on by a small, dangerous and influential fraternity of black men leading double lives.

Ever since the down low story broke, many journalists have been convinced that men on the down low are responsible for the spread of AIDS in the black community. Books have been published that claim to teach women "the signs" to tell if a man is on the down low. Black women have been deputized as down low detectives and told to watch to see if their male partners stare too long at other men. The media and the public have developed a whole new fascination with all things down low.

But is all this hype really necessary? Is the information even true?

We should start with a basic question that needs to be asked at the beginning of any serious discussion about this issue: What is the down low? Before you answer, here are a few examples to help us understand the question. Try to figure out which of these people are on the down low.

Raheem is a twenty-four-year-old black man in northeast Washington, D.C. He looks just like any other young man on the street on a hot summer afternoon. He is wearing an XXXL-size plain white T-shirt, oversized baseball cap, droopy jeans, and sneakers. But Raheem is different. Raheem says he's "on the DL." He only "messes with" brothas, and he has a computer at home that he uses to find them in chat rooms and Web sites on the Internet. Although he has not been involved with a woman since he graduated from high school, six years ago, he still dreams that one day he will settle down with the right woman and get married. Is Raheem on the down low?

David is a thirty-six-year-old black man in Stone Mountain, Georgia. He lives with his wife and two kids in a two-story, three-bedroom house and commutes to work in midtown Atlanta. He wears a business suit to the office but brings his gym clothes to work out at the gym near his job. A few years ago, he started meeting men at the gym and taking them to hotels to have sex with them. Eventually, he worked up the nerve to go home with the men he met. He enjoys his sexual encounters with men, but he has no plans to leave his wife and kids, and they do not know about his homosexual experiences. David has recently heard of the term "down low," but he does not identify with it. He calls himself "straight." David is HIV negative. He doesn't want to run the risk of getting caught, so he always uses a condom with his male sex partners, and he only plays the role of a "top." Is David on the down low?

Jabbar is a twenty-nine-year-old black man in Dayton, Ohio. He's a shoe salesman for a high-end department store, and he prides himself on the way he dresses. He's fashionably conservative and considers himself very masculine. Jabbar's deep bass voice and tall good looks help make him an effective salesman, but Jabbar has a not-so-secret life away from the department store. Once or twice a month, Jabbar drives his BMW to the gay clubs in Cincinnati. He's very popular with the black men there, who see him as a good catch, but he's never allowed himself to be caught. He has sex with men but has never been in a relationship with one. Jabbar loves being single, he loves the attention he gets from men and women, and he loves being so "unclockable" that no one can tell his sexuality. Is Jabbar on the down low?

Joyce is a thirty-eight-year-old black woman in Little Rock, Arkansas. She's the HR director for a major local hospital and has been involved in three long-term relationships in her life: two with men and one with a woman. Joyce's feminine good looks make her very desirable to women and men, but she won't commit to either. She's dating a man right now, but she's also seeing a woman on the side. Her man thinks she's straight. Her woman thinks she's on the DL. Is Joyce on the down low?

Shawn is a twenty-two-year-old white man in Brooklyn. He wants to be an electrical engineer, and he's got a part-time job to help him pay his way through community college. He has a white girlfriend he met at school and a black boyfriend he met in a club one night. Shawn grew up around blacks and Latinos in a racially mixed neighborhood in the Bronx, so he has always been comfortable developing friendships and relationships with people who are different from him. He knows he can never tell his girlfriend about his boyfriend, but he has told his boyfriend about his girlfriend. Shawn considers himself "on the down low." Is Shawn on the down low?

Jerry is a forty-six-year-old black man in Los Angeles. He's a semisuccessful visual artist who made a name for himself fifteen years ago and has continued to grow in popularity in local arts circles. Jerry lives with his wife and their twelve-year-old daughter, but Jerry also has a long-term male lover. Years ago, Jerry told his wife that he was bisexual, and after a heartfelt discussion she allowed him to date men outside of their marriage as long as he was safe. Jerry and his wife have made peace with their living situation, but they haven't told anyone else about it. When their daughter found out about the situation recently, she had a name for their relationship. She told her parents that they were a "down low couple." Is Jerry on the down low?

Luis is a nineteen-year-old mixed-race Hispanic man in Chicago. He planned to join the military until he realized the armed forces did not allow gays to serve openly. Almost everyone seems to know or assume that Luis is gay. He says he's very proud of his sexuality, and most of his good friends are gay or transgendered. But his friends don't know the whole truth. Luis has a girlfriend he's been hiding from them. Is Luis on the down low?

Those are the seven people. Now here's the question again. Which of the people mentioned above are on the down low? The question is not as easy as it seems. To answer the question, we have to start with an acceptable definition of what it means to be on the down low in the first place. And that's the problem. In the years since the media began to hype the down low, no one has ever really defined it. You start to realize the problem when you try to pick which of the seven people are on the down low.

Let's start with Raheem. Raheem raises the difficult issue of self-identification. He doesn't fit neatly into a gay stereotype. He doesn't look gay and he doesn't call himself gay. He self-identifies as "down low," but he has not had sex with a woman since he was a teenager. So here's the question. Can you be on the down low merely by self-identifying as being on the down low? Most of the recent media definitions of the down low seem to assume that you have to be unfaithful to a woman in order to be on the down low. Raheem, however, doesn't even date women, but he does considers himself on the down low. For Raheem, being on the down low simply means being a man who doesn't look gay and isn't public about being gay.

David raises the other side of self-identification. By most accounts, David fits the classic definition of a man on the down low.

He's black, he's married to a woman, and he secretly sleeps with men. But unlike Raheem, David doesn't consider himself to be on the down low. In fact, he's barely even familiar with the term, and he calls himself straight. If self-identification determines whether you're on the down low, then David is not down low, even though most observers would say he is.

David's story raises another issue as well. Since David is HIV negative and always practices safe sex, David's life challenges the assumption that down low men are spreading HIV to black women. In fact, David's wife is actually safer having sex with him than with an HIV positive man who is exclusively heterosexual.

Next there's Jabbar. On the surface, Jabbar seems to be another candidate for the down low, but beneath the surface he raises troubling questions about looks and behavior. Some would say that you can't be on the down low if you go out to gay bars and night clubs. For Jabbar, however, being down low simply means being what he considers masculine and discreet. Most people think he looks like he's straight, and since he never hangs out with gay guys in his hometown, he thinks that makes him down low. Is he right?

Then there's Joyce. Joyce's story complicates the simplicity of the down low formula by introducing the issue of gender. Like the men on the down low, she's cheating on her partner with someone of the same sex. What makes her different is that Joyce is a woman, and her partner is a man. Most of the public discussion about the down low seems to assume that women don't engage in the same unfaithful behavior that men do. Women are portrayed as the victims, not the perpetrators. Joyce's story forces us to reexamine our simplistic stereotypes about female fidelity and male deceit.

Shawn's situation complicates matters even more. If we define a down low man as someone who cheats on his wife or girlfriend with a man, then Shawn perfectly fits the bill. The only issue is that

Shawn is white. If white men can be on the down low, why all the fuss over black men on the down low? Is the down low specific to race? There's no evidence to prove that black men are more likely to be on the down low than white men. Perhaps the focus on black men can be explained because white men on the down low are not spreading the HIV virus to their female partners at the same rate as black men. If so, why not? Is it because white men engage in safer sex, and if so, shouldn't our prevention efforts focus on how to get black men on the down low to take the same precautions?

What can we say about Jerry and his wife? If you knew them as a couple and then discovered that Jerry was sleeping with another man, you might think that Jerry was on the down low. He's black, he's married to a woman, and he's secretly sleeping with a man. What else does it take to be on the down low? Well, in this case, Jerry's secret is not a secret from his wife. His wife already knows. The rest of the world doesn't. Does that make Jerry on the down low? Jerry's life raises the issue of disclosure. Once you tell your wife, does it matter that you keep the secret from everyone else?

Finally, let's look at Luis. Luis is a proud Hispanic gay man. He goes to gay bars, he has gay friends, and he calls himself gay. Doesn't sound very down low. But Luis has a secret. He recently started dating a woman, and he doesn't know how to break the news to his gay friends. If being on the down low means lying to the world about your sexuality, then Luis may very well be a member of the group. But if being on the down low only means lying to your opposite-sex partner about your same-sex partner, we've created a very narrow field of concern.

At the end of this exercise, we still don't have a common definition of what it means to be on the down low. So how is the down low defined in the media? To position this story as a cautionary tale about AIDS, the media seem to have accepted a popular definition of the down low that suggests five basic traits for those on the DL. According to the media, those on the down low are:

(1) black,

(2) male,

(3) HIV positive,

(4) in relationships with women, and

(5) secretly having sex with men.

We've considered seven examples of people who could be on the down low, but each of them challenges the popular definition. Raheem is not in a relationship with a woman. David is not HIV positive. Jabbar is a closeted gay man. Joyce is a woman. Shawn is white. Jerry is out to his wife. And Luis is gay.

Is it possible than none of the seven people mentioned above are on the down low? To resolve this dilemma, I asked several of the most visible black figures who have talked publicly about the down low to answer a simple question: What is the down low?

I began with J. L. King, the author of a book called *On the Down Low: A Journey into the Lives of "Straight" Black Men Who Sleep with Men*. I could not find a clear definition of the down low in his book, so I decided to ask him myself. He responded to each of my four e-mails but never answered the question, so I went back to his book and tried to piece together a definition from his own words. The subtitle of the book presents one possible definition: "'straight' black men who sleep with men." But that definition doesn't require the men to be involved in relationships with women. The dedication for the book seems to explain more. King dedicates the book, in part, to "all the women whose health has been jeopardized and emotional state compromised by men living on the DL," a dedication that suggests men on the down low are responsible for the spread of AIDS to black women. Should we also be concerned about down low men who are HIV negative and always practice safe sex? King uses other terms such as "double lifestyle" and "duplicitous behavior" to give us more understanding of what the down low means to him. The closest definition he provides, however, is in response to a question from an Ohio health official who asks about the secret lives of bisexual men. "The secret," he writes, "is that men who look like me, talk like me, and think like me are having sex with men but still love and want to be with their women. And they do not believe they're gay." King's definition seems to exclude men who date women just to conceal their homosexuality. In other words, men on the down low would be inherently bisexual. But if they are bisexual and not just in denial about their homosexual desires, then why should we vilify these man who are acting out on their natural desires?

I put the same question to Phill Wilson, the director of the Black AIDS Institute in Los Angeles. "Like many slang terms, 'DL' means different things to different people," he said. "Some DL men identify as straight and have wives or girlfriends but secretly have sex with other men. Others are younger men who are still questioning or exploring their sexuality. Some are closeted gay men. And then there are African-American brothers who openly have relationships with other men but reject the label 'gay' or 'bisexual' because they equate those terms with white men."

Many of those black men who do not consider themselves gay would still feel perfectly comfortable cavorting in a predominantly black gay bar. By rejecting the homosexual label, they are not necessarily rejecting the sexual behavior associated with it. Black men often reject the term "gay" to repudiate white social constructs of homosexuality but not to reject their own homosexual sexual behavior. Some black men who openly acknowledge that they have sex with other men have simply found other words to describe themselves, including the term "same-gender-loving." They reject the term "gay" not because of internalized homophobia or because they are on the down low. Instead, they simply want to create their own identities outside of what they perceive to be a racially insensitive white gay world.

The journalist Kai Wright in New York shares Wilson's sense of complexity about the definition. Wright has written extensively about the down low, and he finds the act of defining the term problematic. "It's whatever the person using the phrase wants it to be," he explains.

For black gay men, labeling themselves on the down low is a way to validate their masculinity. Wright mentions an example of a black gay bar in Brooklyn that advertised in a local gay magazine as "Brooklyn's down low choice," despite the fact that "there couldn't be a less down low place," he says. "It's one of the oldest black gay bars in the city, first off, and it's packed with gay-identified men watching a male strip show!"

For white gay men, "the down low has become the latest way to fetishize the scary, roughneck black men of their porns," says Wright. He fears that "this racist fantasy bleeds into the AIDS activism" of some white gay men as well.

For black women, the down low provides an easy way to deal with difficult issues, he says. By focusing on the behavior of men on the DL, black women are not required to reconsider their own behavior and may be left disempowered to protect themselves.

"That's just the problem with this issue," according to Wright. "It's the perfect boogeyman: a group of shady, dangerous men who are, by definition, hidden and unidentifiable." Kai Wright raises an excellent point. How do you define someone who doesn't want to be defined? How do you identify someone who doesn't want to be identified? And once you get the person to be identified, that person is, by definition, no longer on the down low.

Dr. Darrell Wheeler of New York's Hunter College defines the term more broadly than most. The down low is "a term used by some men to describe behaviors that they do not want others to know about," he says. Dr. Wheeler's definition seems to open the door to those who are white, gay, HIV negative, and not in relationships. The down low is also a term used to describe men "or women" who are homosexually active but do not identity themselves as lesbian, gay or bisexual, he adds. In other words, almost everyone who hides his or her behaviors from others can be on the down low.

The Arkansas-based columnist Alicia Banks, who writes an online column called *Eloquent Fury*, says she resents the media characterization of the down low as "an exclusively ethnic moniker to trivialize and exploit a universal issue." Banks also identifies a link between racism and homophobia in the common definition of the down low. All humans cheat, she said, and men of all races creep with women and men. Cheating and lying are both "fatal infections," according to Banks, "whether your partner is creeping with a woman or a man." Her comment implies that the public might not be as concerned about infidelity when practiced in a traditional male-female relationship. But for Banks, the down low is nothing to be proud of. The DL, she says, is both a "damned lie" and a "deceitful life."

Dr. David Malebranche, a professor of medicine at Emory University in Atlanta, provides historical perspective in his definition of the down low. "The 'down low' is a phrase that has been part of the black community for ages, and historically meant something that is 'secretive' or 'covert.'" he says. Dr. Malebranche cites several examples where the down low simply means to keep something—a loan, a love affair—a secret. "Only within the past couple of decades has the term become a more specific catch phrase to describe black men who have wives or girlfriends, but also mess around with other men on the side."

Dr. Ron Simmons, a former professor of communications at Howard University in Washington, D.C., also associates the term "down low" with its history, describing it as "a hip-hop expression meaning something secret or undercover." Today, however, he says the term "is commonly used to refer to men who have sex with men but self-identify as heterosexual." Simmons runs Us Helping Us, a Washington-based AIDS organization for black gay and bisexual men that provides a down low telephone help line, Internet outreach, and barbershop intervention. "Part of the problem," he finds with the definition of the term "is that self-identified gay men also refer to themselves as being on the down low." The situation can be confusing to outsiders, and Dr. Simmons recalls an incident when a reporter called him to find men on the down low. "I told her that down low men do not have a physical place or area where they can be found," he said. "She remarked that she had heard that there was a down low party during D.C. Black Gay Pride. I had to explain to her that this was a party of gay men who were using the term but not the kind of 'down low' men as she was investigating."

The reporter who called Dr. Simmons is not alone. Since the down low story hit the media in 2001, every major newspaper in the country has scrambled to find down low men in their community. Black magazines like *Essence* and gay publications like *The Advocate* have covered the down low story, while many of their reporters have struggled to find men on the down low and others have stretched to define the community they were covering. An August 2004 article in *The Advocate* starts with a visit to a popular black gay bar called The Study, but for black gay men in Los

Angeles, the location—situated on a major street in Hollywood—is hardly a secret. Do "real" down low men go to gay bars? The story quotes a young man named Ezel, who declined to give his last name but is described as a volunteer for the Minority AIDS Project and who is distributing condoms at a table in the bar. He's married, bisexual, and in the closet. But is he on the down low? It is hard to imagine that a man on the down low would volunteer for a gay-identified AIDS organization that hands out condoms at gay bars. It's even harder to imagine that such a man would give out his first name to a reporter. It wouldn't take a lot for a curious reader to piece together the details of his life and blow his cover. If someone like Ezel is on the down low, then just about anyone can be on the down low. And that's exactly the problem. Without a uniform definition of the down low, we are left with no clear boundaries in defining this mysterious group of men.

Dr. Greg Millett, a behavioral scientist in the epidemiology branch of the U.S. Centers for Disease Control and Prevention (CDC), has studied the down low issue for the federal government. To generate a sense of clarity about the meaning of the term, Millett developed his own definition of the down low as a "man who is heterosexually identified and has sex with other men without the knowledge of their primary female partner."

Millett acknowledges "there are many other definitions that people have for the down low that you see in the media. Some people are considering down low [to be] men who are not out about their sexuality. Some people consider down low men just men who are bisexually active. Some people consider down low men many other things—men who are having sex with other men, have female partners and having unprotected sex with their male and female partners," he said.

While Millett's definition may not be universally accepted in the public, his objective was to "define it and operationalize it for the scientific community" so that future researchers could work with the same basic understanding of the population to be studied. That may help settle any scientific disputes, but it does not settle the raging debate in the public.

The down low has become so pervasive in the public discourse that the term has even crept its way into Internet encyclopedias, but the definitions employed by these reference materials often simply repeat popular perceptions. One online encyclopedia explains, "Among some sectors of African-American homosexual sub-culture . . . same-sex sexual behavior is sometimes viewed as solely for physical pleasure. Men on the 'down-low' may engage in regular (though often covert) sex acts with other men while continuing sexual and romantic relationships with unsuspecting women." Another source defines the down low as "men who discreetly have sex with other men while in sexual relationships with women." These are fairly common definitions, but they exclude a large segment of the population who self-identify as "down low" but do not have relationships with women. In addition, the first definition seems to exclude whites and others who are not black, while the second definition excludes women on the down low.

So once again, what is the down low? The answer may challenge everything we think we know about the subject. The only point on which the experts seem to agree is that the down low is about secrecy in our sexual behavior. You don't have to be black, you don't have to be male, you don't have to be HIV positive, and you don't even have to be in a relationship to be on the down low. The down low is everything and nothing. In fact, the down low seems a bit like water. It has no shape, no form, and no color of its own. Like water, it is flexible enough to adapt to the shape and color of any container. It can mean whatever the user wants it to mean.

For closeted black gay and bisexual men, the down low is a way to validate their masculinity. For straight black women, the down low is a way to avoid the difficult issues of personal responsibility. For white America, the down low is a way to pathologize black lives. And for the media, the down low is a story that can be easily hyped.

For a phrase that is subject to multiple interpretations with no uniform definition, the "down low" is a term that is widely used and even more widely misunderstood.

Chapter 2
Since the Beginning of Time

I REMEMBER MY first experience with the down low. The summer before I started law school, I worked out at a Bally's gym in St. Louis and developed an acquaintance with a tall, muscular black man named Mike. I was young and naïve and totally clueless about the culture of the down low. Mike knew the culture well. When I would speak to him at the gym, he would stare into my eyes with a penetrating look that seemed to indicate that he knew more about me than I knew about myself. "We should hang out," he told me shortly after we met. I politely agreed but never followed up with him. There was something about Mike that I found both intriguing and terrifying. He turned me on and turned me off at the same time. Every time I looked into his eyes, I knew at some level that I was looking into my own, and the experience scared me to death.

I did not know why Mike decided to introduce himself to me the day we met, but I'm sure he knew that I was willing to talk. Maybe he caught me studying the curve of his biceps or peeking beneath his tank top to see his chest. There must have been something about me that told him I was safe for conversation. I had never been involved with a man, and I had no intention of ever doing so. I was in deep denial about my sexual orientation, and he knew it before I did.

Mike was also a master at smooth talk. He made me feel safe and comfortable when we spoke, but there was something enticingly mischievous about him. He would wink his eye to say good-bye. He would glance me over from head to toe as though he were contemplating a meal. And then there was his handshake. It was a normal handshake at first, but soon it became more intimate. I noticed it one day when he held my hand for an extra second as his middle finger ever so casually brushed across my palm. I did not respond, a reaction that I thought was appropriately neutral. But instead of sending him a red light signal I had actually given him a green light, or at least a yellow light to proceed with caution. Mike was a master at nonverbal communication. If I had flinched at his gesture, he could have easily dismissed it as unintentional contact. But since I did not flinch, he assumed it was okay with me. The next time we shook hands, he tried it again, this time clearly stroking my palm as he watched for a response. "We should hang out and get together some time," he suggested. I agreed, but we made no plans.

As the summer ended, I paid my last visit to the gym one night and found Mike on the bench press. As we had done before, we worked out together. He spotted me when I did my sets, and I spotted him on his. At the end of the workout, I reminded him that I was leaving town and moving to Boston to go to school. Sensing an opportunity would be lost, he suggested that we get together when we left the gym that evening.

"We've been talking about getting together for the longest time," he said. "What are you doing tonight?"

"Nothing," I said.

"Why don't we hang out?"

"Sure, what do you want to do?"

"We can just hang out. Come on over to my place for a while," he said.

I agreed, and when we left the gym I followed him in my car to his house. We walked through the family room, where he yelled to someone in the kitchen that he was home. He led me to his bedroom, and I asked if the person who answered was his roommate. "No, that's my wife," he told me. I felt strangely comforted by this knowledge, feeling safe that his wife was in the house. But then he locked the door in his bedroom, turned on the television, and sat on the edge of the bed next to a chair where I was seated. His seductive stare made me nervous and confused. I turned my attention to the television, but his eyes remained fixed on me. A few minutes into an awkward conversation, he reached out and touched my hand, caressing my palm with his middle finger once again. I felt guilty and excited all at once. What was I doing in this man's house? And what would his wife think about all this if she saw us together? How do you bring home another man while your wife is at home, lock him in the bedroom, and not tell her about it? I knew he was a smooth talker, but this was hard to understand.

I did not have much time to think about what was happening, and Mike did not have time to waste. He continued touching me, stroking my palm and caressing both sides of my hand. He never said a word. There was no need. He gestured for me to sit next to him on the bed, and I got up and moved closer. He moved his hands up my arm and found a position between my shoulders and back. Then his hands moved under my T-shirt and across my chest, and I felt a guilty pleasure in his touch. The feel of another man's body so close to mine was a new and exciting experience for me, but Mike was not satisfied with a simple touch. He lifted my shirt and threw it on the floor, forcing me back on the bed as he lay on top of me. That was the moment that scared me the most. I could not focus on what he was doing because I could not stop thinking about what I was doing there and how I had allowed myself to get into such an awkward situation. I stopped suddenly and pushed him off of me, clearing my head as I fumbled for my T-shirt.

"What's the matter?" he asked.

"I have to go."

"Why? You just got here."

"No, you don't understand. This is, this is not for me," I said. "I have never done this before, and I'm not about to start right now. I can't do this. I have to go home, right now." He tried to talk me into staying but I was determined to leave. Finally, he relented, but he must have realized the turmoil going on inside of me. No matter how awkward I felt, I had enjoyed the experience at some level, and he knew it. Mike must have known that this would not be my last encounter with a man, and he predicted the future with his final words as I left. "You'll be back," he snapped.

"I don't think so," I objected, and walked out the door.

I met Mike in 1989 when I was a completely different person from who I am now. I had not started law school, had never worked in the White House and had never written a book. I had been involved with a girlfriend and had no intention of ever being with a man. Most important, I did not consider myself to be gay. I had a profound and deep-seated physical attraction to men that I did not understand and did not acknowledge. I never acted on the feelings inside of me, and I did everything I could to repress them. I was so far in denial that I was in the closet even to myself. Had I continued along my path of self-deception, I would have ended up on the down low. I would have been married with children only to wake up one day and realize I was living a lie.

The lie in which I was involved began long before the current down low sensation. In fact, it began long before 1989, when I had my first experience with a man. To tell the truth, the lie began before I was even born. The lie to which I refer is the lie we tell ourselves about who we are as a people. And that lie is what makes the recent obsession with the down low so painfully problematic. Given what we already know or should know, it is hard to believe that anybody with an ounce of real-world experience would think the down low is new. Let's be honest. Men have been secretly sleeping with other men since the beginning of time.

As I said before, this is a book about lies, and one of the biggest lies we have told ourselves about the down low is that this story is new. Sometimes, we passingly acknowledge that the down low has been around for a while, but then we continue on with the discussion as though we are engaged in a bold new conversation. It's not. However you define it, the down low has been going on since the beginning of recorded history. In the Bible's first chapter of the second book of Samuel, a supposedly straight David says to Jonathan, "Thy love to me was wonderful, passing the love of women." Yes, David is speaking to another man. At one point in the story, Jonathan goes to a secret hiding place where he and David "kissed one another, and wept one with another, until David exceeded." That story took place more than two thousand years ago. The down low has been around for a long time.

Just how far back does it go? The writer Cary Alan Johnson has uncovered evidence of homosexuality in pre-colonial Africa. Professor Charles Nero at Bates College has exposed a centuries-old slave narrative that reveals the existence of homosexuality among black slaves. And scores of scholars have documented the influence of black lesbian, gay, bisexual, and transgendered writers, artists, musicians and entertainers in the Harlem Renaissance of the 1920s and 1930s.

Homosexuality and bisexuality have always been somewhat difficult for many of us to understand, but the notion of a married man sleeping with another man seems to be irresistibly scandalous. It seems every generation produces artists who "expose" this drama. Ma Rainey's 1926 song "Sissy Blues" provides an example. Rainey sings:

> *I dreamed last night that I was far from harm*
> *Woke up and found my man in a sissy's arms.*

Two years later, the bisexual Rainey had moved from victim to culprit in her song "Prove It on Me Blues." Exposing the down low culture of the times, Rainey plays the role of the cagey defendant who secretly acknowledges her activity but demands that her accuser "prove it" to the world because "ain't nobody caught me." In that song, she sings:

> *Went out last night with a crowd of my friends,*
> *They must have been women, 'cause I don't like no men.*

Of course, women weren't the only ones who sang about the experience. In 1926, Pinewood Tom (Josh White) seemed to have given up on the hope of finding a "good woman" when he sang:

> *If you can't bring me a woman*
> *Bring me a sissy man.*

And no chronology of the down low is complete without acknowledging what may be the first popular song in history to connect the words "down low" with closeted homosexuality. In the 1930 song "Boy in the Boat," George Hanna exposes a culture among lesbian women who socialize at dimly lit venues designed to protect their identities:

If you see two women walking hand in hand
Just look 'em over and try to understand
They'll go to these parties, have their lights down low
Only those parties where women can go.

There was a name for these women living in the shadows. Bessie Jackson (Lucille Bogan) called them "B.D. women" in her song "B.D. Woman's Blues." The B.D. stood for "bulldagger." Reinforcing socially constructed gender norms, Bessie Smith referred to a "mannish-acting woman" and a "womanish-acting man." Some of the men were simply called "sissies."

The Depression at home and the war in Europe brought an end to the sexual candor of the twenties and thirties, but homosexuality and bisexuality persisted nonetheless. In the 1940s, *Ebony* magazine reported on a Harlem nightclub called Lucky's Rendezvous at 148th Street and St. Nicholas Avenue where "male couples are so commonplace . . . that no one looks twice at them." In 1953, the civil rights activist Bayard Rustin was arrested in Pasadena, California, and convicted of a morals charge for having sex with two men. Three years later, James Baldwin wrote a gay love story in his novel *Giovanni's Room.* And the following year, the young playwright Lorraine Hansberry wrote a letter to *The Ladder,* an early lesbian publication, where she condemned "homosexual persecution and condemnation" as "social ignorance." By the 1960s, Hansberry, Baldwin, and Rustin had become genuine black celebrities. Hansberry had won critical acclaim for her play *A Raisin in the Sun,* Baldwin's books were selling in the millions, and Rustin had won fame as the architect of the famous 1963 March on Washington.

History provides plenty of evidence of black homosexuality and bisexuality, but we don't have to go back in time to find examples of men sleeping with men. We can find them in our own circles. They have always been there, but we did not always talk about them. We saw them leading the church choir. We spotted them on the street. We recognized them at our family reunions, funerals, and weddings, and they were obviously gay. They were the easy ones to understand because they fit neatly into a box that allowed us to reduce and define them into a simple stereotype. They made us feel good about ourselves because they could make us laugh, but, just as important, we felt good because we were not them. We were married with children and trying our best to live the prototypical American dream of happiness while they were perpetually lonesome and single, we thought, and yet they were somehow fun-loving and excited about life.

We liked them, in part, because they knew their place. They knew the role they were supposed to play in our lives, and they performed it on cue. We liked them because they did not threaten us by forcing us to challenge our preconceived notions of homosexuality. And that was the great paradox. By being so different, they actually made us feel at ease. If they had looked and spoken and acted just like us, we might not have been as comfortable. How would we pick them out and identify them if they were just like us? But they were identifiable, or so we thought, and so we could relax because we knew who *they* were. They were not us.

What we did not know, or did not want to know, is that there was never an "us" or "them." We were always the same. They were not just the "flamboyant" florists and the "sensitive" male friends. They were the "masculine" construction workers and the "married" men with children. All of them had been there all along, but we continued to live intoxicated by the narcotic power of a collective lie. Like the characters in the film *The Matrix,* we had swallowed the blue pill that made life simple and easy to understand instead of the red pill that made life complicated and truthful. Unfortunately for us, life is not always simple and easy. But the truth did not matter because our virtual reality had already told us what was true. It was a perfect matrix. Straight women could identify straight men, and straight men could identify straight women, and both of them could identify gay men, who could in turn identify one another. But there was actually a fundamental flaw in the system, and it produced an anomaly. In order for the system to work, everyone had to believe it.

The matrix worked well when most homosexuals were confined to the closet. In that world, a few out gay men were free to be themselves while the vast majority of gay men lived their lives in hiding. Closeted gay men who did not want to risk the disclosure of their sexual orientation would carefully adapt their public lives to society's expectations. Homosexuality was not to be discussed. It was, after all, "the love that dare not speak its name." So as long as we remained hooked up to the matrix, we kept ourselves oblivious to the secret lives and torment in which many gays and lesbians lived.

The matrix functioned most smoothly in a world where oppression was common and expressions of difference were forced underground. While the world tolerated injustice for blacks and women and others, few people had any need to worry about the concerns of homosexuals. But with the rise of the civil rights and women's rights movements, ordinary people began to question the premise of their own oppression and to challenge the notion that one group of people had a right to rule over others. Alice Paul led thousands of women through the streets of Washington, D.C., in March 1913 in a demonstration for women's right to vote. A black seamstress in Montgomery, Alabama, named Rosa Parks sparked a boycott in December 1955 when she was arrested after refusing to give up her seat to a white man on a bus. Martin Luther King, Jr., led a quarter of a million people at an August 1963 civil rights march on Washington. And a quarter of a million people marched through the nation's capital in November 1969 to protest the Vietnam War.

By the end of the 1960s, the vocal defenders of oppression more often quietly slipped into the closet while the oppressed spoke out loudly. A string of assassins' bullets had silenced the most audible voices of the decade and threatened to wake us from the stupor of the matrix. Although some could overlook the murder of four little girls in Birmingham, they could not ignore the deaths of John Kennedy and Malcolm X and Martin Luther King and Bobby Kennedy. Nor could they ignore the thousands of American soldiers who were being killed in the war in Southeast Asia.

America in 1969 was a much different country from America in 1960. Our heroes were dead, Richard Nixon was president, and NASA was making plans to send the first man to the moon. It was in that environment that a group of drag queens and gay men would stage an unlikely revolt at a popular bar in New York's Greenwich Village. On Friday, June 27, 1969, eight New York City police officers raided the Stonewall Inn and ordered the patrons to leave. Many of them had seen police raids before, and they knew the drill all too well. But this time was different. As they congregated outside the bar, some of the patrons began to resist. Some taunted the police. Others threw bricks and bottles. The crowd did not disperse. We have conflicting reports about how the night ended, but the event became legendary in gay history.

A riot at a gay bar may seem like an odd event to mark the beginning of a revolution, but word spread quickly, and protests continued at the bar for several days afterward. It is impossible to know how many gays and lesbians outside of New York even heard about the Stonewall incident during the summer of 1969, but by the 1970s, cities across the country were celebrating something called gay pride on the anniversary of Stonewall.

Suddenly, Americans started seeing large numbers of lesbian, gay, bisexual, and transgendered (LGBT) people who were willing to be visible in public. Thousands of them marched in annual pride parades through the streets of major cities like New York and San Francisco. America slowly warmed up to a campy 1970s version of gayness that had been constructed by cultural icons like Elton John and Peter Allen, while black gays found representation in disco divas like Sylvester and the Village People. Once again, Hollywood was available to help us understand another complicated social issue. The comedian Redd Foxx and the singer Pearl Bailey depicted a black couple coming to terms with their son's homosexuality in the comic 1976 film *Norman, Is That You?* Then there was the actor John Ritter, who deployed every gay stereotype he could summon in his role as Jack Tripper, a straight man pretending to be gay in order to live with two female roommates in the 1970s sitcom *Three's Company*. The gay stereotypes worked quite well for most Americans by providing us a comfortable way to process homosexuality through the lens of comedy, but by the time the AIDS epidemic surfaced in the early 1980s, a problem developed. The matrix was beginning to unravel at its seams.

The matrix had always depended on our faith in a collective lie that gay men were readily identifiable. We believed they could be picked out by their behavior, their dress, their walk, their sense of style. The AIDS epidemic, however, began to challenge our assumptions about homosexuality by presenting us with real-life images of gay men who were not the stereotypes we imagined them to be. As thousands of gay men became sick and died, we realized that many of them were our brothers, our cousins, our uncles, our fathers, and sometimes even our husbands. We realized it, but many of us still denied it. Many of us acted as though the truth was not the truth, and we continued to generate and perpetuate outdated but reassuring images of homosexuality.

As gays became more vocal and visible as the victims of AIDS and the fighters against it, the backlash against them became more strident. Increased gay visibility provided fertile ground for televangelists like Jerry Falwell and Pat Robertson and others to exploit America's discomfort with homosexuality. The televangelists misled Americans to believe that liberal political and cultural changes had produced legions of new homosexuals. Although it seemed that gays and lesbians were suddenly coming out of nowhere, in reality they had always been there. The gay movement did not make them gay; it simply gave them the courage to tell the world that they were gay. Before the movement, they had been invisible and silent. After the movement, they were visible and vocal.

Meanwhile, by the 1980s, gay men had learned to morph themselves from a homosexual stereotype into a heterosexual one. A community that was being destroyed by a deadly new disease now exalted men who fit into a stereotypical image of masculine fitness and health. An extensive gym culture developed, and a new gay icon emerged. The new gay model was not just the guy next door. He was a better version of the guy next door. And that was one of the secrets that had been exposed by the unraveling of the matrix. While the matrix told us that gay men looked a certain way, gay men themselves knew that the matrix was wrong. They could see it in their social circles, and they could see it in the mirror. What's more shocking, however, is that some of the antigay conservatives knew the same thing. While they continued to profit from their perpetuation of a gay stereotype, some of them knew all along that the stereotype was wrong. They knew because they helped to design the system. As lawmakers, ministers, corporate executives, and beneficiaries of the status quo, they were the architects of the matrix.

Ironically, the architects of the matrix maintained the system with the complicity of the very people it oppressed. By creating a utopian vision of heterosexuality, the architects produced a social

norm that helped to push gay men into false and unnatural relationships with women. The men in these sham relationships knew
better than anyone that the matrix was a fraud, but they could never
reveal the fraud without revealing their homosexuality. Their ability
to operate without suspicion in society depended on their silence.
So they persisted in the lie that gay men were simply stereotypes,
and as long as they avoided the stereotypes they also avoided detec-
tion. That is, until the AIDS epidemic.

With their lives in jeopardy, white gay men quickly mobilized to
respond to AIDS in the 1980s. They raised money, created new
organizations, educated the community, provided services to people
with AIDS, lobbied for public policy, and funded research efforts to
produce a cure. The new activism generated concrete results, but it
also exposed deep-seated racial fault lines in the gay community. In
the 1990s, the AIDS infection rates were declining more significantly among white gay men than among homosexual and bisexual
men of color. In spite of all the AIDS education efforts, large numbers of black men who have sex with men (MSM) were still not
being reached. While white gay men were coming out of the closet,
many black gay men were battening down the hatches.

The AIDS outbreak had also mobilized a cadre of trailblazing
black gay poets, writers, artists, and film makers in the 1980s. Many
of these men had already told us about a culture that predated the
down low. Presumably straight black men had been having sex with
one another on the down low for decades. Essex Hemphill's 1991
book *Brother to Brother* included a poem called "The Tomb of
Sorrow" about black men secretly having sex in Washington's Malcolm X Park. But by 1995, nearly all the top black gay figures—Joe
Beam, Steven Corbin, Melvin Dixon, Craig Harris, Essex
Hemphill, Marlon Riggs and Assotto Saint—had died of AIDS-
related complications. The memory of their work disappeared from

the collective consciousness of the black community as the brightest stars in the black gay constellation slowly faded away into obscurity. An old era had ended, and a new one was beginning as a fresh breed of writers stepped forward to represent the changing times.

In the new era, black gay writers were able to break out of the gay label and reach mainstream black audiences with new images of black gay and bisexual men. E. Lynn Harris opened the doors with his immensely popular groundbreaking debut novel, *Invisible Life*. For many African Americans, Raymond Winston Tyler, Jr., became the embodiment of black bisexuality, and suddenly the secret was out. Harris had introduced the nation to black gay men who did not fit the common stereotypes and to black bisexual men who liked sports, held professional jobs, dated women, and looked just like other black men. At the same time, the writer James Earl Hardy rounded out the new image with his depiction of a young black male couple in his first novel *B-Boy Blues*, in which a streetwise Raheim "Pooquie" Rivers negotiated his relationship with a young journalist named Mitchell "Little Bit" Crawford. Black America was slowly waking up from a long slumber of denial about homosexuality and bisexuality. The blue pill was gradually wearing off.

Our history is not difficult to find in our popular culture, so it is hard to understand how we missed the truth all these years. It is hard to understand how we could believe the down low did not exist until now. Unless, of course, we were not awake. And that is exactly what happened. For a long time, we had been hypnotized by the rhetoric of our own alternative reality. We did not acknowledge what we had seen or what we should have known all along. We had been living in a matrix, but the down low was always there.

Whether through popular culture or real life, we have always known that there were men (and women) on the down low. Like the invisible man in Ralph Ellison's famous novel, they have always been there. Often, they have hidden from us, but sometimes there was no need to hide. As long as we believed that our collective lie was the truth, we were unable to see anything but what we believed to be true. For years, we lived in denial. And for years, we ignored the truth that they, like us, possess the free will to see the truth. "I am invisible," Ellison wrote, "simply because people refuse to see me."

CHAPTER 3

Everybody's Doing It

WHEN I WAS a child, I had an uncle on the down low. People in the family never really talked about Uncle Michael, but we knew he was gay. He was a well-known organist at a popular church in St. Louis, and he had a fraternity of male friends whose association with him raised a few eyebrows in the community. Nevertheless, as far as I can recall, Uncle Michael was very well liked and respected. That is, until he was murdered one night in his own apartment. We never found out who killed him, and no one was ever convicted of the crime. But Michael was not the one on the down low. Uncle Larry was. Uncle Larry lived in a beautiful ranch house in the suburbs of St. Louis County. He was married with children and had a successful job as an up-and-coming businessman. From the outside, it appeared that Uncle Larry had the perfect life. From the inside, we knew it was a lie. Uncle Larry was living a double life. He was on the down low.

Before you make any assumptions about Uncle Larry, you should know this. Uncle Larry considered himself to be straight. He did not sleep with men or have sex with them. If anything, he considered himself a ladies' man. And that, actually, was the problem. Uncle Larry was married, but he also had a long-time girlfriend on the side. You see, Uncle Larry not only *considered* himself to be heterosexual; he *was* heterosexual. Uncle Larry was straight in his sexual orientation and in his behavior, and yet he was on the down low. He was on the down low because he cheated on his wife. When his wife found out, she confronted him, challenged him, and ultimately left him. She refused to be married to a man on the down low.

Quiet as it's kept, there is a dirty little secret about the down low that most of the media have not discussed. Here's the secret. The down low is not only about closeted gay men and bisexuals. Straight men and women are on the down low too. In fact, if gay men and bisexuals have now popularized the down low, then heterosexuals might actually have perfected it. Long before the current down low scare, heterosexuals were cheating in their marriages and in their relationships, just like everyone else. History is filled with heterosexual examples of men cheating with women and women cheating with men. From the ancient Greek tragedies to the Christian Bible to Shakespeare, few themes are more constant than infidelity. We have been writing about it, singing about it, and creating art about it for centuries. The only thing that has changed is what we call it.

I learned that lesson when I was driving my car down U Street in Washington, D.C., one day when a new song came on 95.5/WPGC. The infectious beat quickly had me bobbing my head in the car, and I recognized the artist's voice as soon as I heard the words:

> *My body wants you so*
> *For what I miss at home*
> *Nobody has to know*
> *Keep it on the down low.*

The year was 1995, the artist was Brian McKnight, the song was "On the Down Low," and Maxine became one of the first modern poster girls for the DL. Back then, the down low was simply an expression of secret intimacy outside a relationship, and because Maxine yearned for satisfaction that her man could not provide, she was portrayed as a sympathetic figure, the forlorn woman abandoned by her unsympathetic partner. Poor Maxine. Her man "doesn't take her anywhere," McKnight explains. He used to "say sweet things" but now he "acts like he doesn't even care." Who could be upset at a woman rebelling against the heartbreak of a loveless relationship? She was a woman who simply "needed someone to hold" and whose lonely nights were "oh so cold." Brian McKnight, the handsome young man with a smooth voice and sensitive looks, became the perfect paramour for the lonesome woman, able to sweep her off her feet with a song and rescue her from her tragic relationship. When McKnight's song was released, there was little public concern about the decline of moral values or the problem of infidelity in the black community. At the time, the down low was seen as a heterosexual thing, acknowledging the reality that both men and women often go unfulfilled in their relationships and seek comfort elsewhere.

Brian McKnight may have been the first artist to mention the down low in a *title* of a popular song, but he was not the first popular recording artist to sing about the heterosexual down low. The female R&B trio TLC had already introduced us to the down low in their 1994 song "Creep." As in McKnight's story, the lonely woman in "Creep" decides to cheat on her man because she needs "some affection." She suspects her man is unfaithful to her, but rather than confront him, she takes a different approach—she cheats as well. Behind a flaring trumpet interlude and a jazzy sexual overtone, the TLC trio sings the now-famous chorus:

So I creep, yeah
Just keep it on the down low
Said nobody is supposed to know.

The song that played on the radio presented a morally neutral view of the woman's actions, but TLC also released a socially conscious remix of the song that seemed to question the values of the down low. The remix added a new verse that sounds more like a public health warning than a typical R&B song. The added lyrics warned that creepin' could lead to passionate crime, unwanted pregnancy, incest, family breakup, AIDS, and death, and the remixed song explicitly warned that "HIV is often sleepin' in a creepin' cradle."

In the 1990s, "creeping" became a widely used slang term to describe unfaithful behavior. Meanwhile, the down low that TLC sang about was an intangible place or space where secrets were kept, but it was not a description commonly used to identify someone. People were not *on* the down low, but people would *do things* on the down low. The down low was not a description of who they were, it described something that they did. Our early understanding of the heterosexual down low operated in much the same way as our understanding of sexual orientation in the late nineteenth and early twentieth century. In prewar America, homosexuals and bisexuals did not identify themselves based on their sexual orientation. What they did in bed described their behavior, not their identity. But times change, and similarly some words and ideas change their meaning over time. The word "gay," for example, once meant "happy" and "cheerful" but now means "homosexual" as well. The word "black" was once avoided by African Americans but was later embraced by the black nationalists of the 1960s. When Luther Vandross sang about "creepin'" in his 1989 song of the same name, the word had a somewhat positive connotation as Vandross sang to a lover who creeps into his dreams. It was the ultimate expression of loyalty that a man would fantasize about his partner at night. Five years later, TLC had changed the perception of the term by associating it with the disloyalty of the down low.

Even as TLC tried to cover its tracks with its warning about the risks of the down low, the music that they and others created still seemed to romanticize heterosexual infidelity. Brian McKnight's 1995 *I Remember You* CD led with his "On the Down Low" song as the first track. McKnight was pictured on the cover of the CD in a sexy pose with his shirt open and chest exposed, but inside the liner notes he was shown in another photo that portrayed him embracing his two young sons, B. J. and Niko, who actually introduced the down low song. Thus began the contradiction associated with the down low. Here was Brian McKnight, a family man still married to his college sweetheart, but he was singing a song that rationalized cheating. The crooner known for his melodic love ballads was striking a chord as a bad boy. In a CD filled with endearing songs about "crazy love," the down low tune seemed strangely out of place, but the song helped to reposition McKnight in line with the emerging anything goes hip hop mentality of the early 1990s.

In the 1990s, top hip hop performers were becoming the new kings and queens of the music world. The rap group Naughty by Nature glamorized both male and female cheating in their 1991 crossover hit "O.P.P.," an abbreviation loosely interpreted to mean "other people's property." Long before "the down low" term became popular, people were asking each other another question: "Are you down with O.P.P.?" In the words of that song:

> *Have you ever known a brother who had another like a girl or wife*
> *And you just had to stop and look cuz he look just that nice.*

Never mind the girl or wife. The man was going to be "yours anyway," the song claims. In the bold new world of hip hop, men and women could openly celebrate their disrespect for marital vows. Despite a woman's repeated claim that "I Got a Man" in a 1993 song of the same name, the rap artist Positive K nonetheless repeatedly asks: "What's your man got to do with me?"

Hip hop opened up new opportunities and new challenges for women as well. With its provocative female MCs and its sexual depiction of women in rap videos, hip hop had ushered in a controversial new sexual revolution for black women. Perhaps that explains why many of the first songs about the down low were songs *about women* on the down low. One major exception was a song recorded *by women,* as the female group Salt-N-Pepa rapped about a man on the down low. Back in 1993, before Brian McKnight's "On the Down Low" or TLC's "Creep," Salt-N-Pepa released a song called "Whatta Man," recorded with the female group En Vogue, that repeatedly boasts about the virtue of a particularly good man. But rather than praise his faithfulness, the artists appreciate his discretion, while tacitly acknowledging his cheating:

> *Although most men are hos*
> *He flows on the down low*
> *Cuz I never heard about him with another girl.*

The reference to "another girl" makes it very clear that Salt-N-Pepa are thinking about heterosexual infidelity. But more importantly, the lyrics indicate that some women, almost a decade before the most recent down low sensation, were publicly excusing their men for their down low behavior.

In 1993, the down low was, arguably, acceptable, or at least expected, behavior for some men in relationships. Long before J. L.

King was writing about the down low, black women were acknowledging and living with the reality that men cheat. Although Salt-N-Pepa acknowledge "that ain't nobody perfect," the man they applaud in their song seems pretty damn close. When it comes to monogamy, however, he's given a pass. Here's a man who is described in the song as funny, smooth, masculine, muscular, handsome, intelligent, caring, well-dressed, good in bed, patient, dependable, polite, and respectful of his elders. But there's one tiny little glitch: he's a ho. And what's the woman's response? "I don't sweat it because it's just pathetic to let it get me involved in that 'he said/she said' crowd." That's an odd statement, suggesting that monogamy is too much to expect or even discuss with an otherwise good man. But if the man is really as caring and sensitive as he's described, it's hard to understand why their relationship would be hurt by a little candor.

Salt-N-Pepa were not one-dimensional. The group also tried to balance their overtly sexual messages with public education about the dangers of AIDS. The artists even allowed a Boston youth group to record a three-minute public service announcement called "I've Got AIDS" that was included on their *Very Necessary* CD. The PSA, presented as a skit between a young man and a young woman, is introduced by Salt in her speaking voice. "Well, for a long time, me, Pep, and Spin have been involved in the fight against AIDS, and we always say the best cure is not to get it and not to spread it. You should be responsible if you're gonna have sex." Although seemingly at odds with the implicit message of much of their music, the PSA was actually consistent with the idea behind their 1992 hit "Let's Talk About Sex," a song that encouraged America to "talk about all the good things and the bad things that may be." The PSA also communicated the need for safe sex, not for abstinence. "All we had to do was just use protection," says the young woman who learns she's HIV positive in the skit. "I mean, the condoms were right there." It was a valuable public service message, but it underscored a paradox in American sexual behavior. In 1990s America, it was still easier to talk about sex than it was to talk about safe sex. Condom ads were banned from the same airwaves that made TV shows more sexually explicit than ever before. Music videos and cable television programming promoted graphic sexual depictions, and yet Surgeon General Joycelyn Elders was fired from her job because she talked about masturbation as a method of safe sex. In that climate, Salt-N-Pepa would be best known for such hit songs as "Push It," "Let's Talk About Sex," "None of Your Business," and "Shoop," and not for their efforts to promote safe sex and HIV awareness through their PSA.

On the surface, Salt-N-Pepa's most popular music seemed to send a different message from the PSA on their CD, but the predominant message of empowering women remained the same in the PSA as in their music. In "None of Your Business," for example, the rappers present an image of women empowered to make their own sexual decisions without regard to the opinions of others. That sentiment was hardly new in black music and culture. The song was reminiscent of Billie Holiday's legendary recording of "Ain't Nobody's Business If I Do." In the old song, Holiday sang:

> *If I go to church on Sunday*
> *Then cabaret all day Monday*
> *Ain't nobody's business if I do.*

In the new song, Salt-N-Pepa sing:

> *If I wanna take a guy home with me tonight*
> *It's none of your business.*

Hidden behind the lyrics of the two songs was a deeper meaning. At first blush, the songs represented the right of women to make their own decisions about their sexuality. Upon closer inspection, the songs revealed a long held but seldom discussed truth about relationships. Many of us knowingly remain in complex, even problematic relationships. Even when we know our partners are lying, cheating, and abusing us, we find it difficult to admit the truth. And when we do admit the truth, we still find it difficult to make a change. In "Ain't Nobody's Business," written by Porter Grainger and Everett Robbins, Holiday claims that she would rather her man "would hit me" than to "jump up and quit me." Sometimes, stability is more important than peace, but Holiday takes it to a new level when she promises not to call the police even if her man should beat her up. Similarly, although less dramatically, Salt-N-Pepa seem to indicate they won't be filing divorce papers if an otherwise good man cheats on one of them. In reality, we all make different choices about what we will and will not tolerate in a relationship, and many of us compromise our convictions out of love.

Salt-N-Pepa's 1993 song opened the door to the truth about men on the down low, but the next major musical references to the down low focused on women on the DL instead of men. There was TLC in 1994, followed by Brian McKnight in 1995, and then the R&B singer R. Kelly joined the crowd with his popular 1996 slow jam called "Down Low (Nobody Has To Know)." In R. Kelly's song, the featured character is once again a woman in an unhappy relationship. The woman approaches the man and whispers to him to keep it on the down low, and then like every other song of the genre she adds the familiar refrain: "nobody has to know." It's the exact same phrase used by Maxine in Brian McKnight's song ("nobody has to know") and strikingly similar to the phrase used in TLC's song ("nobody is supposed 2 know"). In the highly derivative world of contemporary music, it is not uncommon for artists to sample each other's music or lyrics or even their ideas, but the 1990s down low craze seemed to represent a new extreme as one artist after another jumped into the mix with his or her own version of the down low.

Not content with one song about the subject, R. Kelly decided to milk the down low concept again. In the 1998 song "Down Low Double Life," he plays the role of a down low man cheating on his wife until he's busted by his caller ID. But even before he gets caught, his wife seems to suspect his double life, which becomes clear when she tries to stop him from leaving the house one day. R. Kelly sings:

> *You pulled me to the side and you begged for me to stay*
> *But I was caught up in a life that forced me to walk away.*

In the end, he confesses to his "creepin'" only when he's thrown out of his house and forced to live with his momma, and even then his own mother scolds him and tells him he's pathetic. His response: "Must be because of what my old man did to her." Yes, the down low has been around for a long time.

In some form or another, the down low story has been told for generations. Long before there was a name attached to it, men and women were cheating on each other and singing about it in their music. In a popular 1955 song, Chuck Berry asks his sweetheart: "Oh Maybellene, why can't you be true?" In 1968, Marvin Gaye "heard it through the grapevine" that his woman was cheating on him. In 1972, Bill Withers asked the question, "Who is he and what is he to you?" And in 1985, Stevie Wonder sang about "part-time lovers."

We can learn a lot about the way we see ourselves as a people by taking a look at our popular culture. To the extent that popular music reflects our real-life concerns, we learn about the down low by looking back at the music of various periods in our history. In many ways, music has provided a virtual soundtrack for our lives, where art imitates reality imitating art. Music survives when the public consumes it, and the public consumes what they think is real, which is based, in part, on perceptions that are reinforced by what they hear from their music. Music helps us to realize that the down low is not just about supposedly straight men sleeping with other men. Instead, as we see through our music, the down low is also about men and women cheating on each other. It's about finding outlets to satisfy our needs when our partners cannot or will not do that for us. It's about men sleeping with women, women sleeping with men, men sleeping with men, and women sleeping with women. It's about infidelity and trust, victimhood and blame, and the difference between life as we would like it to be and life as it really is.

Despite the recent narrative of the down low that assumes a male perpetrator and a female victim, the musical history of infidelity—like its real life counterpart—cannot be reduced to simple equations where male equals bad and female equals good. In fact, the complex discography of the down low is filled with examples of men as both victims and participants in illicit affairs. A lonesome Hank Williams warned his ex-lover "your cheating heart will tell on you" in a 1952 song. The Eagles cautioned a young girl, "You can't hide your lyin' eyes" in 1975. Prince asked his woman "What's it gonna be? Is it him or is it me?" in his 1984 song "The Beautiful Ones." In each song, the man is portrayed as the victim of the woman's cheating.

Men, of course, have played the perpetrator role as well. The Doors' lead singer Jim Morrison bragged that he was the "Back Door Man" in a 1967 song of the same name. The back door man was the guy who had sex with another man's wife while the husband was away. Twenty years later, Bobby Womack sang "I Wish He Didn't Trust Me So Much," a song about a man who wants to sleep with his best friend's wife. And in 2000, the reggae recording artist Shaggy counsels a cheating friend "never to admit to a word that she say" in his song "It Wasn't Me." Even when his friend's girlfriend catches him naked with another woman, Shaggy tells him to deny it.

It's not always easy to determine who to blame. Like men, women have also played dual roles in the discourse of the down low. In some examples, women were not only active participants but actually initiated the affairs they had. Bessie Smith, for example, plays the role of a moneygrubbing, love-hungry woman who threatens her man in the 1923 song "If You Don't, I Know Who Will." Portraying herself as both victim and perpetrator, she warns her man that her "other papa" will take care of her if her needs are not met. The country singer Loretta Lynn plays the same dual role as victim and perpetrator in her 1971 song "Another Man Loved Me Last Night." Although Lynn expresses some remorse for her betrayal, she seems to justify her actions because "not being loved" was more than she could take. In contrast, Meshell Ndegeocello unapologetically flaunts her success in stealing somebody else's man in her 1992 breakthrough song "If That's Your Boyfriend (He Wasn't Last Night)." In a schoolyard-style chant, Ndegeocello sings, "Boyfriend, boyfriend, yes I had your boyfriend" and boasts that she's "the kind of woman [to] do almost anything to get what I want."

Women are often portrayed somewhat sympathetically in songs about cheating, but Bessie Smith, Loretta Lynn, and Meshell Ndegeocello provide a different and more complicated image of the woman as an empowered figure making her own choices about fidelity. Perhaps it's significant that a white country music singer and two black bisexual women could present such an image, while many other black women recording artists seem to shy away from such depictions.

One of the lies we tell ourselves about the down low is that women are only the innocent victims of men on the down low. Even when women are the coconspirators in a man's infidelity, we sometimes think of them with sympathy. In many of the popular R&B songs where women sing about their participation in an affair, the women portray themselves as lonely mistresses waiting for their men to come back to them. Gladys Knight plays the role of mistress in the 1970 song "If I Were Your Woman," where she justifies her affair with a married man because the man's wife does not treat him well. Like so many other deluded mistresses, she imagines that the man's cheating would somehow stop if she were his woman. "If I were your woman and you were my man, you'd have no other woman," she sings.

"A few stolen moments" is all that Whitney Houston shares with her fictional man in the 1985 song "Saving All My Love For You." True to the traditional story line, she complains that "it's not very easy living all alone," and she remembers the days when her man told her they'd run away together. Houston's song positions her in the classic victim-as-participant role, a common template through which our society understands women in extramarital affairs. It's no accident, for example, that the guilty female murderers in the musical "Chicago" reflexively revert to the victim-as-participant position in their "Cell Block Tango." When one of their soon-to-be victims comes home and accuses his wife of "screwing the milkman," rather than address his accusation, the wife responds by stabbing him nine times. Nevertheless, she claims "he had it coming," that he deserved his fate, and through the lens of politically correct preconceived notions about gender, the calculated appeal to victimhood may have been perfectly timed. After all, the woman is often seen as a victim, whether it's from domestic abuse, infidelity, or even from previously latent effects of child abuse. It may be true that all criminals can be seen as victims of their environment, but men are rarely afforded the same presumption of victimhood that is sometimes conferred upon women. There is no need to explore the male inner psyche when we have already concluded that "men are dogs."

The truth is that being involved in an extramarital affair can be emotionally stressful for both men and women on both sides of the relationship. Sometimes, the pressure of being "the other woman" can be too much to bear, as Stephanie Mills discovers in her 1987 song "Secret Lady." After struggling in a role behind the scenes, she finally breaks down and announces, "I just can't go on being your secret lady, mystery baby," a chorus that is repeated until the end, as Mills becomes more and more defiant. In contrast, one of the most amusing examples of the victim role comes from Candi Staton's 1978 disco tune appropriately called "Victim," where the woman who counsels other women not to fall in love finds herself in a relationship with a cheating man. As Staton explains, "I'm a victim of the very song I sing."

One of the problems with the caricature of women solely in the victim role is that such roles ignore the obvious inconsistency of typecasting both the wife and the mistress as victims. If the wife is a victim, shouldn't the mistress be a perpetrator or at least a coconspirator with the husband? Instead, the mistress is usually viewed as a coconspirator if the story is told from the wife's perspective, but even then it's not always a critical depiction of the other woman. In "Clean Up Woman," for example, the R&B singer Betty Wright realizes that her own indifference to her man may have "made it easy" for another woman to get him. Still, it's more of a warning to married women than a criticism of the other woman. Similarly, in "All The Way

Lover," the raunchy recording artist Millie Jackson chides married women for their general inattentiveness to their men and warns them that some other woman might come and "steal your man." But even in that song, the other woman is portrayed more as an opportunist than as a predator. Perhaps no song depicts the rival mistress as more sympathetic and complex than Nina Simone's "The Other Woman." Although "the other woman" has time to manicure her nails and do her hair, she's still lonesome most of the time, crying herself to sleep because she "will never have his love to keep" and "will spend her life alone." In other words, she is to be pitied, not condemned.

The image of the sympathetic female culprit is not universal in contemporary pop culture. Compare those earlier songs with Shirley Brown's 1975 single "Woman to Woman." Brown picks up the phone and calls the other woman, Barbara, and tells her, "The man you're in love with, he's mine." In a calm, respectful tone, she appeals to Barbara's sense of dignity as a woman. "If you were in my shoes," Brown asks, "wouldn't you have done the same thing too?" More recent music has taken the woman-to-woman concept and applied it to dramatic face-to-face scenes in music videos such as "Gettin' In The Way," where Jill Scott marches over to the other woman's house, rolls her neck and pulls off the woman's wig. Confrontation is also a major element in musical duets such as Brandy and Monica's 1998 hit song "The Boy Is Mine" or Whitney Houston's duo with Deborah Cox, "Same Script, Different Cast." By presenting both the wife figure (or girlfriend) and the mistress, those songs break new ground by acknowledging the conflict between the two, and yet at some level the listener is left conflicted because the women are arguing over an apparently unfaithful man.

Only a few moments in life compare to the drama involved when a woman confronts her man about his infidelity. It happens every day in real life, and it's often reflected in our popular culture.

Whitney Houston tells her man "My Name Is Not Susan" when she hears him call out the other woman's name in his sleep in her 1990 song. Toni Braxton struggles with what to do in a similar situation when she catches her husband mentioning the other woman in her 1996 song "Talking In His Sleep." Meanwhile, the members of the female musical group Destiny's Child develop a creative way to find out if a man is lying when he's on the phone. "Say My Name," they say in their 1999 song. "If no one is around you, say baby I love you, if you ain't running game."

Some of the most striking scenes about cheating are viewed not from the perspective of the victim but from the viewpoint of the cheaters themselves. In the 1972 song, "Me and Mrs. Jones," Billy Paul seems almost tearful as he sings of his "thing going on" with his married mistress. Back then, artists sang euphemistically about their other "obligations" as an indication that they were already involved in other relationships. The same "obligations" language comes up in The Manhattans' 1976 classic "Kiss and Say Goodbye," where a man meets with his lover at their usual rendezvous to break off their down low relationship. Knowing that the two can never meet again, the man calls it "the saddest day of my life." The same sense of sorrow hangs over Shirley Murdock's 1985 song "As We Lay," as she and a married man wake up to the consequences of a one-night stand.

While some of us were busy making amends for our infidelity and moving forward, Luther Ingram took issue with that view of morality in his 1972 classic "(If Loving You Is Wrong) I Don't Wanna Be Right." Even with a wife and two kids at home, Ingram sings about holding on to his lover, whom he calls "the best thing I ever had." But one of the most memorable examples of cheaters singing about their relationship comes from the tune "Secret Lovers," recorded by Atlantic Starr in 1986. As in earlier songs, the cheating man and the cheating woman are both married to other people, but in this song the cheaters come together to sing to each other. In one verse, the man acknowledges the difficulty of "living two lives" after he sings:

> How could something so wrong be so right
> I wish we didn't have to keep our love out of sight.

Unlike so many other songs about cheating, the "secret lover" songs acknowledge the reality that it takes two people to cheat. The man and the woman are both involved.

We know that many women find it embarrassing when a man is cheating on them. Imagine the response, then, when men discover that a woman is cheating on them. The reaction to being cheated on (or played) begins to change with the increased machismo of modern times, as men feel the need to assert their dominance against newly liberated women. The passive response of Hank Williams, Chuck Berry, and Marvin Gaye started to be replaced by a more vengeful retaliation in the 1980s. Early hip hop music provides an example. At first, hip hop seemed to follow the pattern of its musical predecessors. "If your woman steps out with another man," said Kurtis Blow, "and she runs off with him to Japan," all you were expected to do is "clap your hands" and go dancing because, hey, "these are the breaks." By 1986, however, Oran "Juice" Jones catches his woman "walking in the rain" and "holding hands" with another man and waits till she gets back home to confront her. In the modern male reinterpretation of responding to female infidelity, the cuckold has been taught to respond strategically but forcefully. If he responds with violence, he could end up in jail for abuse, but if he does nothing, he risks looking weak. In this song, Jones's character says he chose not to be violent because he did not want to mess up his $3,700 lynx coat, so instead he goes to the bank, closes her account, cancels her credit cards, and packs her belongings in the guest room, all in an effort to teach her "a valuable lesson." Similarly, in Justin Timberlake's 2002 song "Cry Me a River," Timberlake cuts off his relationship with his cheating girlfriend and plots his revenge against her. "The damage is done so I guess I'll be leaving," the background vocalist sings.

Vengeance works for women too, as we see in Blu Cantrell's 2001 song, "Hit 'Em Up Style (Oops!)," where the woman exacts her revenge by taking her man's credit card on an expensive shopping spree at Neiman Marcus. Angela Bassett follows a more destructive path in the 1995 film *Waiting To Exhale,* based on the novel by Terry McMillan, when she burns her husband's expensive suits in his BMW after she discovers his infidelity. In the accompanying song from the soundtrack, Mary J. Blige promises she's "Not Gon' Cry." Today, it's not unusual to find women who are defiant to unfaithful men. Whitney Houston sang "It's not right, but it's okay" in 1998 as she told her man to pack his bags and leave. In the 2002 hit "Heard It All Before," Sunshine Anderson explained, "Your lies ain't working now" and told her man, "I had to shut you down."

In Carl Thomas's 2000 song "I Wish," one of the most memorable songs about the down low, he tells the story of a deceptive woman. Thomas sings about meeting her, falling in love and spending long days and nights together until one day she tells him that she's married with children. She goes back to her life, while he is left alone and devastated. She's just another woman on the down low.

With all the popular musical references to heterosexuals on the down low, there are considerably fewer songs about homosexuals and bisexuals on the down low. Nevertheless, those references exist too. In 1984, long before the current down low sensation, Barbara Mason released the song "Another Man (Is Beating My Time)," which was a follow-up to a seemingly endless stream of spin-off songs from an earlier tune called "She's Got Papers On Me." But unlike most songs from the perspective of women as victims of cheating, this song actually challenged the man's masculinity. "There was a little too much sugar and you were a little too sweet," Mason sings. Mason also sings of her suspicion that her man borrowed her new dress, she says she saw him "switching" his hips on the steps, and she caught him holding hands with another man. Like many other women who are challenged by homosexuality, Mason describes her man as "a waste," presumably because she believes he cannot fulfill her needs. She thought she had a real man, she says, but instead she had "a facsimile thereof," whose sexual orientation she sees as a "defect" or as evidence that "something went wrong" after he was created.

The scandalous gay song of the nineties was a simple blues tune called "Bill" by Peggy Scott-Adams, where she catches her husband in the arms of another man named Bill and sees them "breathing hard and french-kissing." Describing the pain involved, she sings:

> I was ready for Mary
> Susan, Helen and Jane
> When all the time it was Bill
> That was sleeping with my man.

Her sense of betrayal is directed not only at her husband, but at Bill, who she said was a friend and a god uncle to her son. Then in a particularly demeaning reference to her former friend, she says, "Now it looks like Uncle Billy wants to be his step mom." Her song, like Barbara Mason's before it, is filled with outdated stereotypes about flamboyant homosexuals, but she does raise one very provocative question that vexes other women in her position. In broken English, she asks, "How do a woman compete with a man for another man?" She seems genuinely interested in learning more about bisexuality, but her curiosity is clouded by her prejudice. When she asks her husband why he did not tell her that he was gay, he explains his hope that being with a woman "would change me." Fortunately, she says she does not feel ashamed and does not take the blame, but she does place blame on her man, whom she describes as "just a queen . . . that thought he was a king."

It seems the absence of visible black openly gay recording artists has left a one-dimensional image in the black community's musical depiction of male homosexuality. Since Sylvester kicked down the music industry's closet door with his 1978 hit "You Make Me Feel (Mighty Real)," most black gay recording artists—like their white gay counterparts—have labored in obscurity or hidden in the closet. The black gay performer Carl Bean, who later founded the Unity Fellowship Church, created what some called a "gay national anthem" with his 1985 recording of "I Was Born This Way." In the 1980s, the once and future Prince was confusing everybody with questions about his sexuality. Before Prince, the rock 'n' roll legend Little Richard had generated speculation for years about his sexual orientation. It was always easier to dodge the issue than to confront it directly. Those who have been openly gay have rarely met with the same public success as those who have dwelled in the closet. When the R&B recording artist Tevin Campbell was arrested in 1999 for soliciting a male prostitute, his career was ruined. On the other hand, recent "homo hop" artists like Tori Fixx, Tim'M West, Rainbow Flava, and DeepDickCollective have become legendary in the underground scene but have not been introduced to the public at large. The drag queen RuPaul seemed to open up new possibilities with her early 1990s anthem "Supermodel (You Better Work)," but her visibility, without other balancing images, merely confirmed popular beliefs that gay men wanted to be women.

Among today's major figures in the industry, Meshell Ndegeocello stands alone as an openly bisexual black recording artist, and much of her music explores the complexity of sexual identity. When Ndegeocello remade Bill Withers's classic "Who Is He (And What Is He to You)," she complicated the formula of the song without changing a word. When Withers had asked the question in the title of the song, it seemed clear he was asking his woman about a man they had just passed on the street. But when Ndegeocello sang the exact same verse, it automatically introduced a homosexual relationship into the picture. If she was asking the question to her man in the traditional heterosexual equation, then the man must have been involved with the other man who was walking down the street. In order to make that illicit relationship into a heterosexual affair, Ndegeocello's partner would have to be a woman, meaning that Ndegeocello was in a homosexual relationship. Either way, whether it's two men or two women, somebody was sleeping with someone else of the same gender.

Ndegeocello introduced another form of sexual nuance in her 2002 song "Berry Farms." In front of a slow go-go beat, she raps about an ex-girlfriend who "liked to flirt with me, and act like she didn't know me when her friends came around." After people begin to wonder about their relationship, the girl stops talking to her and starts dating a man. Then one day the ex-girlfriend spots Ndegeocello, approaches her and confesses that she misses her. Oh really, Ndegeocello asks, "What do you miss?" The ex-girlfriend replies in a whisper: "Can't nobody eat my pussy the way that you do."

Meshell Ndegeocello is not impressed by the obvious attempt at flattery, and she knows exactly what is going on—her ex-girlfriend is on the down low. As Meshell explains in the chorus to the song:

She couldn't love me without shame
She only wanted me for one thing
But you can teach your boy to do that.

Ndegeocello's music tells us that men are not the only ones who have been having secret same-gender relationships without telling their opposite-sex partners. Just as there have been men who have sex with men but do not identify as gay, there have also been women who have sex with women but do not identify as lesbian. These women rarely get talked about in the recent media hype about the down low, but they have been discussed from time to time in music. In Michael Coleman's 1987 blues song "Woman Loves a Woman," he confesses that he's in love with a woman, and then he drops the catch line: "She's in love with a woman too." Listeners to the blues have always known the real deal. Even as far back as the 1930s, "the blues reflected a culture that accepted sexuality, including homosexual behavior and identities, as a natural part of life," according to the historian Eric Garber in an essay called *A Spectacle in Color: The Lesbian and Gay Subculture of Jazz Age Harlem*. While the mainstream media were documenting an official company line about America, the blues became the real paper of record that told us who we were, not just who we wanted to be. Thank goodness for the blues.

In the end, the down low in popular culture is almost as complicated as the down low in real life. There are women on the down low as well as men. They are black and white, straight, gay, and bisexual. Film makers, authors, song writers, and recording artists have romanticized, scandalized, and fantasized about it. And whether they called it cheating, creeping, O.P.P. or something else, it's the same old song that's been playing for generations. As we see from our culture, we've heard it all before. We just weren't listening.

Chapter 4
It's Not Just a Black Thing

I MET YVONNE in my first year of law school. She was almost everything I thought I wanted in a woman: attractive, intelligent, articulate, spiritual, and physically fit. She didn't drink too much. And she didn't smoke cigarettes. She was a modern woman. She would have made a perfect wife. A perfect wife for someone else, that is. When Yvonne and I started dating, we were at a difficult point in our lives, trying to sort our way through the maze of the first year of law school. Harvard was a whole new world for both of us, and we were each looking for ways to bring stability to the otherwise chaotic experience.

Before I started Harvard, everyone had told me not to worry about dating. Those who had been through law school warned that I would have little time to do anything but study. Law school, they told me, was not at all like college. In most college courses, professors give you midterms, final exams, and papers to write. In law school, however, your entire course grade is based on a single exam you take at the end of the semester. If you're not prepared or if you have a bad day, three months of course work can go down the drain in a three-hour exam. In order to do well, you have to keep up with the reading, attend classes, and form study groups. Several people advised me to do *nothing* but study. I listened carefully to what they said, but I could not follow their advice. I knew I would go crazy if I spent three years of my life in the library. That has never been my style.

I thought I would function well in school if I followed the same strategies that had worked for me in college. That meant trying to maintain balance in my life, which I found by going to the gym, hanging out with friends, joining organizations, and dating Yvonne. Yvonne and I had a wholesome relationship. We went out to dinner, spent time at each other's apartments, and went to church from time to time. One Sunday after church, however, I made an important and dramatic discovery about our relationship. I realized I was not in love with Yvonne.

The streets were bustling with activity as Yvonne and I walked down Massachusetts Avenue from St. Paul's A.M.E. Church to the subway stop at Central Square. Yvonne reached out to grab my hand while we walked. I recoiled for a split second and then returned my hand back to hers. I had hoped she had not noticed my reaction but the gesture was far too obvious for her to miss. She waited a few seconds as we walked and then turned to me with a smile and called me on it. "You don't like holding my hand, do you?" I smiled back, trying to think of what to say, so I asked a dumb question in response. "Why do you say that?" Yvonne knew I was stalling. "You just pulled your hand away from mine," she said. Seconds had passed, and I still hadn't thought of what to say. To be honest, I did not know what to say. I did not know why I had pulled my hand away from hers. I knew I liked her, and I was not the least bit ashamed to be seen with her. But I guess, deep down, something told me not to hold her hand at that moment. Something about the intimacy felt fake.

"I'm not a very touchy-feely person," I told her. That was true. My family was never physically expressive, and I guess I had picked up their behavior. I had dated a couple of girls in high school and one woman in college, and I don't recall ever really holding hands with any of them. Yvonne seemed to accept that explanation, but I knew she suspected there was more to it than I was telling her. She was very perceptive, and she was right. Yvonne could see things about me that I was unwilling to see, and shortly after that day our relationship began to fizzle out. We stopped talking as much, then we stopped hanging out, and soon we just stopped dating.

A few months after Yvonne and I broke up, I started to feel burned out from school and life. I felt as though I had been on a treadmill from grade school to junior high to high school to college to law school, and I was exhausted. Like the unnamed protagonist in Ellison's *Invisible Man,* I had been running all my life from one task to the next, and suddenly it had all caught up to me. I was tired of going to school, tired of being involved in extracurriculars, and tired of living my life in confusion about my identity.

In the spring of my second year of law school, I decided to resign from my position as an editor of the *Civil Rights–Civil Liberties Law Review,* and I withdrew from my role as a spokesman for the campus Coalition for Civil Rights. For the first time in my life, I was pulling back from the activities that had defined my existence. I realized suddenly that my whole identity had been wrapped up in my work and not in my relationships. My work had become my life, and my life had become my work. Then one day, I decided to step off the treadmill and live, and that was the day I realized I had been living a lie. I had never lied to my girlfriends. I had never lied to my friends or my family. I had not lied to the rest of the world. Instead, most tragically, I had lied to myself.

In April of 1991, I finally stopped lying to myself and acknowledged the sexual orientation I had tried to repress my entire life. I called my mom and came out to her, and the next day I told a friend on campus. Coming out to my family and friends was liberating and frightening at the same time. It felt good to finally speak the words, "I'm gay," but it was difficult to repeat the monologue over and over again with each person I told.

That's why I decided not to tell everyone. I realized it would be easier to *be* out than to come out, and I quickly discovered one of the first rules of coming out. That is, if you tell the right people, you don't have to tell everyone else. It worked. Within days of coming out to a few friends at school, it seemed as if everyone on campus knew I was gay. One of my professors even asked me about it. "I heard you came out recently," he said. "Yes," I replied, "but how did you hear about it?" His response shocked me. "One of the other professors told me," he said. It was an unusual admission of academic gossip. For a long time, I had labored under the delusion that professors at Harvard Law School had more important things to do with their time than to speculate on the sexual orientation of their students, but apparently I was wrong. It was fitting irony, especially since many of my classmates had spent our time speculating on the sexual orientation of our professors.

Except for a few close friends I spoke to directly, everyone on campus found out through the grapevine that I was gay. Everyone, including Yvonne. She and I had almost stopped talking by that time. We would see each other in passing and speak to each other briefly, but we had not hung out since the day we broke up months earlier. I heard from a friend that Yvonne felt betrayed when she found out I was gay. I never spoke to her about it, and she never asked me, but I imagine she felt a sense of awkwardness in being the last person to date me before I came out of the closet.

It took me thirteen years to understand exactly what Yvonne

must have felt. That was the day when I realized the real meaning of the down low. I was visiting my family in Chicago one day when my friend Maurice called on the cell phone. "Are you watching TV?" he said. It was the middle of the day, so I had no reason to be watching television. But the urgency of the question suggested that something was happening that was important enough to be broadcast live on several different networks. Immediately, my mind sped back to September 11, and I remembered the call I got early that morning. "Are you watching television?" a friend had asked that day as well. What could it be this time? Another terrorist attack in Manhattan? Had the White House been attacked? Could it be another hijacking? A thousand different thoughts raced through my head before I could answer the question. I fumbled for the remote and clicked on the television as I asked what happened. I could see the image slowly brighten on the screen as Maurice spoke. "Governor McGreevey is holding a press conference," he said. "I think he's going to announce that he's gay."

It was hard to believe at first, but here was the governor of New Jersey holding a press conference that was being televised on MSNBC. I switched to CNN and to other networks, and there he was again on almost every channel. "He hasn't said it yet, but I can just feel it," Maurice told me. "He said something about grappling with his identity since he was a child. And he talked about having some 'feelings' that made him different from the other kids. I really think he's gonna come out," Maurice said. I was still doubtful—no governor of any state had ever come out before—but I could not deny the obvious code language in the words Maurice had quoted to me. Separated by thousands of miles, Maurice and I watched the television together in stunned silence as McGreevey finally reached the climax of his speech. "At a point in every person's life, one has to look deeply into the mirror of one's soul and decide one's unique truth in the world, not as we may want to see it or hope to see it, but as it is. And so my truth is that I am a gay American."

I was shocked. I had never seen or heard anything like this before. It all seemed surreal. Flanked by his parents and his wife, the governor of the ninth-largest state in America had just told the world that he had been living a lie. He had been married once before to a woman named Kari. They had a daughter together and then, as McGreevey delicately put it, Kari "chose to return to British Columbia." After their divorce, McGreevey married Dina Matos, and the new couple had a daughter as well. It was a perfect rebound. From the outside looking in, they were an ideal family. On the inside, known perhaps to no one but James McGreevey himself, there was a secret that could ruin everything.

Like many observers of the scene, I tried to stare into the soul of Dina McGreevey as her husband made his announcement. I wondered if her eyes would betray her disappointment, or if she would reveal an inner peace that suggested she had known all along. Was this an arranged marriage, a marriage of convenience, a marriage of love, or perhaps some combination of all of the above? I could not tell. In the end, it was not important for me to know. It was a matter between the two of them, and Dina McGreevey appropriately kept it that way. Nevertheless, I wondered what it must have felt like to stand there while her husband told the media that their marriage was not what it appeared.

Then I remembered Yvonne. It was not the same thing, of course. Yvonne and I had never gotten even close to marriage. But the public nature of my own decision to come out made me realize how hurtful it might have been to Yvonne. Fortunately, I did not come out in the middle of a scandal, but I did come out in a very public setting. I had been a leader in the movement for faculty diversity at Harvard, and I had been quoted frequently in the newspapers. I took part in student sit-ins, vigils, and other protests to register our support for women and minorities to be hired as professors. We had occupied the dean's office, taken over the administration building, marched to the president's office, and demonstrated outside faculty meetings. But my claim to fame was as one of several students who filed a lawsuit against Harvard for discriminating in the hiring of its faculty. We lost the lawsuit but won the war to bring national attention to the issue. I was quoted in newspapers around the country talking about the issue, and my picture showed up more than once in the *Boston Globe*. A few weeks after I came out, I gave a speech on campus at an outdoor rally where I announced that I was speaking as a "black gay student." Anyone on campus who had not known by that time surely knew then. Some of those watching the speech might have thought I was still dating Yvonne, and that, I'm sure, only made matters worse.

For a long time, I felt guilty about coming out so publicly, but slowly I realized that I had to be true to myself. Truth was the common element here. Yvonne had to be true to herself as well. No doubt, dating someone who turns out to be gay, lesbian, or bisexual can produce feelings of self-doubt and guilt. "Did I do this? Did I cause this person to be gay? Was there something I could have done?" Those are the questions that are sometimes expressed but more often simply held inside. Women who have been involved in relationships with men who are gay or bisexual must negotiate their way through a complex series of issues that often reach the core of their own sense of identity. SaraKay Smullens, a family therapist, explained more about the challenges involved in a column in the *Philadelphia Daily News* shortly after McGreevey came out. Smullens, who has worked with a number of women who have been married to gay men, said the names used to describe these women ("cover girls" or "beards," for example) are "cruel and humiliating." Women who are attracted to gay men are described as having "the curse of the pink wand" and those who have gay male friends are often called "fag hags," she explained. Smullens tells us that women in these situations go through a range of emotions in deciding whether to continue in their relationships, and all of us could be a little more understanding.

Governor McGreevey's wife must have been going through a full range of emotions the day she stood next to her husband at his press conference. The governor's disclosure of his sexual orientation was not the end of the issue. McGreevey also admitted to "an adult consensual affair with another man," which he said "violates my bonds of matrimony." That was the real bombshell McGreevey dropped that day. Many of us were already surprised to hear him announce that he was gay, but we were more shocked to learn that he had carried on an affair. Yes, the governor of New Jersey was on the down low.

By announcing his affair with another man, Governor McGreevey immediately provided a clear example of the reach of the down low. He was young, attractive, masculine, successful, powerful, and married with children. And he was white. With one stunning example, McGreevey proved that the down low is not just a black thing.

In hindsight, we should not have been surprised. Surely, we must have known that white men lived on the down low as well. We should have known that black men were not the only ones who cheated on their wives. Or had we bought into the myth of black male identity that constructs black manhood solely as pathology? Did we really believe that black men were the only ones?

James McGreevey provides an ideal example of the white down low, but he is only an example. He is not the only white man on the down low. He is not even the only white politician on the down low. He is just one who got caught, in public. We perpetuate a lie to ourselves if we believe that McGreevey is simply a rare exception. White men on the down low are everywhere. They are professional athletes, famous entertainers, powerful businessmen, and influential elected officials. More important, they are our coworkers, neighbors, and friends. Perhaps what makes the McGreevey case stand out is that it seems so new and different. When was the last time a prominent married politician came out and announced that he was not heterosexual? Well, actually, it was just a few years before.

With degrees from Stanford and Harvard and a career as vice-chairman of his family-owned energy business, Michael Huffington seemed to be on the rise when he decided to run for Congress as a conservative Republican in the early 1990s. He had a prominent wife, Arianna, and he had already accumulated impressive experience in federal government when he served as a deputy assistant secretary of defense in the Reagan administration. After spending $5 million on his campaign, it was not a surprise when Huffington was elected to Congress from California's Twenty-second District in November 1992. But Huffington was not finished. He had not even completed his first term in the House of Representatives when he agreed to run for the U.S. Senate, a race in which he spent $28 million of his personal wealth to try to beat Dianne Feinstein. In what was then the most expensive nonpresidential election in American history, Huffington lost by less than 1.6 percent of the vote. Afterward, his career in politics survived, but he could not shake the personal demons that haunted him about his sexuality. Finally, in 1998, Huffington came out of the closet. In an interview with David Brock in *Esquire* magazine, Huffington explained that he once had homosexual feelings years earlier but had renounced them after watching a critical discussion about homosexuality on Pat Robertson's *700 Club* television show. So the path he decided to follow at the time was one of self-deception. "I am straight. I will get married. I will have children. I will never sleep with another man again," Huffington told himself.

But no matter how hard he tried over the years, he could not deny the truth inside of him. Huffington had been living on the down low.

And then there is the case of Edward Schrock, an investment broker, retired Navy officer, Vietnam veteran, and loyal family man who was married with one son. Schrock was born and raised in Middletown, Ohio, and married a school teacher from Long Beach, California. The couple settled in Virginia Beach and became active members of the Atlantic Shores Baptist Church. After a few years in Virginia politics, Schrock decided to run for Congress. Elected in 2000, he was chosen to be the chairman of the Republican Freshman Class and quickly became one of the most conservative members in the U.S. House of Representatives. He cosponsored the Federal Marriage Amendment, which would have amended the U.S. Constitution to prohibit same-sex marriage, and he sought to block gays and lesbians from entering the military. From all outward appearances, he was a classic social conservative. But others had doubts about his personal life. When a Web site called Blogactive.com released an audio recording of what it said was Schrock calling into a gay telephone sex line, the congressman never admitted his behavior. Instead, Schrock announced he was leaving the Congress and would not seek reelection.

It happens outside the world of politics too. The entertainment industry is filled with stories of white men and women on the down low. One of the most famous relationships of the 1970s involved a pop recording star and a music mogul on the down low. It was September 1973, and Neil Young was headlining at the opening night of the Roxy nightclub, a new Los Angeles spot on Sunset Boulevard. David Geffen, the owner of the new club, had made a name for himself by working with some of the top talent in the music industry and had recently sold his new music company, Asylum Records. On the opening night at the Roxy, Geffen met Cher. They seemed to like each other, and the two soon started dating. While

Cher waited for her divorce from her husband and business partner, Sonny Bono, she and Geffen became a Hollywood item and reportedly planned to get married. But Cher abruptly called it off in early 1974 and decided against the marriage. Geffen, meanwhile, kept his reputation as a ladies' man, dating Marlo Thomas and other women over the years. By the early 1990s, however, Geffen's homosexuality had become an open secret, and Geffen had been a very generous contributor to numerous ostensibly gay-related AIDS causes over the years. In 1990, he sold his company, Geffen Records, to MCA and became a billionaire. Then in November 1992, Geffen said the words that shocked the industry. He publicly came out of the closet in a speech at AIDS Project Los Angeles. David Geffen had been on the down low.

Like Geffen, many of Hollywood's leading men were also on the down low. None was more famous than Roy Harold Scherer, Jr., of Winnetka, Illinois. Scherer moved to Hollywood to become an actor, and his agent, Henry Willson, promptly renamed him. It was to be one of many contrivances to advance his career. When rumors circulated that Scherer was homosexual, Willson quickly arranged for Scherer to marry Phyllis Gates, Willson's secretary. The marriage lasted three years, but it may have salvaged Scherer's career. Scherer, known publicly as Rock Hudson, became even more successful the following year when he played opposite Doris Day in the film *Pillow Talk*. For decades, Rock Hudson (Roy Scherer) became the veritable embodiment of heterosexual masculinity. Men wanted to be him, and women wanted to be with him. But like so many other Hollywood celebrities, his life was a lie. While he played the role of the heterosexual playboy on screen, he was a closeted homosexual off screen. When Hudson died of AIDS-related complications in October 1985, his lover, Marc Christian, successfully sued his estate because Hudson had not informed him of his HIV status. Hudson had been married to a woman and maintained his heterosexuality, but he slept with men, and he was HIV positive. Even by today's definitions, Rock Hudson might be a poster boy for the down low. Except for one inconvenient fact. Rock Hudson was white.

When black men become involved in fake relationships, we process the issue by ascribing negative characteristics to an entire group of people, and we tend to think in global terms concerning the breakdown of the black family and other such nonsense. When white men become involved in fake relationships, we simply call it what it is and move on. We don't make sweeping generalizations about all white men, and we don't try to study the pathology of their behavior.

When Peter Allen married Liza Minnelli in 1967 or Elton John married Renate Blauel in 1984, there was no public outcry about celebrity men on the down low. But when ordinary black men marry ordinary black women under similar circumstances, suddenly we are told we have a crisis in the black community. Black men are dishonest, irresponsible liars, cheaters, pimps, and thugs—if you believe the rhetoric. But similarly situated white men are just white men, and they are relieved of the unrealistic burden of bearing the responsibility for an entire race.

We should have known decades ago that white men were doing the same things that black men were doing. It never made sense to assume otherwise. Remember the story in the 1982 film *Making Love*? The relationship between a happily married heterosexual couple (Kate Jackson and Michael Ontkean) begins to unravel when the husband comes to terms with his homosexuality and falls in love with another man (Harry Hamlin). That was a warning sign that white men were also on the down low.

In fact, we knew the truth all along. For years, both black and white America convinced each other that homosexuality was merely a "white thing." When the gay rights movement grew in the 1970s, we pretended that it only concerned the rights of white gays and lesbians, and we continued to deny the existence of lesbian, gay, bisexual, and transgendered people of color. Then, as white gays and lesbians emerged as public figures, we assumed that black openly gay and bisexual public figures would never emerge because homophobia was too widespread among blacks, as if homophobia did not exist in the rest of America.

The truth is, we created this lie, and now we have to find our way out of it. Homosexuality, like homophobia, is widespread in the black community and in the white community. White men do not live in a parallel universe where homosexuality is widely accepted. They live in the same country as everyone else—a country where no federal law prohibits workplace discrimination against gays and lesbians and where a president of the United States has tried to write antigay discrimination into the U.S. Constitution. White men make many of the same compromises and false choices that black men do, and because they tend to have access to power and opportunity that elude most blacks, they may have more to lose by coming out. White men are on the down low just like black men, and since we live in a country with far more white men than black men, it stands to reason that there are far more white men on the down low than black men. They, too, are secretly sleeping with men while they plan their lives with their wives. Some of them may even bring home sexually transmitted diseases to their unsuspecting partners. But if more white men are doing it than black men, where is the outcry about white men on the down low? And why aren't more white women being infected with HIV from these white men on the down low? How do we reconcile the black infection rates with the white infection rates? Those questions never even get asked. Instead, we find it much easier to continue using a racial typecast that confirms our preconceived beliefs about black male guilt.

I know what it feels like to live with the burden of proof always resting on your shoulders. Ever since the day I was fired at Sears, I have carried that burden. I do not claim to be perfect, and I am not always innocent. But I do believe that those who make scurrilous accusations against black men bear the burden to prove their assertions with facts. Instead, what we usually get is the same old tired circumstantial case built on the same old racial stereotypes.

We know this much. The down low is not just a black thing. We have packaged it as such because it provides a simple and convenient mechanism to understand a complex issue. But for every black man on the down low, there is a Jim McGreevey, a Michael Huffington, a David Geffen, a Rock Hudson, or a no-name white man who is also on the down low. So we are left with this possibility to consider. If the white down low is not leading to a new outbreak of AIDS in the white community, then maybe, just maybe, the black down low is not responsible for the spread of AIDS in the black community either.

CHAPTER 5
When a Disease Becomes an Excuse

BY CHANCE OR fate, I found myself in the thick of the down low story when it first broke in the media in 2001. I had little interest in exploring the story at the time, but the universe had other plans for me. I had known, or come to know, all the major players involved in the story—the reporters, the advocates, and the critics. I knew Linda Villarosa, the reporter for the *New York Times* who wrote about the down low in the most influential paper in America. I knew Phill Wilson, the founder of the Black AIDS Institute who introduced the down low at a mainstream black AIDS conference. And that was the year I met J. L. King, the chief advocate and poster boy for the down low. It was not my intention to be involved in this story, but it happened. On the day when the story first developed, I was there.

Linda Villarosa's presence was striking. A thin, fair-skinned woman with long curly hair, she radiated energy and charisma. I met her at a writers' conference in Boston in March 1995. She was executive editor of *Essence* magazine and had recently published a book about black women's health, but her real claim to fame was from an *Essence* article she had written in May 1991. In that article, Linda, with her mother Clara by her side, told the world that she was a lesbian. It was the first time that any prominent black woman had come out so publicly, and it happened on the cover of the nation's leading black women's magazine. Linda quickly became a lightning rod for attention, provoking hate mail and angry phone calls from detractors and enormous praise and encouragement from supporters. Personally, I was impressed that *Essence* would even publish an article about a black woman coming out, and more impressed that the subject of the article was an editor at *Essence* as well.

Essence was also breaking down barriers about black women and AIDS. A few months before I met Linda, and years before the current down low hype, *Essence* had published a dramatic cover story of a heterosexual black woman with AIDS. Her name was Rae Lewis-Thornton, and she was a well-educated, drug-free, thirty-two-year-old self-described "Buppie." Lewis-Thornton said she had "never been promiscuous" and "never had a one-night stand," but she was "dying of AIDS." Like so many other women, she had contracted the virus from unprotected sex.

Many of us in the black community had enormous respect for *Essence* and especially for Linda for pushing the envelope on issues that were difficult for black people to understand and accept. The gay community was also eager to embrace Linda. As the keynote speaker at a gay and lesbian writers conference in 1995, Linda drew attention from nearly everyone as she entered the main room in the Park Plaza Hotel. I was excited to see her as well, but the hall was packed, and I had no special privileges, so I took a seat far away and squinted my eyes from the balcony. I was writing my first book and wanted to interview Linda, but I was not sure I would ever get a chance to speak to her one-on-one, so I tape recorded her speech from the audience.

Linda had a fast-pitched conversational speaking style that was part educational, part inspirational, and part comical. It was almost like listening to someone talk in a living room after dinner. But despite her disarming appearance, her speech was hard-hitting, especially when she challenged the way majority cultures typecast minorities to justify their oppression. "Black men and women were told that we were hypersexual in order to justify slavery," she said. To prove her point, she read from the journal of a seventeenth-century slave trader who once wrote that "negro nature is so craven and sensuous in every fiber of its being, so deeply rooted in [the] immorality part on negro people, that they turn in aversion from any sexual relation which does not invite sensuous embraces."

I thought I might have missed a word in the transcription from the tape recorder, so I went back and did some research on Linda's point, but I could not find the quote. I did find, however, a strikingly similar statement made by a different person at a different time. In the book, *The American Negro,* William Hannibal Thomas wrote that "Negro nature is so craven and sensuous in every fiber of its being that a Negro manhood with decent respect for chaste womanhood does not exist."

The words were almost identical, but there were two significant differences between Thomas's statement and the statement from the slave trader. Thomas wrote his words in 1901, not in the seventeenth century. And unlike the slave trader of centuries past, Thomas was black. Not surprisingly, Thomas was roundly criticized by the black community for his comments, but the fact that he made them at all, and that they were widely published, demonstrates three important points.

First, black people have been trained to internalize and repeat the very prejudices used against us. Second, a few opportunistic blacks are all too willing to tell white America exactly what they want to hear about us. And third, white America is all too willing to publicize and promote controversial black figures who are severely ill-informed.

Those thoughts came to mind when I met with Linda at a trendy Washington restaurant called Jaleo in February 2001. As I mentioned before, this was the dinner when I first heard about the down low. Linda was in Washington for an African-American AIDS conference she was covering for the *New York Times*. Two of our mutual friends, Phill Wilson and Maurice Franklin, were also in town for the conference, and the three of them invited me to join them for dinner. I had interviewed Linda in 1995 after I met her at the Boston writers' conference, but I had never had the chance to sit down with her for a meal. Phill, on the other hand, I knew very well. We had met at a White House meeting in March 1993, in the early months of the Clinton administration. In an effort to involve the gay and lesbian community in the administration, the White House Office of Public Liaison set up a series of meetings between LGBT leaders and administration officials. As an openly gay staff member, I was eager to participate in the discussion when I walked into the ornate board room in the Old Executive Office Building. I sat down at the long wooden table just as the meeting began. A few minutes later, Phill walked in.

He was a handsome, well-dressed black man in a room filled with white gay men, so my eyes immediately focused on him. I learned during the meeting that Phill was the public policy director of AIDS Project Los Angeles and the founder of the National Black Lesbian and Gay Leadership Forum. After the meeting, we spoke and agreed to stay in touch. Our friendship developed quickly when Phill invited me to dinner a few days later. When I returned the favor and invited him to the White House Mess for lunch, Phill surprised me with a kiss in the entrance foyer to the West Wing. I suppose most of the staff already knew I was gay, but the Secret Service agents who stood guard at the door did not, until then.

The following month, Phill returned to the White House with a group of seven gay and lesbian leaders, including Nadine Smith, a black lesbian activist from Florida, for a meeting with the president. The gay community was preparing to hold a massive march in Washington in April 1991, and they wanted President Clinton to speak at the event. Clinton had been elected as a friend of the gay community, and they expected he would speak at their rally, but I knew that would never happen. Hundreds of groups hold marches and rallies in Washington every year, and presidents rarely, if ever, attend these functions. At the most, the president might send a statement to be read at the event, but the White House had no interest in seeing the president too closely identified with the gay community.

As I sat across from Phill during the meeting in the Oval Office, I could not help thinking about the significance of that moment. Although the White House tried to downplay the meeting by scheduling it on a Friday afternoon when the media were winding down for the weekend, everyone in the room knew it was the first time *any* president had ever met with leaders of the gay and lesbian community in the Oval Office. That made it historic. But there was another thought on my mind that day. It was also historic for African-American involvement. Alexis Herman, the straight black woman who ran the White House Office of Public Liaison, and I, a black gay man who served as special assistant to the president, sat in the room on behalf of the staff. Along with the other two African Americans in the room, it had to be the first time in history when two black openly gay men, an open black lesbian and a straight black woman all met with the president of the United States, in the Oval Office of the White House, on any civil rights issue.

Some people merely watch history while others make it. Phill and Maurice, who were on the front lines of the battle to educate America about AIDS and sexuality, seemed to be making history and had been at the center of several historic events, from the thirtieth anniversary of the March on Washington to the Million Man March. But neither of them knew that the discussion at dinner that night with Linda would also mark a historic turning point in the black community. That may have been the night when the down low media story was born.

George W. Bush had just been sworn into office, and there was a bitter sense of acrimony in the capital. At the dinner table, I griped about the changing political scene with the Republicans in town. After eight years of living in D.C., I was ready to go somewhere else. I had decided to leave politics and move to New York, and I was eager to learn about my new city from Linda, who was then a reporter for the *New York Times.*

The four of us had ordered *tapas* and were comparing notes about New York, Washington, and Los Angeles when the conversation turned to the down low. I had heard the term before, but I had never heard it connected to AIDS policy, so I was a little confused. "What is the down low?" I asked.

"It's about these black men who sleep with men but don't identify as gay," Maurice replied.

"Oh, you mean MSM," I said, using a term I knew for "men who have sex with men."

"Well, these men on the down low are MSM, but not all MSM are on the down low," he explained. It took me a second to register what he meant. Researchers had long ago replaced the term "gay" with "MSM." Under pressure from minority activists who felt the word "gay" was too limiting for men of color, the CDC started using "MSM" in its 1991 *HIV/AIDS Surveillance Report.* Although it sounded clinical, "men who have sex with men" more accurately identified the range of men who engaged in same-sex behavior. It also shifted the focus of AIDS prevention away from "identity" and toward "behavior." A large number of these MSM, even those who were open about their sexuality, had never identified with the more white-oriented and political term "gay."

I asked another question. "So are you talking about men who have sex with men but who are in the closet?"

"They wouldn't necessarily consider themselves in the closet," Maurice said.

"So you mean they're in denial?"

Maurice paused. "I guess you could say that," he said with a smile. I wasn't sure if he agreed with me, or if I had just worn him down with my persistent questions, but I had more to say.

"So what else is new? That's been going on since the beginning of time," I said. Maurice seemed to agree, but there was one aspect of the story that did seem to be new. Black women were being infected with HIV at alarming rates, and no one had a good explanation for why it was happening. No one except for James L. King.

Linda had her reporter's cap on that night. She wanted to write a story about the conference, and the down low angle provided the most promising opportunity. Earlier in the day, a lively exchange had taken place at the conference when Phill, Maurice, and a former down low man named James L. King (later known as J. L. King) took part in a luncheon. Phill, who was then the director of the Los Angeles-based Black AIDS Institute, moderated the panel, while Maurice and James were the two panelists. Maurice let us know at dinner that he felt King was an "ill-informed black gay man masquerading on the down low." That was a strong indictment, but I had no reason to distrust Maurice. King seemed to have little real experience in AIDS policy, while Maurice had been involved in the trenches for years.

When I met Maurice back in 1993, he was a young civil rights activist who had worked for Dr. Joseph Lowery at the Southern Christian Leadership Conference. A veteran of the Navy, he had come to Washington as a lobbyist for the newly formed Campaign for Military Service, an organization that was fighting to lift the ban on gays in the military. But with his attractive chocolate face, muscular body, and medium-length dreadlocks, Maurice stood out like a sore thumb among the bland legion of gray-suited lobbyists in Washington. After the campaign ended, he became intensely involved in AIDS policy work and had recently become a director at New York's Gay Men of African Descent (GMAD).

Based on what Maurice and Phill said that night, I was a little wary of Linda's plan to write a story about the down low. I knew that other reporters would cover the down low angle even if Linda did not write about it, but I felt that a prominent *New York Times* article might give the story credibility it did not deserve. The *Times* had already mentioned the down low once in an article a few weeks before, but there was a big difference between writing an article that mentioned the down low and writing an article *about* the down low. It also made a difference that the new article would be written by Linda Villarosa, who was one of the most respected black women in journalism. But Linda seemed to be genuinely intrigued by the story. She knew that black women all over America were clamoring for information, and this story could help them sort through the confusing issues involved with the epidemic. It seemed like a perfect story. It combined the public health issue of AIDS with a new angle that could get people to wake up and pay attention. In addition, the down low seemed to provide an obvious answer to lingering questions about the alarming HIV infection rates among black women.

There was one big question that black women wanted answered in 2001. Could the down low be a bridge that brings the virus from closeted black gay and bisexual men to straight black women? The idea seemed reasonable. If men on the down low were secretly sleeping with other men and then bringing HIV back to their female partners, that could explain the infection rates among black women. But there was not much evidence to support the theory, and I was concerned that focusing attention on the issue would divert our energy from the factors we already knew were responsible for the problem, including unprotected heterosexual intercourse and intravenous drug use with infected needles.

Maurice and I were also concerned that the down low story might have the potential to divide the black community into a battle of the sexes, to demonize black gay and bisexual men, and to distract the public's attention from the personal responsibility to protect themselves instead of expecting someone else to protect them. Little did we realize that our conversation would serve as a harbinger of the public dialogue to follow.

Part of what concerned me was that the connection between the down low and black women seemed a bit illogical. There were two ways to look at it. Either the down low was new or the down low was old, but either way it did not make sense. If the down low was new in 2001, it could not have been responsible for an epidemic that was twenty years old. On the other hand, if the down low was old in 2001, then we should have been alarmed about high HIV infection rates among black women ten to fifteen years earlier when the epidemic was raging out of control.

AIDS had not just arrived in black America in 2001. We had been affected by it since the early days of the epidemic, but we did not always pay attention. For a long time, the African-American community responded to AIDS as if it were somebody else's disease. In the first few months of the epidemic, the virus was thought to be limited to a notorious group known as the four Hs: homosexuals, hemophiliacs,

Haitians, and heroin users. But in June 1982, just a year after the beginning of the epidemic, the U.S. Centers for Disease Control (CDC) reported that 23 percent of initial AIDS cases were among African Americans. We were just 12 percent of the population, but we accounted for nearly a quarter of the first AIDS cases.

Just two years later, the CDC reported that African Americans accounted for 50 percent of all new AIDS cases among children. And two years after that in 1986, CDC reported that black women accounted for half of all AIDS cases among women. Right from the beginning, in the first five years of the outbreak, African Americans were put on notice about the reach of the epidemic, but instead of reacting with action, we continued to pretend that it was a white gay disease.

In December 1988, it became harder to deny the truth when ABC's Max Robinson, the first black man to anchor a network news broadcast, died of AIDS-related complications. A year after Robinson passed away, the dancer and choreographer Alvin Ailey died of AIDS as well. Then in February 1991, the gospel recording artist James Cleveland died of AIDS-related complications. By the time the basketball superstar Magic Johnson announced that he was HIV positive in November 1991, we had no reason to be surprised anymore. But then, five months after Johnson's stunning announcement, the tennis legend Arthur Ashe announced that he too had AIDS.

At the dawn of the nineties, black America knew that the epidemic had crossed over to the black community. Some experts suspected the problem was related to drug users transferring HIV to one another by sharing dirty needles. Others felt that convicted felons were a major source of transmission after being infected in prison and bringing home the virus to their unsuspecting partners upon their release. While black America struggled to explain the heterosexual AIDS cases, far fewer people seemed concerned about the thousands of black gay and bisexual men who were already dying in cities all across the country. At the end of 1991, the CDC reported that more than 30,000 black men had died from AIDS, and only a tiny percentage of them reported that they had acquired the virus solely from heterosexual contact. That posed a challenge in getting straight black men to pay attention to an epidemic that did not appear to affect them.

The Marketing of An Epidemic

The AIDS community of funders, researchers, activists, and sympathetic government officials had a problem. In the early 1990s, some AIDS activists knew that Americans would not pay attention to the growing epidemic if they thought the disease primarily affected black drug users and black gay men. That's when some activists apparently decided to market the epidemic for middle America. As a result, in their well-intentioned desire to motivate the country to do something about AIDS, the activists provided the media with a more palatable story line that was technically accurate but misrepresented the greatest impact of the disease. Phill Wilson confirms this strategic decision. "There definitely was a concerted effort to make AIDS more compelling to the black community," he recalled, "and that process entailed a de-gaying of the epidemic." Perhaps as a result, we saw stories about children with AIDS and women with AIDS and other "innocent" victims of the disease. In fact, African Americans might have gotten the impression that women and children were the primary black victims of AIDS. But they were not. At the end of 1993, 52,259 black men, 12,875 black women and 1,517 black children had died from AIDS. In the black community, AIDS was still a disease of black gay men and black drug users.

While the media presented a cleaned-up version of the black AIDS epidemic, there was a dramatic shift in the demographics of the international AIDS problem. AIDS became a black disease in the 1990s. Not a black American's disease. Not a black gay disease. Not a black drug user's disease. Not even a black ex-convict's disease. AIDS became a black disease, period. Early in the decade, the World Health Organization estimated that two-thirds of the 15 million people who were infected with HIV were sub-Saharan African. That meant that AIDS was killing black people all over the world.

Meanwhile, in this country, AIDS had become the leading cause of death for black men between the ages of twenty-five and forty-four and the second leading cause of death for black women in the same age group. The primary difference between the AIDS epidemic in Africa and in black America was the method of exposure. In Africa, AIDS was primarily a heterosexual disease. In black America, it was not. But there was one other sobering fact that should have caused alarm. In 1995, the CDC reported that the AIDS incidence rate for blacks had surpassed the rate for whites. For the first time, there were more new black AIDS cases than white AIDS cases. Twelve percent of the population was driving the entire nationwide AIDS epidemic. We knew that in the nineties.

Despite the trends in the epidemic, much of the mainstream media continued to ignore the issue of AIDS in the black community. Thus, the decision to focus on media-friendly AIDS stories may seem understandable when you consider the lack of coverage given to minorities and AIDS.

Cathy J. Cohen, a political science professor at Yale, researched the media's coverage of AIDS in her 1999 book, *The Boundaries of Blackness: AIDS and the Breakdown of Black Politics*. She looked closely at the coverage in the *New York Times*, widely considered the American "newspaper of record" for its extensive coverage of national and international news. In her analysis of all *Times* articles written about AIDS from the beginning of the epidemic in 1981 to the first year of the Clinton administration in 1993, Cohen discovered that the *Times* published just 231 articles focused on African Americans. That may seem like a high number until you consider the fact that the *Times* published a total of 4,671 articles on AIDS during this time period. In other words, only 5 percent of all *Times* articles about AIDS focused on African Americans.

Even more disturbing, Cohen found that 62 percent of the articles about blacks focused on just two celebrities, Magic Johnson and Arthur Ashe. That meant that only 1.9 percent of all *New York Times* stories about AIDS focused on ordinary black people, even though blacks made up 32 percent of all AIDS cases during that period, according to Cohen.

Stories about gays were almost as rare. In the thirteen years of her study, Cohen found only 369 stories that focused on gay men. That amounts to 7.9 percent of all *New York Times* stories on AIDS, even though the CDC reported that men who had sex with men made up 60 percent of all AIDS cases during that period. If ordinary blacks made up 1.8 percent of the AIDS news coverage and gay men made up only 7.9 percent of the news coverage, we can expect that even less coverage was devoted to those double minorities who were both black and gay. Never mind the fact that 80 percent of all AIDS cases in America at that time involved either blacks or men who had sex with men, and in many cases the two categories overlapped.

Unfortunately, the racial disparity between the epidemic and the media coverage has not been limited to the *New York Times.* Kai Wright has done more to separate fact from fiction about AIDS than almost any reporter on the beat. He's traveled the world and written about AIDS in Africa and in black America. In the spring of 2004, Wright wrote an article in the *Columbia Journalism Review* that analyzed a media survey conducted by the Kaiser Family Foundation. The results were shocking.

The Kaiser study looked at twenty-two years of media coverage on AIDS from 1981 through 2002. They examined more than 9,000 new stories from four major national newspapers (*New York Times, Wall Street Journal, Washington Post,* and *USA Today*), three major regional papers (*San Francisco Chronicle, Miami Herald,* and *Los Angeles Times*), and three major network news programs (*ABC World News Tonight, CBS Evening News,* and *NBC Nightly News*). Amazingly, they found only 3 percent of news stories in the major media outlets focused on U.S. minorities. Just 3 percent.

Why was the number so low? The study offered an explanation. The media tend to operate with a pack mentality that focuses primarily on specific and dramatic episodes in the AIDS epidemic instead of the ongoing challenges. "In the early years," Wright explained, "it was the effect on the blood supply and debate over San Francisco bathhouses being shut down. Next came the public infections of Rock Hudson and Magic Johnson, followed by a pair of very large events, the discovery of the drugs that have staved off death for so many people, and, finally, by the AIDS devastation in Africa." In other words, the media were covering episodes, but they were not really covering the epidemic.

Ironically, the new HIV drug treatments and the proliferation of AIDS in Africa may have actually hindered the possibility of generating sustained media attention for AIDS in black America. Just when black America started paying attention to AIDS in the mid 1990s, the powerful new drugs that were released in 1996 began to extend the lives of people living with AIDS. As a result, the media stopped covering the old story about people dying and started reporting the new story about people living. In November 1996, for example, the *New York Times Magazine* published a cover story by Andrew Sullivan, a prominent white gay conservative, who suggested the AIDS epidemic had been won.

In his article, "When Plagues End," Sullivan told the world "this ordeal as a whole may be over." Yet even Sullivan knew that prediction did not apply to everyone. In a single paragraph at the beginning, he passingly acknowledged the enormous socioeconomic disparities that separated him from most others. "The vast majority of H.I.V.-positive people in the world, and a significant minority in America, will not have access to the expensive and effective new drug treatments now available," he wrote. "And many Americans—especially blacks and Latinos—will still die." Despite that caveat, the tone and title of his piece was unmistakably optimistic. A few weeks later, *Newsweek* magazine followed suit and declared "The End of AIDS" on its cover. That was in 1996.

Given the media hype about the end of AIDS, it's no wonder that America, including black America, stopped paying attention. Most African Americans get their information about AIDS from the media, so many of us in the black community allowed our attention to drift elsewhere—or return our focus to other urgent matters in the black community—as the news coverage declined. In 1995, 56 percent of African Americans considered AIDS to be the nation's most urgent health problem, according to a Kaiser study. By 2000, that number had dropped to 41 percent.

Black America, like the rest of America, simply let down our guard. We still knew that AIDS was affecting significant numbers of black people, but the black people who were affected did not engender our concern. For the first time in the history of the epidemic, people with means could buy their way out of much of their suffering, so those who were left were the ones who could not afford the expensive drugs to save their lives. They were gay, bisexual, drug users, sex workers, and low-income people. Middle-class black America was not as directly affected in the same way that marginalized blacks were.

But blacks were still bearing a disproportionate burden of the epidemic in the late 1990s, and black activists and journalists were rightly concerned that America was not paying attention. The easiest way to get the story back in the headlines and generate community sympathy and action was to create an image of law-abiding, middle-class, heterosexual black people facing AIDS.

The "Bisexual Bridge"

In January 2000, the CDC issued a press release noting that HIV infection had "increased significantly in women of color over the last decade." Researchers at CDC suggested a possible answer. They suspected that men who had sex with men might be bringing the virus from the gay community to heterosexual women. Since black men who have sex with men often do not identify as gay, CDC speculated that "these men may not accept their own risk for HIV, and therefore, may unintentionally put their female partners at risk." Notice the language used by the CDC. The word "unintentionally" suggests that the men involved were not necessarily guilty of doing anything purposefully harmful. The language from CDC was typically nonjudgmental, but the language used in the black community would be a different story.

By July 2000, Linda Valleroy (not to be confused with the *Essence* magazine editor Linda Villarosa), a researcher at the CDC, coined a name for the theory that black men were bringing AIDS to black women. Valleroy called it a "bisexual bridge for HIV." The idea was that black men who have sex with men were also having sex with women and therefore might be acting as a bridge for the virus to cross over into the black heterosexual community. The bridge theory coincided with new information about the AIDS epidemic among black gay and bisexual men. Earlier that year, the CDC reported for the first time that gay and bisexual men of color made up more AIDS cases than white gay and bisexual men. Even more alarming, 24 percent of HIV-positive black men who had sex with men identified as "heterosexual" in a separate CDC study. For some observers, that was all the proof they needed. Black men who had sex with men were becoming infected, and since a quarter of them considered themselves heterosexual, they were *probably* taking the virus back to black women. That seemed logical, but it did not tell us everything we needed to know.

The problem with most of the media analyses about the down low is that they were based on circumstantial evidence. A more thorough analysis might have approached the story from the perspective of a homicide detective. Think about it this way. Imagine finding a suspicious weapon in the course of a murder investigation. What looks like a smoking gun from a distance may appear more innocent upon closer investigation. If the gun is actually smoking, does that mean it was used to kill anybody? Even if the gun was used to kill, does that prove that it killed the victim in the investigation? And if it did kill that victim, does it tell us who pulled the trigger? Those are the questions you need to ask in a criminal case. Who? What? When? Where? Why? How? And the same basic level of analysis used in a homicide investigation should be used in examining the down low theory. Yes, there is definitely a bridge between men on the down low and black women. That has never been in dispute. The real question is how large is that bridge, and that we do not know. To show that the bridge is wide, as most of the media stories assume it is, you would have to prove several different assumptions from various studies.

First, you would have to prove that the black women in question were becoming infected by heterosexual sex and not from injection drug use. Given the legal ramifications and social stigma attached to drug use, some women may not want to admit, or may not know, that they were infected by drug use.

Second, you would have to prove that the women who did become infected by heterosexual sex were not having sex with drug users. Just because a woman contracts the virus from male-female sex does not mean the man was initially infected by another man.

Third, you would have to prove that the same women were becoming infected by black men, not men of other races. This seems likely given the racial segregation in American dating, but you would still have to prove it.

Fourth, you would have to prove that the MSM who identified as heterosexual were actually having sex with women. Social stigma against same-sex behavior might discourage many of these men from admitting that they only had male partners. Just because they claim they are heterosexual on a survey does not mean they really are in practice.

Fifth, you would have to prove that the men involved were HIV positive. Obviously, HIV cannot be transmitted across the down low bridge unless the person has HIV.

Sixth, you would have to prove that the same men were having sex with the same women who were becoming infected. It may seem a reasonable assumption, but you still have to prove it.

And then seventh, you would have to prove that the men were having *unprotected* or *unsafe* sex with the same women. Even if a bisexual man is HIV positive, it is very difficult to spread the virus to anyone unless he engages in unprotected sex.

That was the logical challenge. All seven elements had to be proven. But no CDC study had ever been able to answer all those questions at once. No study had ever told us what percentage of black men who had sex with men were HIV positive. Nor had the CDC told us what percentage of black bisexual men were HIV positive. Those had always been complicated questions. But in early

2001, there was a deceptively simple answer waiting across the horizon.

One Out of Three Black Gay Men

In February 2001, CDC's Linda Valleroy announced the preliminary results of a major new study. Speaking at a conference in Chicago, Valleroy announced that one out of three young black gay men were HIV positive. Well, that's not exactly what she said, but that's how the media reported it. What she said, of course, was more nuanced. But here's how it happened.

From 1998 to 2000, the CDC conducted a survey of young men who have sex with men (MSM) in six cities (Baltimore, Dallas, Los Angeles, Miami, New York, and Seattle). The CDC recruited the men at gay bars, nightclubs, bookstores, shopping areas and other locations that gay men visited in those cities. They found 2,401 MSM between the ages of 23 and 29. They tested the men for HIV and 293 (12 percent) of them tested positive. The more troubling number was that 30 percent of the African-American men in the group tested positive. That was the number that sent headline writers into a frenzy.

Newspapers across the country printed the story the next day. *USA Today*'s headline said, "1 in 3 young gay black men are HIV-positive." The *Milwaukee Journal* headline read, "HIV hits 30% of gay black males." The *Boston Herald* simply said, "Gay black men hit hard by AIDS virus." The *Washington Post, Los Angeles Times, Chicago Sun-Times,* and *Atlanta Journal* all ran stories, as did several radio and television news programs. It seemed to be a breakthrough moment—the first time the major media seriously addressed the issue of black gay men and AIDS. But the breakthrough was not what it appeared, and it was very short-lived.

Despite the flurry of news stories, many of them were not exactly accurate. Take the *USA Today* article, for example. That paper claimed that "1 in 3 young gay black men are HIV-positive." But the CDC never really said that. Instead, what they said was that 30 percent of the black gay men in the survey *of those six cities* were HIV positive. It was important to understand the distinction between those six cities and the rest of the nation. Five of the six cities in the study were among the hardest hit by the epidemic, and the sixth city (Seattle) did not have a large enough African-American population to provide many black participants. That meant most of the blacks surveyed came from Baltimore, Dallas, Los Angeles, Miami, and New York, the same cities where the AIDS epidemic was at its worst.

We know that 73 percent of blacks living with AIDS are located in just ten states. Since the survey relied heavily on those states, that meant that the places chosen for the survey were not necessarily representative of the rest of America. The black AIDS epidemic in New York and Los Angeles, for example, was always much worse than it was in smaller cities. That was the problem with the *USA Today* headline. The CDC never said that 1 in 3 of *all* young gay black men were HIV positive. It was only about the people in the survey from those six cities.

Of course, surveys routinely use small sample sizes to determine a larger picture of the country. Public opinion polls do that every week. A thousand people are interviewed by telephone and then an anchorman on the network news tells us that 60 percent of Americans feel this way or that way about something. We're used to that, but most of those surveys that purport to represent American public opinion do so by sampling a wide cross-section of people from various backgrounds. The CDC survey, however, was never designed to give us a complete national picture. It was only a snapshot of the places hardest hit.

The headline in the *Milwaukee Journal* was also problematic, but for different reasons. The *Journal* claimed that 30 percent of black gay males were HIV positive, but once again, the CDC never said that either. Remember, the CDC only surveyed people who were between twenty-three and twenty-nine years old, one of the age groups hardest hit by the epidemic. The results would have been dramatically different had the CDC taken a survey of black gay men who were fifty-three to fifty-nine, a group with a much smaller AIDS incidence rate. The point is that we cannot draw conclusions about all black gay men based on a survey of twenty-three- to twenty-nine-year-olds. What the *Journal* did was like going to Harlem to get a sample of New York City and then drawing the conclusion that 90 percent of New York is black. Certainly, 90 percent of Harlem might be black, but that's not the case in the rest of New York City. That's why any time you draw broad conclusions from a survey, the survey has to be wide enough to include the diversity in the community.

The *Boston Herald,* in comparison to the other two papers, played it safe with its headline: "Gay black men hit hard by AIDS virus." That was a lot more accurate. But there was one tiny little problem. The men in the study were not necessarily "gay." The term that CDC used was MSM, which in this case meant "men who have *ever* had sex with men." As used here, MSM is a broad term that could include gay men, bisexual men, men on the down low, or men who had only one sexual experience with another man. In other words, the men in the study were not all gay.

There appeared to be one other flaw in the reporting about this study as well. It was very basic. Most of the news stories did not tell us how many people in the survey were black. We knew there were 2,401 men in the study. We knew they were drawn from public venues in six cities. We knew that 293 of the men tested HIV positive. And we knew that only 85 of the 293 men knew they were infected before the testing. That's a lot of numbers to digest. But the numbers that were curiously missing were the number of black people in the study and the number of blacks who tested positive. That was critical. Say, for example, there were only three blacks in the study. In that case, a shift of just one person would cause a dramatic difference of 33 percent in the statistics. It is much harder to make accurate generalizations from small numbers than from larger numbers, which is why we needed to know how many blacks were in the study before we could draw any broad conclusions.

Despite the absence of this critical piece of information, the *USA Today* article on February 6 never mentioned the number of blacks in the study. Neither did the *Milwaukee Journal* article on February 6 or the articles in the *Los Angeles Times* or *Washington Post* on February 7. That information was even missing from the *New York Times* article on February 11. Did the reporters simply forget to mention the numbers? No, the real story is actually more complex than that. The media did not report the numbers because the CDC did not tell them. It's not that the CDC purposefully hid the information, but they certainly did not make it easy to find.

Journalists often develop their stories based on news releases provided to them by reputable government agencies such as the CDC. (The CDC, for example, was very helpful to me in the writing of this book.) The communications department of the government agency usually helps the reporters by giving them press releases with the basic information they need for their stories. These press releases are extremely valuable to guide reporters who cover conferences where there are many different events going on in a short period of time. That's exactly where the story about young black men was released, during a CDC conference in Chicago on February 5, 2001. Unfortunately, the CDC press release never mentioned the number of black men in the study. The release did mention the number of total study participants (2,400) and the number of HIV-positive men (293) in the study, but it failed to mention the number of black men who were in the study or the number of black men who tested positive. That was crucial information that could have helped provide context for the headlines that screamed across the nation's newspapers the next day.

Day-to-day reporters seldom have time to dig deeply into the numerous issues that come across their desk, but beat reporters who cover a specific topic or beat often have more time to develop their stories. Many of these beat reporters wanted to know the story behind the story. Why were so many young black gay and bisexual men becoming infected? Eager to find explanations for the statistics, reporters called on the usual suspects to interpret the study. Here's what they said.

Cornelius Baker, the director of Washington's Whitman-Walker Clinic, said the study's findings were "no surprise." Other AIDS activists blamed the high infection rates on the "stigma" of being black and gay. Doug Nelson, the executive director of the AIDS Resource Center of Wisconsin said the study confirms "how vital it is to repeat and reinforce the AIDS prevention message." The director of Boston's AIDS Action group said the problem is that many black gay men are afraid to "come out."

The problem with those answers is that the experts were saying the same thing that they had been saying all along, and reporters wanted something new to explain the new infections. Cleo Manago, the head of the AMASSI Center in Inglewood, California, offered one perspective that seemed to be fresh and different from what the rest of the experts were saying. "The CDC and the public health departments need to reevaluate who they're funding and why they're funding people to do this work, because clearly it's not working," he told the *Los Angeles Times*. But even Manago's provocative comments were not necessarily new. Many members of the community in Los Angeles had heard him deliver that same message several times before. Reporters were still stumped. No one—at least not one of the usual suspects—could provide a new or definitive explanation for the infection rates.

Then came the down low.

A Star Is Born

Just two days after the CDC study was released about black gay men, there seemed to be an answer ready to be served. That was the day the down low first appeared in the mainstream media. The first major media reference to the down low took place on February 7, 2001, in the *Los Angeles Times*. The *Times* article—the same article that quoted Cleo Manago—came up with a possible new answer to the infection rates. The article featured a twenty-eight-year-old black man named Charles. Described by the reporter as "young and attractive," Charles said he had a steady girlfriend but occasionally slept with men. Five years earlier, Charles had made a fateful decision that changed his life when he had decided not to use condoms while having sex with someone who he later discovered was HIV positive. But despite his pattern of sleeping with men and women, Charles did not consider himself to be gay or bisexual. Charles was on the down low.

Jocelyn Y. Stewart and Sharon Bernstein had introduced America to a new lifestyle and a new term: "the down low." The two reporters had also introduced other phrases that were rarely seen in newspapers at the time. They described terms like "homo thug" and "same-gender-loving" and used these words synonymously with "down low." As discussed previously, in the early days of the DL, the term "down low" had a much broader meaning than it often does today. By today's standards, homothugs (gay men who dress and act like hip hop thugs) would not be down low. Likewise, men who call themselves "same-gender-loving," a politically conscious term associated widely with Cleo Manago, would not be considered down low either. But back then, any man who had sex with men who did not look gay or talk gay or call himself gay might have been labeled on the down low. That was also the impression given by a *New York Times* article four days after the Los Angeles article appeared. The *New York Times* piece quoted two mysterious men (Walter and Jay) who were supposed to be on the down low, but without last names and photographs we were left to our imagination to visualize them.

A good reporter can smell a story before it develops. Linda Villarosa was one of the best health reporters, and I think she knew something that Maurice and Phill and I did not realize the night we had dinner. She knew the down low story had to be told. Somebody was going to tell the story, so she might as well tell it in a candid, nonsensationalized way. So on April 3, 2001, Linda's article finally appeared in the *New York Times* under the headline "AIDS Education Is Aimed 'Down Low'." Not surprisingly, hers was one of the most thorough stories about the down low, and it teased out the complexity of the term itself. In Linda's story, James L. King had described the down low as "men who have sex with men but do not identify themselves as gay or bisexual," according to Villarosa. That was a definition that did not require the men to be involved in relationships with women. But Linda also interviewed our mutual friend Maurice Franklin, who said that half of the men in the focus groups conducted by his organization, Gay Men of African Descent, described themselves as being on the DL. Men who were willing to identify themselves at a focus group run by a gay organization were calling themselves down low. That posed a major challenge for the down low story from the beginning. Nobody had a clear, universally accepted definition of what it meant.

There was also a problem with the timing of the down low story in the news. "It has long been known that men of all races have sex with men but prefer not to be labeled gay or even bisexual," Linda wrote in her article. Maurice echoed that sentiment in his quote: "There has always been a secret society of men who were undetectably gay and continued to live in the black community," he told Linda. That begged an obvious question. If the down low had "long been known" and these men had "always" been there, why was this suddenly becoming an issue in the spring of 2001?

Perhaps it was because of the CDC study that showed that one fourth of the HIV-positive black men who had sex with men identified themselves as heterosexual. Linda mentioned the study in her article, but that information had been released more than a year earlier. Then, maybe it was because 54 percent of women newly reported with AIDS had acquired the virus from heterosexual relations. Linda mentioned that study as well, but the information came from 1998. In fact, the only major new information that had been released about AIDS in the black community was the CDC study that showed 30 percent of young black gay and bisexual men were HIV positive. But that study had nothing to do with the down low. It was a study of men in six cities who were found at gay-identified venues and other locations where gay men tend to go. "There were very few down low guys in this sample," the study's author Linda Valleroy told *Gay City News*. "Down low guys don't tend to appear at the more obvious type places [where men who have sex with men go]," she said.

The study may have raised more questions than answers. Nobody could explain the high prevalence of HIV among young black gay and bisexual men. The CDC researchers could not explain it. The AIDS activists could not explain it. And the reporters could not explain it. The only thing we did know is that they were *not* becoming infected because of the down low. After all, the men in the study were self-acknowledged "men who had sex with men" who had been recruited at public venues. By King's own definition, they were not on the down low.

So if there was no new information about the down low, how did the media leap from black gay and bisexual men to men on the down low?

At least four factors may have played a role in the shift to the down low. First, the twentieth anniversary of the AIDS epidemic was coming up in June 2001, and many reporters were looking for ways to understand the past two decades and predict the challenges ahead. Second, the statistics about black gay and bisexual men were staggering, but they were not entirely surprising, and since no one had a clue what caused the numbers, those statistics could still be used as a springboard to talk about other black AIDS issues that were easier to discuss. Third, HIV seemed to be increasing among black women, and a story line that incorporated black women was more likely to generate public concern than a new batch of stories solely about black gay and bisexual men. Fourth, although the down low may have been around forever, no one had any personal investment in pushing the story until James L. King came along at the conference in February 2001.

A Story with No Proof
After the February conference, dozens of stories about the down low appeared, and many of them quoted King. What the stories did not provide, however, was any proof that the down low was responsible for the black AIDS epidemic. I did a Nexis search of all the articles I could find about the down low from 2001. I found articles in the *New York Times, Los Angeles Times, USA Today, Chicago Sun-Times, Atlanta Journal, San Francisco Chronicle, St. Louis Post-Dispatch, San Diego Union-Tribune, Columbus Dispatch, Village*

Voice, VIBE, Essence, and *JET.* All the stories referenced the down low, but not a single article mentioned a black woman who had been recently infected with HIV by a man on the down low. Not one case. Here's what I found.

February 7: The *Los Angeles Times* runs the first article that mentions the down low, but the story never cites any women who had been infected by a man on the DL.

February 11: The *New York Times* runs a story that mentions the down low. It quotes five men, but not a single woman is mentioned.

March 15: *USA Today* runs an article about "the danger of living 'down low'" with a subtitle about how these men "can put women at risk." The story quotes six men and one woman but provides not one case in which a man transmitted HIV to his female partner.

March 19: An extensive article about the down low runs in the *Columbus Dispatch* in Ohio. The article quotes seven men and four women, and mentions several others. Two of the men had passed HIV to their female partners, but they were not necessarily on the down low. The first man had "experimented" with homosexual sex before his marriage but never did so while he was married. The second was an African exchange student who had infected his female partner in 1993, but the article never said that he engaged in any homosexual or bisexual behavior.

April 1: An article in the *St. Louis Post-Dispatch* quotes a man named Tyrone who had been married for ten years and had two daughters before he divorced his wife and came to terms with his sexuality. Tyrone, however, was not HIV positive.

April 3: A *New York Times* article quotes five men and two women. All of the people quoted were experts, and not a single person mentioned in the article had given HIV to his partner.

April 22: The *Chicago Sun-Times* runs an article about a new film called *Kevin's Room*. The film includes a "church brother who's having sex with men on the down low" and the article concludes that "secrets are endangering our lives." However, not a single person in the article had passed HIV to a partner.

June 3: A columnist in the *Atlanta Journal* explains that men on the down low "stubbornly resist the safe-sex messages that have helped to curb the epidemic among whites." Nevertheless, the article never mentions a single example in which a man on the down low passed HIV to his partner.

June 4: An article in the *San Francisco Chronicle* quotes six men and one woman. The woman is HIV positive, but "she believes she contracted the virus through unprotected sex with someone she met through a singles telephone line." Once again, there is no evidence of the down low.

June 6: A *Village Voice* article titled "The Great Down-Low Debate" profiles a twenty-five-year-old down low man named Tevin who has a relationship with a man and a woman. However, there is no evidence that Tevin is HIV positive or that he has passed any viruses to his female partners. In fact, Tevin says "he always uses condoms."

July: *VIBE* magazine runs an article called "A Question of Identity" about homothugs and men on the down low. The article never mentions any women who were infected by men on the down low.

July 3: A lengthy *New York Times* article about the toll of the AIDS epidemic on black women never mentions anyone on the down low. Instead, it quotes a doctor who specializes in AIDS and identifies other problems for women such as the absence of fathers, the lack of insurance, alcohol, drugs and a history of sexually transmitted disease.

September 8: An article in *JET* magazine explains "why AIDS is rising among black women." It is the first article I can find that actually mentions a woman (identified as Hannah) who was given

HIV by a man on the down low. But there's one catch. The story took place in 1991, ten years before the down low hype began.

October: An article in *Essence* magazine quotes six men and two women to prove that "brothers on the down low pose a serious AIDS risk to black women." Despite that claim, not one black woman mentioned in the article was even HIV positive. The closest case was Julie Posey, a San Francisco fashion merchandiser who discovered that her ex-husband was living with HIV and on the down low. Two paragraphs later, we learn that Posey herself was HIV negative.

December 2: A story in the *San Diego Union-Tribune* mentions a man on the down low who passed HIV to his female partner. Ava Gardner, a minister's wife in Sacramento, learned just before her second wedding anniversary that her husband had AIDS and had infected her. On his deathbed, her husband told her: "Ava, I did what I did to you purposefully because I didn't want to die by myself." It's definitely a story about the down low, but when we look closer at the article we see the story took place in 1996, five years before the 2001 down low craze.

December 7: A *Los Angeles Times* article profiles Tony Wafford, a community activist who has set up an innovative HIV testing facility in a local beauty salon. The article mentions men on the down low but never mentions a case in which a man on the down low passed the virus to his partner.

At the end of the year, out of all the articles I could locate, not one of them mentioned a woman who had been recently infected with HIV by a man on the down low. Most of the articles did not even come close. The only two articles that were close involved stories that were five to ten years old.

The argument for the down low has always rested on a very shaky circumstantial case. Without statistical evidence to back up the claim that the down low was spreading AIDS in the black community, the media had to rely on anecdotal evidence. It found plenty of stories about black men on the down low and black women who had been infected, but almost none of the stories ever connected the men on the down low with the women who were being infected. In most cases, there was a missing link. In some examples, the man was on the down low, but he was not HIV positive. In other examples, he was HIV positive, but he always practiced safe sex. In a few examples, the woman was HIV positive, but she was not infected by a man on the down low. Or if her man was on the down low, he had not infected her. If the down low argument had been introduced in a court of law, any good lawyer would have found plenty of reasonable doubt, and a judge might have dismissed the case before it even got to the jury.

After a year of media hype in 2001, the media could not produce a single example of a man on the down low who had recently given HIV to his female partner. That is not to say that it didn't happen. Of course, there were men on the down low spreading HIV in 2001. But how many? The media never told us. Perhaps the full story was too complex to explain or not as dramatic as the down low sensation, but the public had a right to know the truth.

The real issues around AIDS are very complex, sometimes boring, and not easy to follow. I know. In the months I spent researching AIDS issues for this book, I had to talk to scientists and researchers and translate their techno-speak into plain English. I had to pore over dozens of dry research documents with titles about "prevalence, predictors and presumptions" and "noncordant HIV serostatus." And then I had to study the CDC's own HIV surveillance data for every year from 1982 to 2002. Twelve years of primary and secondary school, four years of college, and three years of law school were all more interesting than reading through the CDC's raw data and statistics. But it had to be done. There was no other way to make sense of the down low story and AIDS.

One of the first statistics I read led me to question the whole principle behind the down low. Here it is. In 1991, 51 percent of AIDS cases among black men (24,118) reported homosexual contact as a method of exposure. In 2001, the figure had dropped to 33 percent (4,605). In other words, the number and percentage of black men exposed to AIDS because of homosexual contact had declined sharply over that decade. Why is that important? Because those men were the primary potential source of the down low infection "bridge," and if there were fewer of them around in 2001 than in 1991, there should have been fewer black women becoming infected as well. In other words, the "bridge" should have been much wider back in 1991 when there were five times as many black MSM AIDS cases than in 2001.

What could explain the discrepancy? The answer was remarkably simple but rarely revealed. The number of black female AIDS cases from heterosexual contact *did not* rise from 1991 to 2001. It actually fell. In 1991, there were 3,784 adult and adolescent black female AIDS cases from heterosexual contact. In 2001, the number had fallen to 2,606, a reduction of 1178 cases per year. So despite the media frenzy that gave us the impression of skyrocketing numbers, the number had actually decreased.

Much of that drop was due to the life-sustaining AIDS drugs introduced in 1996 that enabled people with HIV to live longer, healthier lives. But even when we look at the *percentage* of black women exposed by heterosexual contact, the change is not dramatic. In 1991, the CDC reported that 34 percent of black women with AIDS were exposed by heterosexual contact, and in 2001 the figure had increased to 37 percent. A year's worth of media hype had been based on an increase of 3 percent over 10 years, and there was almost no evidence that the increase was connected to men on the down low. In fact, out of the 7,023 total black female adult and adolescent

AIDS cases reported in 2001, only 111 (1.6 percent) reported sex with a bisexual male as the method of exposure. No wonder it was so hard for reporters to find people to interview for their news stories.

Anatomy of a Media Frenzy

Facts are rarely as important as impressions when we talk about black men, and the down low story would not be stopped because of lack of statistics. This was a story with several ups and downs over the years, beginning with its dramatic launch in February 2001. The story died for a few months following the September 11 terrorist attacks but picked up again in 2002 when the television show *E.R.* unveiled a plot involving a rapper on the down low who was diagnosed with HIV. Then the story died again.

Like a cat with nine lives, the story resurrected itself in August 2003 when the *New York Times Magazine* ran a controversial cover article called "Double Lives On the Down Low." That story also took me by surprise. I had been reading the *New York Times Magazine* since college, during the height of the AIDS epidemic, but in the years since that time I had never seen a cover story about black men who have sex with men. It seemed the first time the *New York Times Magazine* took any interest in the lives of black gay and bisexual men was in the context of a scandalous story about the down low, and that story was written by a white reporter, Benoit Denizet-Lewis, who did not seem to have all the facts. Early in the story, Denizet-Lewis made an incredible and completely unfounded claim that caught my attention. "There have always been men—black and white—who have had secret sexual lives with men," he wrote. "But the creation of an organized subculture largely made up of black men who otherwise live straight lives is a phenomenon of the last decade." The last decade? Was he joking? Black men have been on the down low for as long as black men have been getting married to women. I knew black men in my family who had been on the down low in the 1970s. But the reporter offered not one shred of evidence to back up his outrageous claim.

I continued reading with skepticism. The article begins at a bathhouse in Cleveland, where the reporter acknowledges that he is one of the few white people in the facility. That, too, raises a troubling question. Given the racial dynamics in America, it seems plausible that black men on the down low might be reluctant to open up to a white reporter trying to expose them. The story goes on to reveal one of the many contradictions about who is and is not on the down low. "Most DL men identify themselves not as gay or bisexual but first and foremost as black," writes Denizet-Lewis. That may be true, but how does the reporter know this? No studies have ever been conducted about men on the down low, so we cannot really say how most of them identify. If, on the other hand, you claim that a *real* down low man would not identify as gay or bisexual, then you have constructed a circular argument. It goes like this. How do we know men on the down low do not identify as gay? Because only men who do not identify as gay are on the down low. That is the circularity.

In fact, the story itself, like much of the down low hype, is one big contradiction. Some, like King, claim that men on the down low do not go to identifiably gay places, but throughout the *New York Times Magazine* story Denizet-Lewis reports finding men on the down low at gay places, including bathhouses and gay nightclubs. In Atlanta, Denizet-Lewis goes to a nightclub for "young guys on the DL." In one scene, two men on the DL are driving around Atlanta with a third man who is openly gay.

In another scene, the reporter visits the office of a Cleveland Web site that produces live video of down low men having simulated sex "for anyone who cares to log on." No one points out the obvious contradiction as to how a man on the down low can have sex in front of a camera for public consumption. Writing in New York's *Gay City News,* Duncan Osborne said the reporting in the *Times Magazine* article was "sloppy." Osborne directly challenged Denizet-Lewis on his assumptions. "He never tells us why he chose to believe [the men who said they were on the DL] when they claim to have sex with women while he also asserts that these men were lying to those women. These men may be lying when they say they have girlfriends," writes Osborne.

Although the *Times Magazine* story is fascinating and extensive, it does not even attempt to prove that men on the down low are spreading HIV to their female partners. It was one of the longest articles ever written about the down low, and yet it never mentions even one woman who was infected with HIV by a man on the down low. Ostensibly, that was the whole rationale for the down low story in the first place. Or was it?

The public obsession with the down low from 2001 to 2003 was fueled, in part, by a well-intentioned but completely irrational media frenzy. The same energy that had been spent on uncovering a story that wasn't there could have been spent on breaking down stereotypes by showing black gay and bisexual men who were in healthy relationships, or exposing the problem in the assumption that all blacks are straight and all gays are white, or educating the public about how to prevent the spread of HIV/AIDS. Apparently those stories were not as exciting.

Black gay and bisexual men have been living with HIV and dying of AIDS for a quarter of a century now. The HIV infection rates for this group are among the highest in the country. But the media and the black community have never treated this crisis with the same energy now devoted to the down low. Ironically, a story that began because of alarming statistics about black gay and bisexual men had somehow evolved into a completely different story about straight black women. And after all the media attention, we still could not explain the cause of the high infection rates among young black gay and bisexual men. The media did not stick around long enough to answer those questions. Instead, they moved onto sexier topics—straight black women and the implicitly guilty black men who infect them.

If we seriously care about the spread of HIV, we cannot isolate our concern and efforts on one segment of the community and ignore another. We have to create a climate of love instead of fear, where black men who have sex with men are not stigmatized by the church, the media, their families, and their friends. In fact, the whole DL mythology at some level acknowledges the struggle of the black man on the down low. The legend tells us he does not identify with the white gay community, and he is not accepted by the black community, so he goes underground and creates a secret fraternity of sex partners.

But if that is true, then our solutions are way off base. If we accept the premise that black homosexuality is that difficult, then why not break down those barriers? Why not use the media to portray the black gay and bisexual men who are out of the closet, living openly in their relationships, and who have reconciled their careers, their families, and their faith with their sexuality. If it is really that hard to be black and gay and out, then those who are black and gay and out are the true heroes who deserve recognition. The *New York Times Magazine* should profile that group of people. Black media should tell their stories.

Instead, the down low story sailed on and picked up more steam after the *Times Magazine* piece. The subject had fascinated reporters in 2001, provided story lines for television shows in 2002, and then provided a major magazine cover story for 2003. Then, like clockwork, it rose again in 2004.

In the spring of 2004, the down low reemerged. The *New York Times* reporter Linda Villarosa wrote another story about the down low in the *Times*. The comedian Mo'Nique was featured on the front page of a special edition of *POZ* magazine talking about the down low. Even the television show *Law and Order: SVU* aired an episode about the down low during this time. Then, the story made the biggest splash yet. It made it to *Oprah*. The story was about to become big news.

The down low had legs, as reporters would say to describe a story that could go on for a while. For that reason, it could not continue on disembodied. Stories with legs need a voice, a look, a visual. They also need to have a face. To sell the down low to the public, it needed someone who was willing to be the image. It needed a real-life human being who could speak on the record and on camera about this underground movement. It needed a book to generate new media hype and to validate the old media hype. But most important, it needed a poster boy.

CHAPTER 6
Down Low Detectives

THE PHONE RANG, and I sat down at my desk to see the caller ID. I value my privacy, so I rarely answer the phone without knowing who is on the other end. There was no phone number on the screen, so I waited. The phone rang again before the message finally appeared on the caller ID box. "OUT OF AREA," it said. I was not expecting anyone to call, but I answered the phone anyway. "Hello," I said cautiously. Then I heard the voice on the other line.

"Keith Boykin?"

No one ever called me by my full name except for telemarketers and bill collectors. Nevertheless, after a brief moment of suspicion, I responded.

"Who's calling?" I said. I wanted to get the other person's name before I would confirm my own identity.

"This is J. L. King," the voice replied. I was surprised to get the phone call. I had heard of J. L. King before, and he surely must have known that I knew him. In fact, I knew a lot more about him than I could say in the phone call. I knew people in Ohio who knew him, and I knew people in Chicago who knew him. I knew men who had

113

dated him, and I knew men he had tried to date. I had never seen him in person, and I had no idea what he looked like. All I had was his voice on the other end of the telephone.

King introduced himself and told me about a new project of his. I listened intently, but I was not quite sure why he was sharing this information. He told me he was writing a book about the down low, and he wanted to reach out to me. He had heard positive things about me, he said, and he respected the work I had done. I was honestly flattered by the praise, but I still did not know why he had called me. I was not on the down low, and I did not have much to say about it. I was openly gay, and I had been quoted in a *Village Voice* article that Kai Wright had written about the down low. "It doesn't mean that we have to go out carrying rainbow flags," I was quoted as saying. "But we do have to acknowledge sexual orientation." That message contradicted everything I thought I knew about the down low. So why me?

What King told me next floored me. He had signed, or was about to sign, a huge new book deal to write about the down low. He had another deal with ABC News that was going to generate major publicity and exposure for him and the book. He was getting offers to speak at conventions and conferences and schools all across the country. He had so much going on with these new career developments that he had to be selective about what he chose to do.

I was impressed by his accomplishments, but, I have to admit, I was also shocked. To listen to him on the telephone, I did not get the impression that he was the most articulate communicator, but I had to question myself for thinking that. Perhaps I was imposing my own biases on his experience. Maybe I needed to be more open-minded, I thought. But that led me to the central question of the conversation. Why would he contact me?

That's the part that floored me. He had not called simply to chat about his achievements. He had called with a purpose and a proposal. Then he told me the purpose. He wanted me to help him write his book. I must have expressed some noticeable reluctance to accept his offer because he immediately started selling the idea to me as if I needed to be persuaded, and at the same time he backtracked a bit from the offer. He mentioned one or two other names of writers he thought might be suitable to help him with the book, which I took as a convenient exit sign for both of us to think about different options. I threw out a few names of writers for him to think about, and he seemed to take them seriously. But I needed to know more about what he wanted the writer to do.

"Do you need a ghost writer or a co-author?" I asked. Ghost writing (writing without any credit) is much less interesting than co-authoring. Many authors would be reluctant to devote the time and energy it takes to write a book without some hope of recognition for their work. There was, however, one advantage to ghost writing, especially since I expected that King and I would have different perspectives on the down low. If I were to ghost write the book for him, no one would ever know that I had anything to do with it. But, of course, I would know the truth, and if I did not like the final product, I would feel partly responsible. With that in mind, I told him I was reluctant to accept his offer.

King was not finished. He had another card to play, which he had mentioned several times already in the conversation. That may have been his ace in the hole. He had money. He let me know repeatedly and in no uncertain terms that he would be making a lot of money off the deal. That part I understood. But there was more. Not only had he signed a deal that would make money for him, he had also expected that the co-author or ghost writer of the book would make plenty of money as well. He never said exactly how much money was at stake, but he repeatedly let me know that I would be well paid for helping with his book. In fact, as the conversation ended, it seemed to me that money was the primary, if not the sole, motivation behind the book, the media appearances, and the lucrative speaking engagements he was doing. It was as if money was everything to him.

I can't lie about it. I felt a mix of emotions after I hung up the phone. At first, the conversation felt sort of slimy. I had no desire to become a literary mercenary to be sold off to the highest bidder. The conversation felt even worse when I thought about the message that King was communicating about the down low. It was not my message at all. I did not want to trivialize and sensationalize the lives of black men, no matter how they identified (or chose not to identify) their sexuality.

A part of me remained deeply suspicious about the whole transaction with King. I wondered if he had really gotten a deal with a publisher and a television network. He had mentioned ABC's *20/20,* but I could hardly imagine Barbara Walters wanting to do an interview with him. But maybe I was wrong. After all, J. L. King was providing a perfect iconic image for white America to understand. It was the stereotypical image of black men as pathological liars, surreptitiously satisfying their primitive sexual cravings by cheating on their wives. That would have been an easier image for white news anchors to swallow than the image of black men who accept their sexuality and are comfortable with it. To promote positive images of black gay and bisexual men might actually help some black men to deal with their sexual orientation. And soon there would be no scandal to cover.

But another part of me wondered if I should give some serious thought to King's proposal anyway. It was 2001, and I had just moved to New York. I had not written a book in two years. I was self-employed, and the cost of living in Manhattan was much higher than it had been in Washington, D.C. I was $60,000 in debt from college and law school and paying $1,000 a month for a one-bedroom apartment in Harlem that had no air conditioner, dishwasher, or washer and dryer. And I lived on a block with half a dozen abandoned buildings.

Part of me felt it was time to give in to reality and give up the pipe dream of working for myself. My last nine-to-five job was in the White House, and since that time I had struggled to support myself, first while working for a fledgling nonprofit organization and then teaching at a local college. I had once heard "if you do what you love, the money will follow," but fourteen years out of college the money had still not found me. It was all my fault, of course. Over the years, I had turned down several high-paying jobs so I could spend my life in public service. My first job out of college paid me just $250 a week, before taxes, but I was working for Mike Dukakis's presidential campaign, and I loved it. When Dukakis lost, I moved in with my father in Stone Mountain, Georgia, so that I could save money while I taught at a nearby high school. Then, a few months after I graduated from law school, I quit a lucrative position working for a San Francisco law firm, and moved to Little Rock, Arkansas, to work on Bill Clinton's first presidential campaign. And rather than stay in the comfortable White House job I landed, I eventually left the Clinton administration and signed up with a black gay organization that had no money to pay me.

Yes, it was my own fault. I was happy with my life experiences, but I had plenty of reasons to question the economic wisdom of my decisions. My grandmother was particularly persistent in questioning me. How could anyone turn down six-figure job opportunities, she wanted to know. And how could someone with an Ivy League college degree and a Harvard law degree leave a prestigious job in the White House to go work for the black gay community?

She suggested that I move to St. Louis, where I could live like a king if I practiced law. Or if I insisted on writing books, I should write something more interesting. "Why don't you write one of those books like E. Lynn Harris?" she asked. "It's not that easy," I told her, but something about her message stuck with me. Maybe she was right about one thing. Maybe it was time for me to make some money instead of trying to save the world.

I finally hit rock bottom one day when I drove almost an hour in traffic out to Jacob Riis Park, a beach in Brooklyn, and realized I did not have enough money to pay the toll to get across the bridge. There was no money in my wallet. No money in my checking account. No money in my savings. And my credit cards were maxed out. I drove back to the nearest gas station, searched through my car for stray quarters and then worked up the courage to ask someone at the gas station to lend me the last dime I needed. Once I got over the bridge, I realized I needed more money to park the car and to cross the bridge back to the mainland. Again, I had to find a gas station where I could "borrow" some money. When I got back to my apartment that evening, I knew it was time to change my life, and working on King's book seemed to offer an easy way out.

The drive back to the house had given me plenty of time to think about the book, but I still wanted to know more about J. L. King. I remembered that King had encouraged women to be down low detectives, so I decided to do a little detective work of my own to find about him. Was he credible? Did he know what he was talking about? What did other people think about him? My friend Maurice would surely have something to say. I remembered the strong words Maurice expressed about King when we were at the restaurant in Washington, so I called him on the phone to get his opinion. "What do you know about J. L. King?" I asked. Maurice told me that he and King had both been on a recent television segment on *The News*

Hour with Jim Lehrer. I looked it up on the Internet and found the transcript. King's comments on that show concerned me. They played right into the media hype about the down low and set him up as the sole person who could speak on the topic.

"Most down low brothers look at themselves at being nothing but a heterosexual man—with a twist, every now and then wanting to have sex with another man," King told the reporter on the show. "To a down low brother, [sex is] more gratification and not orientation. It's all about, let's get together do the sexual thing, then I'm outta here. Don't ask me any questions whatsoever. That's what makes it so dangerous."

That was an incredible statement filled with generalizations and unprovable assertions. *Most* down low brothers? How did King know what *most* down low brothers wanted to do? Had he met all the men on the down low? Had he done a survey or a poll? How could he possibly know what *most* of these men thought, especially if they prided themselves on maintaining their secrecy and privacy. It was a ridiculous claim, but no one challenged him on it. He was the only one who was actually speaking from the perspective of the down low, so reporters listened uncritically to what he said. But how did one individual's personal experience become the basis for a cultural obsession?

"When I look at gay men, when I look at what they call their culture, how they have their own churches, and they have their own clubs, and bars, and they do their own thing—I don't relate to that," King said. "You will not find a down low brother in a gay bar—a real, true down, bona fide low brother," he said. That statement indicated that King himself knew very little about black gay and bisexual men. Many black men who have sex with men do not identify with the "gay community" either, but they do not necessarily consider themselves down low. A 2002 study conducted by the

National Gay and Lesbian Task Force found a significant percent of black men surveyed at black gay and lesbian pride events did not identify as gay. Some said that they were "same-gender-loving," "in the life," "open to love," "questioning," and "curious," while other respondents simply wrote in "I like what I like." It's also true that some bona fide men on the down low do go to black gay clubs and bars. I have met some of these men myself. They may not go out in the same town where they live, but they will go out in other places. I have also met a number of men on the down low—men with wives and families—who have socialized among black gay men. What I would not do, however, is generalize from my own experiences and then declare that most men on the down low are exactly like the down low men I have met.

J. L. King has also criticized traditional AIDS prevention messages. "The message so far has been to the gay community," he said. "They have not sent those messages out to where 'down low,' or men who don't relate to or are labeled," he said. Wait a minute. That statement made no sense either. By his own testimony, down low men did not go to any special place to meet each other, so how could you target a message for a particular place if they were not going to be there? King talked about the absence of "safe sex messages" at barber shops, shopping malls, and gyms, but once again, he was off base. Was he saying that men on the down low do actually go to certain places? If so, then those places would not be very down low. And the places he mentioned were the exact same places where all men, including gay and bisexual men, could be found.

The story gets more convoluted if you listen closely to the contradictions in the message. If we take King's suggestion and target barber shops and gyms, would that reach men on the down low? Not if you follow King's other logic. Maurice reminded me about the exchange that he and King had at the African-American AIDS conference earlier that year. When asked how to change the behavior of men on the down low, King told the audience, "You can't." I found the transcribed notes from the conference on the Internet, and they confirmed Maurice's description of King's response. But King's defeatist attitude seemed to contradict his message about going to barber shops and gyms. What would be the point of doing outreach to men on the down low if, as King suggested, these men could never be reached? For that matter, what was the point of raising the issue of the down low in the first place if there was nothing that could be done about it?

My next call was to Phill Wilson. I told him about King's offer and asked him if he thought I should accept it. Phill was characteristically evenhanded in his response. On the one hand, working on the book might give me the opportunity to help shape and influence King's message in a positive direction, Phill said. On the other hand, working on the book might prove to be a frustrating experience if the book did not turn out well. Phill's response was so impartial that I wondered if he felt responsible for creating the whole down low monster in the beginning. It was Phill who had given J. L. King his first national platform when he invited him to speak at the African-American AIDS Conference back in February, and Phill moderated the panel where King launched his down low profile. During the panel, King had described the typical attitude of men on the down low when he said, "I don't go to gay clubs and I don't talk to gay people. I go to straight clubs. The pickings are better there." That statement made little sense either. Obviously, some men on the down low had to talk to gay men. They may not have done so openly, but they still talked to them. How else could these men meet their sexual partners, unless King was suggesting that men on the down low only slept with other men on the down low. But that could not be the case either. If they were only sleeping with each other, then it undermined the whole argument that they were bringing back HIV from the gay community into the straight community. How could they bring a virus from the gay community if they had no contact with that community?

The statement was also confusing because King said the "pickings are better" in straight clubs than in gay clubs. That begs an obvious question. How do you know the pickings are better if you have never been to the gay clubs? It didn't add up. In fact, almost nothing he said made sense. It reminded me of the words Phill had spoken at the beginning of the down low panel where J. L. King was first introduced. Likening the situation to Lewis Carroll's *Alice in Wonderland,* Phill described the scene in which Alice finds herself in a place where "What is, is not, and what is not, is." That seemed a fitting description of J. L. King as well. The more I learned about him, the more questions I had.

I had not been following the public down low discussion since I had dinner with Linda, Phill, and Maurice months earlier. I had been finishing my last semester teaching at American University and spending every weekend of the spring driving up to New York to find an affordable place to live. While I was making a transition in my life, J. L. King was making one of his own. Following the African-American AIDS Conference, King had been deluged by reporters who wanted to know more about the mysterious world of the down low. He gave several interviews, and a string of articles appeared in major newspapers across the country.

USA Today's article on March 15, 2001, was the first to focus exclusively on the down low. But that article shifted the focus away from the high infection rates facing black gay and bisexual men and instead focused on black women who were victims of certain deceitful black men. I realized that something was missing, and I quickly figured out what it was. Black men were victims too. They were being infected at an alarming rate, and the overwhelming majority of black AIDS cases were among black men, not black women. But black men in crisis was an old story, and the idea of black men as victims did not fit into our preconceived image of black men as perpetrators. Every few months, somebody was releasing a disturbing new study about black men who were supposedly unemployed, in prison, abandoning their children, or dropping out of school. America knew that story line well. The down low, however, provided a sexy new vehicle to drive home a more predictable message about AIDS in the black community. With hints of closeted sexuality and talk of double lives, it played right into our stereotypical image of black men, and it conjured up the secrecy of a mysterious underground lifestyle. King called it "a culture that represents probably millions of men . . . from the pulpit to the police force." And that made the story exciting.

The *USA Today* article helped to initiate the dramatic change in public concern from black men to black women. The headline read: "The danger of living 'down low': Black men who hide their bisexuality can put women at risk." And with that message, a story that began from a study about black gay men had been transformed into a story about the risk to straight black women. The soon-to-be repeated statistics about HIV among black men became a mere mechanism to show why black women should be concerned. Twenty years after the epidemic began, we were finally starting to engage in the fight against AIDS, but even as we approached the battlefield, we seemed reluctant to fight the full war.

The *USA Today* story began with an imaginary black "Prince Charming" figure who was "well-paid, well-educated, nicely dressed, active in church and devoted to family." But despite his other virtues, we were told, he was "secretly having sex with men" and "might bring home an unwelcome guest—HIV, the AIDS virus."

Unfortunately, that story was a scare tactic for black America. The image of the well-paid, nicely dressed, churchgoing black man on the down low played right into the fears of middle-class black women all across America. But the image was not supported by any evidence in the scientific research. To bolster the claim in the article, the story cited a CDC study that showed that 25 percent of young gay and bisexual men surveyed had unprotected sex with both men and women. True, but that study was conducted with men from fifteen to twenty-two, they were not all black, they came from just seven urban settings, and they were recruited at "venues frequented by young MSM." In other words, they were not the middle-class black men in stable relationships. Most of the men in the study were adolescents who were way too young to be well-paid, well-educated, nicely dressed family men. And since many of them were recruited at gay bars and other places where down low men supposedly fear to tread, they hardly fit J. L. King's description of the DL. All the men in the study were comfortable enough with their identity that they were willing to tell a total stranger that they had sex with men. That was not the down low.

Even for middle-class black men who were on the down low, there was no evidence that they were HIV positive. Often, we make the assumption that all, or most, down low men are HIV infected, but that assumption has never been proven and seems highly unlikely. Nor has it been shown that large numbers of middle-class men on the down low were having unprotected sex with their male partners. In fact, it seemed illogical that they would, given their need to protect their secrecy. Middle-class down low men might be more inclined than others to use condoms. If you don't want your wife to know that you're sleeping around, then you would probably want to use a condom with your outside sex partners so you don't bring home any diseases and end up getting caught.

The stories of the two bisexual men quoted in the *USA Today* article actually undermined the connection between men on the down low and HIV infections among women. The article quoted King, who described himself as "a life member" of the down low but never said anything about being HIV positive. The other bisexual man quoted in the story was Raenard Brown, a forty-nine-year-old man who had a four-year relationship with a woman when he was HIV negative. It seems that neither of the bisexual men quoted in the article ever passed HIV to his female partner. That is an important point to make because the premise of the down low obsession is that DL men are spreading the virus to black women. Nobody would doubt that there are men on the down low who pass HIV to black women, but, again, not one of the men *in the article* had done so. There was not one iota of evidence in the *USA Today* article to prove that large numbers of down low men were infecting black women with HIV. It was all speculation.

The *USA Today* story was the first major newspaper article that mentioned J. L. King, and I was still trying to withhold judgment on him when I read it. The article was already troubling, but there was one part that finally helped me decide what to do about his book proposal. The article said the title of King's new book would be *Secrets: The Official Handbook of the Lifestyles of African-American Men Who Have Sex with Men.* That sensationalistic title was not a good sign, but I would not judge his book by the cover. After all, book titles often change, and King might be willing to change the title and focus of his book. Next, I read King's description of the personality types for men on the DL. There was the "Rough Neck Player," a thuglike figure who King said was the most popular down low type. Then there was the "Brooks Brothers Brother," a professional man who refuses to deal with men below his level. And finally there was the "Bi-Curious Brother," the ex-convict who, out of curiosity, lets men perform sex acts on him.

I chuckled at the descriptions. I had certainly met all three types of men in my life experiences, and I suppose the descriptions were amusing. But I soon realized that the personality types were amusing because they were simply broad, meaningless generalizations. His whole argument was internally contradictory. On the one hand, he claimed that down low men were so secretive that they could not be picked out in a crowd. But on the other hand, he was writing a book to tell black women how to pick them out in a crowd. That was more than I could take.

I spoke to King on the phone and told him that I could not do the book, and I gave him the names of two other writers who might be interested instead. He seemed prepared for my decision but did not give up entirely. He had some other writers in mind anyway, he said, and he thought it might be better to have a female writer since the book would be marketed toward black women. As the conversation ended, however, I got the impression that the door of opportunity was still open as he tried to sweeten the pot. "We're gonna make a lot of money off this," he said, almost enticingly. At first, I was skeptical of that claim. You can't fool all the people all the time, and King's plan seemed so transparently venal that I expected his publishers would see right through him. If not his publishers, then the public would surely challenge him, and King might self-destruct from the weight of his own contradictions. But deep in my heart, I knew he was probably right about the money. After all, no one ever went broke exploiting the fears of the American public. I knew King would do well by exploiting our fears, and although I could have used the money he was offering, I could not be a part of his book. We said our good-byes, I hung up the phone, and I hoped that would be the end of it. But, of course, the down low story did not end with that phone call.

Instead, the down low became increasingly ridiculous. Bloggers on the Internet started writing about it. Women on Internet message boards and listservs started trading secrets on how to spot a man on the down low. Some even started spying on their own men. A few weeks after the *New York Times Magazine* story appeared in the summer of 2003, I heard about a book called *How to Tell If Your Man Is Gay or Bisexual.* The author, Shahrazad Ali, was once the queen of controversy with her book *The Black Man's Guide to Understanding the Blackwoman* (1989). In that book, she provided ridiculous advice on how to deal with a black woman. "Soundly slap her in her mouth," she told black men. Her follow-up book, *The Black Woman's Guide to Understanding the Blackman* (1992) was just as dumb. There, she claimed that her research showed that black gay men became homosexual because of unsuccessful relationships with females, that 95 percent of them grew up in homes with either no father or a weak father, that "they feel no special connection or responsibility to other Blacks" and that they "can cook, sew and bake and are determined to be a better woman than all the women they know." If all those stereotypes were true, then Ali would have a hard time explaining the "unclockable" black men on the down low. Many of them were in relationships with females, grew up in homes with strong fathers, were very connected to the black community, and couldn't or wouldn't cook to save their lives. Given everything I knew about Ali, I could not allow myself to buy her new book without doing some basic research online. There I found one reviewer had retitled it *How to Tell If This Book Is Flammable* and urged readers to light it on fire. With that said, I decided to save my money.

A few months before J. L. King's book was published, an article about him in the *Chicago Sun-Times* raised even more concern. Early in the piece, the article claimed that "the Centers for Disease Control and Prevention connected black men on the down low with the rise of HIV infection rates among black women." In reality, that never happened. By its own admission, the CDC had never made any connection between men on the down low and HIV infections among black women.

As I read through the article, something else concerned me. It seemed as though King had not changed much over the years. I recognized the same J. L. King I had met on the telephone years earlier. He talked about his $4,000 lecture fee, his publicist in New York, and his lecture agent. He also mentioned a media consultant and said, "She's working with me to help me refine my whole image." Even the sympathetic reporter noted that King had "plenty of handlers." To read the story, it seemed as if King was more interested in making money off the down low hype than helping the community with honest information. He told the *Sun-Times* reporter that he was using his speaking opportunities to push a new brand of condoms and was actively looking for paid endorsement deals. And his comments suggested that the book might not actually help black men and women learn to trust each other. Instead, King promised his book was "probably going to set back black male-female relationships."

Black women "finally got somebody who looks like them or their husband, and doesn't act like a sissy," King said of himself. But he never really explained his own identity. "I no longer want to be promoted as this DL person," he acknowledged. "I look at myself as going through a transformation of acceptance." That may be true, but what exactly did he accept? A few months after the article, his identity was much less clear when he appeared on *Oprah*. He was not gay, he was not bisexual, he was not on the down low. He simply refused to be labeled. A few months after that, when *A&U* maga-zine featured him on a cover story, his story changed again. "All my life I was a bisexual man who was living on the DL," he said.

Perhaps it is difficult for reporters to challenge King, because it is was difficult to understand where he stood. In a May 2004 inter-view with *The Advocate,* for example, King complained that "the media needs to show two strong black men in a committed rela-tionship, living together and being positive in their community. Instead, you see sissies, faggots, and clownlike characters." But when asked about his own sexual orientation, King replied, "If I could settle down today, it would be with a woman. My life will be easier if I have a woman in my life, living the American dream. I don't see myself with a man, growing older, being with him for the rest of my life. No way. It's easier to be heterosexual in our culture." Appar-ently, King did not even see the contradiction in his own words. How did he expect the media to show black men in "committed relationships" when he disparaged those relationships in the very next sentence out of his mouth? And when he did talk about black gay men, he talked about sissies, faggots, and clowns.

What is, is not, and what is not, is.

After a life spent deceiving everyone around him, King may now feel the need to make amends for the lies of his past, but that has not stopped him from sensationalizing serious issues into dramatic parody. When a reporter from *The Advocate* asked King about a story line on the television show *Law & Order: SVU* involving a black man on the down low who murders his white male sex partner, King had a ready answer. "I know a brother right now who's fucking a white guy, and if [the white guy] ever outed him, he'd kill him," said King. If nothing else, reporters can always count on J. L. King for a good quote.

So how does a story based entirely on anecdotal and circumstantial evidence become a mainstream media sensation big enough to generate headlines in the *New York Times* and *Washington Post* and to be discussed on the nation's most respected daytime television talk show?

First, it helps if you have a major publicity budget from Random House. The media feed off the other media. If the *Wall Street Journal* runs a story, then the *New York Times* is more likely to run a story, and if the *Times* runs a story, then the *Washington Post* may run a story, and the cycle continues on and on. By the time the down low subject got to *Oprah,* it had been vetted and filtered through every respected newspaper in the country, giving it the pedigree of a serious story. If the nation's most respected journalists were writing about it, then there was no reason why Oprah Winfrey shouldn't talk about it as well. But Oprah was not the problem. The problem was that the mainstream media had never really challenged the logic behind the down low in the first place.

Second, if you want to start a media frenzy, it also doesn't hurt to have a provocative spokesman who is willing to make controversial remarks about a taboo topic. "The reason why this makes *Oprah* is because of the homosexual story line," according to Phill Wilson of the Black AIDS Institute. He may be right, and yet the fascination with homosexuality and bisexuality can blind us to other realities, including the possibility that men who are not on the down low can also spread HIV to their partners.

The worst part of the down low story is that it is being promoted by a black man who is using America's fear of black men to advance his own agenda. Few black figures are more compelling to white America than the black man who is willing to criticize his own people. Remember the example of William Hannibal Thomas who wrote the 1901 book, *The American Negro.* Thomas, you may recall, said that "Negro nature is so craven and sensuous in every fiber of its being that a Negro manhood with decent respect for chaste womanhood does not exist." In Thomas's case, the Macmillan Company was willing to publish multiple printings of his incendiary book despite the fact that Thomas lived "a life shrouded in ambiguity, controversy and secrecy," as he was described by his biographer John David Smith in *Black Judas*. But controversy sells books. If you add ambiguity and secrecy to the mix, you could easily have a best-seller.

It's even easier when you are demonizing black men. Perception is more important than reality when it comes to black men. In 1901, it was easy for Thomas to portray black men as indecent sexual creatures because people in society already saw us that way. Since that time, it has been easy for others throughout history to portray black men as sexual predators because many people in society still see us that way.

When nine black boys were wrongly convicted of gang raping two white women on an Alabama train in 1931, the "Scottsboro Boys" were portrayed as sexual predators. When fourteen-year-old Emmett Till was lynched in Mississippi in August 1955, the white men who murdered him imagined him as a sexual predator because he had whistled at a white woman. And when black men are discussed today in the context of the down low, we too are portrayed as sexual predators.

"The thing that makes this down low story a major media issue is that fact that these men are sleeping with other men," says Phill Wilson. "That's why it's so easy to totally exclude from the conversation the fact that black women might be at risk because their male partners might be sleeping with HIV positive women," he adds. That message is more difficult for us to hear. It may be easier for us to understand the image of the closeted black gay man as the evildoer who is coming into our lives to break up our happy homes. A commentator named "Blackbrit" on the *New York Times Magazine* Web forum put it this way: "Too often the DL brother is constructed as the vessel of contagion." He blamed this perspective on a "hetero-sexist assumption that AIDS is born and bred in gay communities then venomously spread to pure, sterile black communities." In reality, he reminded us, "straight black people are HIV-positive and spreading the disease among themselves without any help from 'evil' black gay men."

The down low story also appealed to us because J. L. King offered answers that no one else would. AIDS rates were relatively high in black America, and King, at least, offered an explanation. Men on the down low, he said, were responsible for the spread of the AIDS epidemic to black women. No one else in America seemed willing to say that. The CDC wouldn't say that. The leading researchers wouldn't say that. The AIDS advocates in the field wouldn't say that either. Of course, no one denied that there were men on the down low. Everyone in the AIDS field already knew that. But they did not know who they were, how many they were, how many were in relationships, how many were HIV positive, or how many were using protection. The down low story only made sense if we could answer those questions, but it would have been very difficult to do so. The only way to verify any information about this group was to ask the people who were on the down low, which was already complicated. First, you would have to find them, and how do you find people who are trying not to be found? Next, you would have to trust them. The same people who would admit that they were habitual liars would have to be trusted to tell the truth about their lies. It was very convoluted, but it was a perfect oppor-tunity for a smooth-talking "expert" who had admittedly spent his adult life deceiving people.

J. L. King had an answer that no one could challenge. As the only one who was talking publicly about this secret lifestyle, anything he said was taken as fact because no one could repudiate it. He had constructed quite a clever ploy. If he said certain people were on the down low, how could anyone prove that they were *not* on the down low? The "suspects" could never admit it because that would blow their cover. If, however, they denied it, King could still argue that they were on the down low. Thus, without any other evidence to back up his claims, King skillfully turned his individual life stories into a public, and soon to be profitable, truth.

It's not clear whether all those handlers paid off. On the *Oprah* show, King "misquoted HIV statistics" and provided "sensational- istic rhetoric," according to Dr. David Malebranche, a doctor, HIV specialist, and professor at Emory University in Atlanta. When Oprah asked King how he could tell who is on the down low, he told her, "we do it by the eyes" and said "I could make a connection in this room." That may be true, but that is not specific to the down low. In fact, gay men have been doing the same thing for centuries. Some call it "gaydar." In a culture that represses open expression of homosexuality, men with same-sex attraction often find other men simply by looking at them and seeing if they look back. It's not complicated, it's not rocket science, and it's not a mystery. It's the same technique that many heterosexuals use to gauge interest from those they find attractive. But King's comments on the *Oprah* show made me more concerned about his book.

The book was not yet in the stores when King appeared on *Oprah,* so I went to his Web site to try to find out more. There, I found his list of the "top questions" asked about the down low, and the first question listed was an indication of what to expect: "How can I tell if my man is on the DL?" I was not surprised by the response. "The answers to these questions and much more will be in the book. Please make sure you get your copy on May 10, 2004."

A few weeks after the *Oprah* appearance, I finally picked up

King's book, *On The Down Low,* and read it on a flight to Seattle. In some ways, the book was better than I expected it to be. The writing, in particular, was much better than I expected and seemed clearly different from King's own voice. He had obviously found an excellent ghost writer. Some big-time celebrities do not write their own books. Many don't have the time, some don't have the knowledge, and others simply don't know how to write. Celebrity ghost writers can be valuable for artists, athletes, and entertainers who want to tell their stories in print, but they can also useful for non-celebrities if they have the money. J. L. King was not yet a celebrity, but he was not an author either. However, he was smart enough to pick one of the best celebrity biographers in the business—Karen Hunter.

Karen Hunter had written celebrity biographies and autobiographies for several of the leading figures in black America. She co-authored LL Cool J's bestselling book *I Make My Own Rules* in 1997. She co-wrote Queen Latifah's bestselling book *Ladies First* in 1999. And when the rapper Mase published his book *Revelations* in 2001, he too chose Karen Hunter to help him out. Even the Reverend Al Sharpton's book, *Al on America,* was co-authored by Karen Hunter.

One of Hunter's most valuable connections was with New York's popular radio personality Wendy Williams. Williams had often spoken on the radio about homothugs, gay rappers, and closeted performers in the entertainment industry, and she had a reputation for dealing with hot topics. With access to A-list celebrities and a huge media market, Wendy Williams could help to make or break a new artist, entertainer, or author. The guests on the highly rated *Wendy Williams Show* were some of the same entertainers who had come to Karen Hunter to write their books, so it was no surprise that Williams chose Hunter to co-write her own books, *Wendy's Got the Heat* in 2003 and *The Wendy Williams Experience* in 2004. And perhaps it should come as no surprise that J. L. King chose Karen Hunter to write his book as well.

Parts of King's book were informative and entertaining, other parts seemed unrealistic, and much of the book was, quite frankly, contradictory. In many ways, the book, like the author, was the proverbial riddle wrapped in a mystery inside an enigma. Every answer seemed to raise at least two questions, which never got answered. The more you peeled away, the more confused you became. Even in the introduction to the book, King claims that his success was "ordained by God" and describes how speaking engagements and media appearances found their way to him "seemingly out of nowhere." As King said, "I had no connections to help me get invited to speak. Nor did I have a public relations professional promoting my message to the media." Yet in the first chapter of his book, he tells a different story. There, he explains that he resigned from his job in 2001 and had a friend put together a brochure called "Secrets of the African-American Bisexual Man." That wasn't all. "I had been in marketing for my entire professional career," King wrote, "so I knew how to do this part of it." King then acknowledges that he sent his brochure to fifty-two health departments throughout the country. Given that extensive marketing campaign, it's hard to understand his claim that the speaking engagements came "out of nowhere."

In another apparent contradiction, King admits his lack of knowledge about AIDS issues when he first started talking about the down low in 2001. "I wasn't a health expert," he wrote. "I didn't know much about HIV and AIDS or the statistics." But on the back jacket of his book, he identifies himself as "an HIV/STD prevention activist, educator and author" whose "expertise" has been cited in various national publications. That's fine. If he is now an expert, then he should be expected to know the basic research to support his argument.

But in the very first chapter of his book, King completely misquotes important CDC statistics that any expert should know. For example, on page 10 of his book he claims that "sixty-eight percent of all new AIDS cases are black women." That's just plain wrong, and anyone who calls himself an AIDS expert should know better. Based on the latest statistics available when King published his book, black women made up just 18 percent of all new AIDS cases, not 68 percent, as King claimed. That's a huge difference, but King did not appear concerned about facts and statistics when asked a question by a reporter for *Southern Voice* newspaper in August 2004. "King brushed off criticism from public health experts about his lack of data, saying he has done more for introducing blacks to safe-sex education in the past year than anyone else in the past two decades," the reporter wrote. That is an insulting statement that shows just how little King really knows about the work of HIV/AIDS activists who have been fighting the epidemic for decades without the publicity of a major book tour.

King is unashamed of his newfound fame and talks about it frequently. A woman would "have to be from another planet by now not to have heard of me," King told the *Houston Chronicle*. "I travel with bodyguards because there are so many people who want to silence the messenger," he added. And he is not afraid to take credit for saving the black community. "I'm making the everyday common folks hear about this epidemic," he told the *Southern Voice*. "Now there's more of a demand for everyday people to learn about it, and that wasn't happening before me." Finally, in an interview with *Salon.com*, King confessed his real agenda. "I want people to say thank you, J. L., for forcing us to take a look at sexuality and sexual orientation. Hopefully when the [HIV/AIDS] numbers start decreasing, people will say it's because of this guy who stepped forward and put a face on this behavior—that it's because of his vision that we're seeing a decrease." In other words, it's all about J. L. King. One man spreading misinformation wants to get credit for saving the entire black community. Apparently, it does not matter to him that the conversation that is now taking place—the conversation that he says he started—is based on fear instead of facts.

King may have been right about one thing. His book may actually set back black male-female relationships, just as he predicted months before its publication. As the author Darryl James observed in an article about the down low, "This issue has not provided any intrinsic awareness, and has not served to create more open discussions about sex, sexuality or sexually transmitted diseases. What it has done is to drive a wedge between the already divided pools of single Black men and women." And there are consequences. A black woman in Tampa told the *St. Petersburg Times* that the book frightened her to the point that she looks at the men in church differently. "It made me not want to date," she confessed. Stephanie Edgecombe in Washington, D.C., expressed similar feelings in an interview with *Salon.com.* "When I first heard about the DL, fear immediately set in . . . Now you have to be an FBI agent? This is what is so frightening to me."

It's hard to believe that those are just some of the minor problems and contradictions in King's book. The other contradictions call into question the seriousness of his "research" and the purpose of his message. For example, in Chapter 2 of his book, King says that down low men are in "denial" about "being a homosexual." Then he adds, "If they tell the truth and say they're gay or bisexual, they will be called a 'fag.'" In essence, King is admitting that down low men are gay or bisexual. But in several other places in the book, he claims that DL men are *not* gay or bisexual. He never clarifies the contradiction.

On one page King says "the DL man is indistinguishable from every other man in the crowd. And that's the way he likes it." Four pages later, he says a DL man is "the first one to stand up in church and shout, 'Get the homosexuals out of here!'" It's hard to figure out how standing up and shouting against gays in a church would make someone "indistinguishable" in the crowd, but that's the kind of inconsistency we see throughout King's book and his message.

The third chapter of King's book is even more perplexing. In that chapter, King reveals a salacious homosexual affair that supposedly ended his seven-year marriage to his wife, Brenda. When she found out about the affair, she locked him out of his own house and cut him off, he says. In describing that affair, King makes a big deal about not using a condom with his male sex partner. "We never even talked about safe or safer sex," King wrote. "We never used protection. Never." Seems like a clear problem until you get to the very end of the chapter. That's when King tells us that the story took place when he was twenty-seven years old. And when was King twenty-seven years old? He does not tell us. It is difficult to be exactly sure of King's age because a number of newspaper articles about him curiously skip over that fact, but there is some reliable information out there. *USA Today* reported that King was forty-four years old in March 2001. In August 2004, an article on King in *Salon.com* reported that he was forty-nine years old. I don't understand how someone jumps from forty-four to forty-nine in just three years, but let's assume the more recent article is correct.

If King was forty-nine in 2004, then he would have been twenty-seven in 1982. His marriage would have taken place from approximately 1975 to 1982. In other words, the melodramatic unsafe sex story that King details in his book actually took place long before *anyone* knew about HIV. The first cases of AIDS were reported in June 1981, and the government did not even create a name for it until 1982. At that time, there were no safe sex messages about using condoms. Nobody was using condoms to stop HIV because nobody knew how it was spread back then. Most men were only using condoms to prevent pregnancy, not to stop a virus that they had never heard about. King's failure to disclose the year in which his affair took place seems purposefully designed to mislead the reader not only about his own safe sex practices, but also about the safe sex practices of other men on the down low. A story about a man not using condoms from 1975 to 1982 is completely irrelevant to the down low today.

The 1982 story raises questions about King's credibility, but it also raises questions about the credibility of the down low story itself. For example, if black men were on the down low twenty years ago, why are we just now talking about it now, especially since King's own marriage provides a clear example that the down low has been around for decades. And here's another question. If black men on the down low have been sleeping around for twenty years, why are black women only now becoming infected by these men? King never answers those questions in his book.

Of the many troubling questions and contradictions in King's book, the most disturbing are the questions about what he calls "DL behavior types" and about "the signs" to tell if a man is on the DL. King claims to have conducted extensive "research" involving "DL focus groups" and has used that research to develop five DL behavior types. King never explains the methodology used to conduct the focus groups or to select the participants, nor does he explain what exactly constitutes a "DL focus group." By his own definition, men on the down low would have nothing to do with anything—especially a focus group— that identified them as being on the down low. Maybe King recruited some of his own down low friends from his secret society. That's a plausible explanation, but it seems unlikely that one person's network of contacts could be broad enough to draw conclusions about what he claims are "millions of men." It seems even less plausible when the men are consciously trying not to be detected. Of course, he might have met some of the men because they wanted to hook up with him, but that would not necessarily create a diverse pool for a focus group unless we assume that men of all ages, lifestyles, and backgrounds wanted to hook up with him. But at forty-nine years old, King is probably not as connected to men in the younger age range who are most affected by the epidemic. The participants in the CDC studies of young black men, for example, were fifteen to twenty-nine years old, not the group of people who typically hang out with forty-nine-year-olds.

The five personality types in King's book were similar to the three types I had read about years before. In addition to the "thug brother" and the "curious brother," King also included the "mature brother" and the "I have a wife/girlfriend brother." He also renamed the "Brooks Brothers Brother" the "professional brother." At the beginning of the chapter, however, King zeroes in on the major flaw in his own research. The behavior types are so broad that they describe "every man in our communities." King says that's the point because "DL men don't stand out." But if that's the case, then why go through the whole exercise of writing a chapter about the five behavior types? He never answers that question. Instead, he provides a litany of stereotypes under the guise of research. The mature brother, for example, "knows how to get what he wants and keep what he has." He's older than the other types, but don't expect much more analysis from King. This character type gets just four paragraphs of text in the book.

The "thug brother," on the other hand, gets several pages. King calls him a "homo-thug," a term most often used to describe black gay and bisexual men who dress in "thuggish" urban gear. But homo-thugs often go out to gay clubs, as Malcolm Venable explained in his groundbreaking July 2001 *VIBE* magazine article "A Question of Identity." In a gross generalization about a whole group of people, King says the thug brother "has little knowledge" about HIV because "he doesn't read." And just to make it easier to spot the thug from a distance, King says the thug brother "might have braids or dreads or sport a baldie." That narrows the field to about half of all black men.

King's "professional brother" is described as a metrosexual who is "always dressed very GQ." But this brother "will tend to have safer sex and may take an HIV test every time he has sex with a man," King says. Safer sex? HIV tests? Those words contradict almost everything the public has been told about the down low. Furthermore, that message actually acknowledges that the stereotypical middle-class professional black man at the very core of the whole down low frenzy is more likely than others to practice safe sex. If that is true, then it calls into question the hysterical media frenzy about middle-class black women becoming infected by their down low partners, and it undermines the whole point of J. L. King's book—that all women are at great risk from the down low.

King dispenses with the "'I have a wife/girlfriend' brother" in just three short paragraphs and then moves onto the personality type that gets most of his attention—the curious brother. Men in this group are described by King as "the only one of the five types of DL brothers I've met who will go to a local gay bar, party, or event." That is a perfectly fair statement because King limits his assertion to the extent of his own knowledge, but in so doing he demonstrates the very limits of his knowledge. Malcolm Venable's article in *VIBE* found homo-thugs in a black gay nightclub in the Bronx, and King himself admitted in Chapter 12 of his book that some other types of DL men may go out to gay bars. In the end,

King's five behavior types do more harm than good by alarming black women with little or no basis in evidence.

As a result, he has helped to create a culture in which women are learning to be "down low detectives." They are trading tips on how to spot men on the down low and posting messages on Web sites to find the tricks of the trade. "I am new to figuring this out," writes one woman on a Yahoo group for women "betrayed" by men on the down low. "But I think there are hand gestures involved such as scratching a part of the face." Another poster encourages women to slip a finger or two up their man's ass. "If he accepts two fingers up his butt then he surely is DL." On a different message forum on Bravenet, women are also upset but they are fighting back by posting photographs of men who they say are on the down low.

It's happening in the mainstream media as well. A counselor quoted in a September 2004 article in the *Detroit News* tells women to look for "low sexual appetite," gay friends, or homophobia. It seems a bit of a circular argument. If the man is homophobic, then he is probably gay, but if he is not homophobic and has gay friends, then he is still probably gay.

In his chapter on the signs, King reprints a letter to the editor written to *USA Today* in which a woman asks a gay friend to make a pass at her husband to see if he responds. The scheme worked for the woman, and based on her experience she offered a suggestion. "My advice to women is get you a gay man and have him come on to your man," she wrote. And if a woman has no gay friends, King has some simple advice to help them as well. Watch the eyes, he says. Men communicate with their eyes, he warns. But of course they also communicate with their mouths, so if your man says the word "S'up," that should cause some suspicion as well, King suggests. "The signs are very subtle," he insists. It could be a "hug that is just a second too long" or if your man wants to have anal sex in your heterosexual relationship. In fact, King's signs are so broadly constructed that just about anything a man does might raise a red flag.

This is where King's message gets muddled in its own contradictions again. To his credit, King says "a woman should not automatically label her man 'on the DL' when his actions change." He also admits that "not every black man is on the DL" and "not every black man in your life is on the DL." That is an accurate and important message to deliver. But at the same time he counsels caution, he tacitly encourages the very behavior he supposedly discourages. He does tell women not to "overdo" it, but he never tells them not to do it—not to spy on their partners. Instead, in two consecutive pages of his book, King seems to deliver repeatedly conflicting advice. First, on page 129, King says that women might hire a private investigator or find a "masculine-looking gay man" to try to seduce their man. But then on page 130 he says couples "should strive to have a relationship where they can talk freely about sex, where they can have the power of choice through open, honest discussion." Later on the same page, he changes his message again and says a woman "can't just approach her man and ask, 'Baby, are you fooling around with another man?'" Instead, he says women should follow "their intuition" and "start playing detective" to find out if their man is on the DL.

How does a couple create an open and honest relationship in this climate of distrust? According to King, just pretend that you're doing good things while you're discreetly checking up on your man. Get to know your man's schedule, King says, and change your own schedule while you're at it. "Drop in on him at work and take him to lunch one day out of the blue. Come home early from work one day; surprise him." King says it's more difficult for men to get away with DL activity if their women keep surprising them. No doubt that's true, but it's also horrible advice for managing a relationship. If your man really wants to be with another man, it's just a matter of time before it happens. It probably doesn't matter how many times you come home early from work to interrupt him. If he's going to do it, he's going to do it somewhere, somehow, away from you.

Men and women in relationships cannot form healthy bonds if they create patterns of distrust. Instead of becoming down low detectives, we need to get to know our partners before we enter relationships with them. Once in those relationships, we have to learn to trust one another and communicate to each other. If you need to snoop around to check on your partner's e-mails and cell phone messages, then maybe you shouldn't be involved in a relationship with him in the first place. Maybe you need to find someone you can trust.

Of course, many women are legitimately concerned about dishonesty from their men, but the way to change the culture of untruthfulness is to practice honesty in your own behavior. Deputizing yourself as a down low detective will not make your man heterosexual if he is not, and it will not save your relationship if it is built on mutual mistrust. You can spend the rest of your life going to down low seminars and reading the latest magazine articles on how to tell if your man is gay, but the truth is there is no way to tell. There are no real "signs" to spot a man on the down low, and there are no real "behavior types" of these men. Despite the contradictory messages in his book, King himself admits that men on the down low do not look a certain way or act a certain way.

If you want to protect yourself, you cannot make assumptions based on appearances, sexual orientation, performance in bed, marital status, or old test results. If you don't want to be infected with HIV, then you have the responsibility to protect yourself. Nobody else can do that for you. The best way to know the truth is not to spy on your partner but to create an environment where sexuality can be discussed openly.

The truth is, you cannot tell if a man is on the down low, and you should never trust anyone who says you can.

CHAPTER 7
Victims and Villains

AS I WALKED off the plane, I could not remember the last time I had been to Atlanta. The city had changed a lot since I had lived there. My father and sister relocated to Atlanta in the 1980s and had moved between Stone Mountain, Marietta, and Smyrna. Between semesters at school and in between jobs, I bounced back and forth to the Atlanta area as a place of refuge. In one of my early jobs during a semester away from college, I sold jeans and things at the Gap at Cumberland Mall. Although they called it the New South, I still felt a bit of the old when some of the elderly white customers would come in shopping. With their strong southern accents and years of wrinkles, I could not help wondering which side they had chosen during the civil rights struggles of the past. Were these the same people who had screamed racial obscenities at my parents and grandparents, and if so, how did they reconcile the passionate beliefs of their past with the racial realities of integration?

That racial history was inescapable in Atlanta. It left its imprint on nearly every institution, and it forced future generations to decide whether to forgive or forget. From Auburn

Avenue to Stone Mountain, I felt connected to the past almost everywhere I traveled. But after my years of absence, the city had been reduced to a kaleidoscopic blur of images in my mind. I remembered working on a political campaign, teaching eighth grade social studies, and hiking to the top of Stone Mountain. And I could never forget the time when I marched with Mrs. King as an honorary grand marshal in the annual King Day Parade. But the most profound image in my mind was the sight of a small band of KKK leaders marching through the streets of downtown Atlanta in 1989 under the protection of black police officers who kept them separated from hundreds of counter demonstrators. That was the paradox of Atlanta. Surrounded by some of the most conservative places in the south, the Atlanta metropolitan area was an oasis of culture and diversity where you could forgive but you could never forget.

I had come to Atlanta to make a presentation about the down low at a CDC HIV Prevention Conference. I was a little nervous about speaking to a group of experts about a topic they all knew well, so I decided to talk about what I knew. I talked about victims and villains, wherein I questioned the need to assign blame to men on the down low. Instead, I suggested that we create a culture that destigmatizes homosexuality and bisexuality so men will not feel the pressure to enter into duplicitous relationships.

I thought I had offered a fairly innocuous recommendation, but after I spoke I was peppered with questions from the audience. Most of the questions were fairly straightforward, but o\ne question shot right through me. A black woman stood at the microphone and looked me directly in the face as she spoke. "It figures they would get a gay man to come up here and speak," she said. "All I hear from you is blame," she continued. "You make it seem like black women are the perpetrators. Until you've been in a relationship with a man for fourteen years and had three kids and had him leave you for another man, then you don't understand," she said.

It seemed as if the room stood still when she finished speaking. Maybe we were all stunned. With one single question, the entire tone in the room had changed. She was definitely right about one thing. I could hardly imagine the pain involved in learning that my partner had lied to me for fourteen years. But, unfortunately, that was not the issue. The subject of the panel was not about infidelity and relationships. It was about HIV and AIDS. The two issues were connected, but they needed to be understood in context. No one would dispute the importance of honesty in relationships, but dishonesty does not spread AIDS. An honest man with HIV can still spread the virus to his partner, but a dishonest man without HIV cannot.

I think the woman who asked the question came to the panel to hear from someone who could affirm her pain rather than question her rage, and my presentation must have been a big disappointment to her. I was unable to provide the comfort she needed. Even as I tried to respond diplomatically, I may have made things worse with my reply.

"Thank you for your comment," I said. "I have three thoughts I'd like to share. First, I did not select the panel, so I cannot take responsibility for who is or is not on the stage. Second, I do hear your frustration, but I am not going to apologize for being a gay man. Third, the purpose of my remarks is not to blame black women. But I am also not here to blame black men. My whole point," I said, "is that we need to get beyond the blame game."

I had hoped that my answer would help resolve the question, but I sensed that it had encouraged more frustration among a few members of the audience. After the session ended, another black woman confronted me and told me that my comments were "insensitive" and "disrespectful." With a half-completed evaluation sheet in her hand, she listened carefully as I tried to explain my position. I got the sense that my comments might dictate her evaluation, but I could not hold back what I felt. "The down low is not responsible for the AIDS epidemic," I said. "It's time we recognize that HIV is spread by behavior, not identity. And it's time to stop pitting female victims against male villains in this discussion. We're all in this together, and we can't afford to have a battle of the sexes in the middle of an epidemic."

On the plane ride home, I thought about what I had said and how I could have handled the situation better. Some of my friends have accused me of responding to life rationally instead of emotionally, and I realized that was the disconnect in my message. I was providing facts and figures and information, but some of the people affected by the down low wanted emotion instead. I was explaining why blame was a counterproductive emotion that would not change reality, but that explanation missed the point for some listeners. Their reality was that they needed someone to blame. They had been lied to and cheated on, and they needed someone to be responsible. They needed a villain.

The man on the down low was the perfect boogeyman. If the subject was AIDS, somebody had to be responsible for transmitting the virus, and if the subject was relationships, the one who cheated was the obvious wrongdoer. It made me think of a conversation I had with J. L. King in 2001. I called to interview him for a story I was writing about AIDS in the black community. I asked him how to reach men on the down low, and what he thought about the trend toward demonizing those men. "As far as DL brothers being demonized, yeah, I think that's what it's going to take in order for women to know that they are sleeping with the enemy," said King. "A lot of guys who are on the DL who are doing this, they have no shame," he said.

Dr. David Malebranche, professor of medicine at Emory University, has a theory about all this. In an essay called "Black Dick as a Weapon of Mass Destruction," Malebranche compares the demonization of men on the down low to the vilification of Arab enemies in the war on terror, and he even provides a formula for how it works. "You identify a group of people in the midst of tough emotional and economic times (the American people or heterosexual black women), and you give them a face or profile of someone they can blame (any Middle Eastern Muslim man or the "Down Low" brutha). 'He is the reason for your problems. He is the cause of your sickness. He is the one we are fighting against.' And *voilà!* Instant fear, instant outrage, instant division, instant war, instant excuses."

The down low fit perfectly into larger cultural dynamics because it confirmed stereotypical values that many of us already believed. For some whites, it confirmed their hypersexualized perception of black people, and for some blacks it confirmed their hypersexualized perception of gay men. Given society's stereotypical view of black men combined with societal beliefs about homosexuality, the story became more believable because it vilified a group of people we did not understand and many of us did not want to know. And for those of us who had been victimized by black men, it gave us a way to express our grief and our rage.

In her classic book *On Death and Dying,* Dr. Elisabeth Kübler-Ross defined five common stages of grief—denial, anger, bargaining, depression, and acceptance. The stages apply to other forms of grief besides dying, and they operate fluidly to allow us to move back and forth as we try to cope. Similarly, the Straight Spouse Network in San Francisco identifies five steps for heterosexuals to cope with the news that a partner is gay—shock, face reality, let go, heal, and reconfigure. But I realized on the plane trip home that many of those most affected by the down low are still struggling with Kübler-Ross's first two stages. Denial and anger are normal human responses to tragedy, and we should definitely be understanding to those women and men in those stages, but we cannot allow emotion alone to dictate our public policy.

When friends of mine are angry and call me for advice on how to confront a friend or a partner, I usually ask them a question and give them two choices. The question is this: What outcome do you hope to achieve by your behavior? If you want to vent and release your frustration, then an angry confrontational approach makes perfect sense. However, if you want to change someone's behavior, you have to be more strategic about how you approach them. That advice applies to the down low as well as to friendships and relationships. If we simply want to vent, then by all means we should get it off our chest with as much anger as necessary. If, however, we want to encourage people to change their behavior, we need to think about the best way to reach them.

Demonizing men on the down low will not change their behavior. It may make us feel better about ourselves, but it will not make those men straight. Nor will it make them come clean. Instead, the anger involved in the demonization process may cloud our judgment as we try to think of rational solutions. Despite that reality, the tone of the down low story has become considerably angrier since the media frenzy began in 2001. The first stories talked about men who were unknowingly spreading HIV to their female partners, but by 2004 the women in the stories were portrayed as being much more upset about it. For example, a September 2004 article in *POZ* magazine begins with the line "Patricia Nalls is mad as hell." Nalls is the founder of a Washington, D.C., AIDS agency for black women called The Women's Collective, and she is HIV positive. According to *POZ,* she was infected in 1984 by her late husband, an IV drug user.

Although Nalls was not infected by a man on the down low, she has seen women who were. "I can't tell you how many married women we've served, some of whom were infected by husbands sleeping with the best man from their wedding or the baby's god-father. I can't believe these men are being so selfish," she said. It is important to understand what she is and is not saying. Her agency has served a number of married women, but not all of them were infected by their husbands, and of those who were, not all of their husbands were on the down low. Some were likely to have been drug users like her own husband. And some may have contracted the virus in prison or from women.

The article quotes another woman who was infected with HIV, but she "isn't sure whether the man who gave her HIV got it from sex with another woman or with another man or from sharing nee-dles." As a heavy drinker, a crack user, an injection drug user, and an incarcerated felon, her former boyfriend fit into numerous risk groups that have nothing to do with the down low.

The story that looked like a condemnation of men on the down low actually turned out to be a broader analysis of complex social phenomena in the black community. Perhaps there is a lesson in that experience. If we allow our anger about the down low to guide us into obsession—however righteous and well intended the anger may be—we may miss the numerous other factors that determine behavioral risk that have nothing to do with the down low. When we approach the issue from the assumption that the down low is the problem, we tend not to see the other problems out there, or we may misunderstand how those problems really affect our behavior.

An August 2004 article in *Essence* magazine provides an example. The article is titled "Deadly Deception" and the pull-out quote on the first two page sets the tone: "Men on the down low view dis-honesty as survival. Problem is, their lies are killing us." Writer Taigi

Smith acknowledges the burdens faced by men who have sexual desires for other men but argues that "shame and social stigma don't make it okay for men on the DL to cheat on their female partners, especially when those liaisons are infecting black women with HIV." Of course she's right. Few people would dispute the argument that cheating or infecting someone with a disease is inappropriate behavior in a relationship, but Smith never cites any evidence to prove how commonly this occurs. Instead, she develops an analysis that seems to be influenced by her anger.

> Why now does it seem that so many more Black men are secretly choosing to have sex with other men? Part of the answer has to do with the oversexualization of American culture in general. Today any child old enough to reach for the remote can be bombarded with sexual images of video girls shaking their booties, showing their boobs or otherwise displaying sex set to music. . . . By the time a boy reaches 18, he is already desensitized to both the sexual act and the feelings of women. It's no wonder that as our men become sexually desensitized, it takes more to stimulate them physically. They start to crave sex that is a bit more risky and a lot more lewd as the ante is upped on what will satisfy them.

Smith's critique is based entirely on the assumption that more black men are having sex with men now than ever before. Of course, there is no way to measure that claim, and Smith does not even attempt to do so. The truth is that black men have been secretly having sex with men since the beginning of time. If it seems that more of them are doing it now than ever before, you can thank the media for creating that impression. There may be more black men talking about it now, but there is no evidence that more black men are actually doing it. Besides, how do you measure a secret? Smith argues that more black men are "secretly choosing to have sex with other men," but if they are really doing it secretly, how do we know how many are doing it? And how do we know how many were doing it before? The evidence we do have seems to contradict Smith. As I mentioned before, 52 percent of African-American male AIDS cases resulted from homosexual contact in 1991 but in 2001 the percentage had dropped to 33 percent, suggesting that homosexuality is less prevalent among black men in this decade than it was in the early 1990s.

Statistics are easy to overlook, so it is not a surprise that reporters would think that the reach of black male homosexuality is a relatively new phenomenon. Smith's other argument, however, is dangerously misinformed. Her claim that black men *choose* homosexuality over heterosexuality because music videos have desensitized them to women is ridiculous and insulting. That statement feeds into the misapprehension that homosexuality is simply a convenient lifestyle choice, like which peanut butter to buy, instead of a fundamental reality for some humans. Moreover, it seems patently illogical that straight men would no longer want to have sex with women after watching music videos with sexy women in them. If anything, we should expect the videos would stimulate their heterosexual desires, but Smith assumes that straight videos actually turn straight men gay.

Unfortunately, Smith's article illustrates the danger in allowing emotion instead of reason to dictate our thinking on the down low. Smith confesses that she is "terrified" after reading an article about the DL in the *New York Times* and she admits: "I no longer make eye contact with attractive men because I'm afraid that perhaps they're living life on the down low." And despite the evidence to the contrary, she is "incensed by the dramatic numbers of African-

American women becoming infected with HIV, mainly from men who sleep around with other men."

Lynn Norment makes a much more reasonable argument in the August 2004 issue of *Ebony.* "Come out of the closet, out of the basement," she tells down low brothers. "Face up to who you are, and let us live." An April 2004 comment from a visitor on Oprah.com conveys a similar sentiment. "We can sit and talk about this for years to come but we should constantly pray that these people can get deliverance from this lifestyle. This epidemic is out of control and souls have to be saved. Be true to the ones you so call love and be true to yourself. Be honest!"

Those are powerful statements that convey the real-life concerns of black women. Black women have a right to be outraged by the deception of the men in their lives who lie to them about their sexual behavior. Outrage is a perfectly understandable emotion, but unfortunately it seems unlikely to change the behavior of the men who lie. In fact, men on the down low may become more resistant to being honest in an environment where they feel hostility and anger directed at them.

Black male-female relationships have already become a casualty in the war on the down low. We have created a new black version of the battle of the sexes in which black men and women fight about who is to blame for the AIDS epidemic. The problem with this battle is that it misleads us about the identity of the enemy. The real enemy is not black men. Nor is it black women. The real enemy is AIDS, and we cannot afford to allow this disease to defeat us with a divide-and-conquer strategy that pits black men against black women.

Unfortunately, we are headed in the wrong direction. On a message board on BET.com, one writer blames men on the down low for spreading AIDS. Another responds angrily: "That's not the reason why black women are infected with HIV." Then the conversation continues with a different post: "We all need to shut up and take responsibility for ourselves." Then: "sad how U dont care what black men do to U." Then another writer: "So many black females with aids n U still say its not black males." Followed by another: "you a fool with a capital F, the reason black people is getting aids is cause women like you who will sleep with my best friend & his best friend & his best friend the whole neigborhood."

For many of those who are angry, the down low is not just about men who cheat. It's about men being cheaters. It fuels a discussion that some believe to be anti-male, not just anti–down low male. Part of that results from the nature of the cheating. When a man and a woman are involved in an affair outside a relationship, it is harder to make negative generalizations by gender than when *two men* are involved in an affair. With a male-female liaison, both a man and a woman are engaged in inappropriate conduct, but with two men it is just two men, and suddenly it is easier to frame the issue through the lens of a gender war, where all the men involved are seen as perpetrators and the women left behind are viewed as victims.

Our obsession with the down low unnecessarily pits black men against black women and reinforces existing negative public perceptions of black men. Black men are constantly portrayed by society as the perpetrators of pathology. We are repeatedly studied and examined for what we are said to do wrong, but these analyses rarely attempt to understand the root causes of our behavior. That is not to say that black men are blameless. In fact, some of us seem to have no shame in the lies we tell or the deception we practice. Women have every right to blame us when we do wrong by them. But blame alone will not solve the problems in our community.

That's why the effort to vilify men on the down low is a mistake. Vilifying men on the down low will not solve the problem with the down low. Pointing fingers will only make the problem worse. I know that some women and some down low educators are heavily invested in demonizing these men, but our resources would be better spent on creating an environment where black women and men can talk candidly and openly about sexual expression. Even if you accept the premise that men on the down low are chiefly responsible for the spread of HIV among black women, it's hard to understand how pushing these men further into denial about their sexuality will help solve the problem. Instead, it's likely to exacerbate the problem as men on the down low become so vilified that they avoid testing, counseling, treatment, and any serious effort to address their HIV status, not to mention their sexuality.

One of the problems in looking at the down low in terms of villains and victims is that the characterization of victims may actually discourage women from taking personal responsibility. Webster's defines a victim as "one that is acted on and usually adversely affected by a force or agent." There is no doubt that some women are real-life victims of men on the down low, but when you think of all black women as victims or potential victims you run the risk of disempowering them as well. If we label women as being "acted on" by outside forces, we assume incorrectly that women are not strong enough to stand up on their own to these deceptive men. Those labels create an unflattering image of women as helpless victims instead of powerful agents of change.

Blame is usually reactive, not proactive. To blame someone for infecting us with HIV means we are already infected. All we can do is react. On the other hand, to stop someone from infecting us with HIV requires us to be proactive, not reactive. The most important lesson that all people need to learn about AIDS is that the disease is entirely preventable. It is our behavior, not our identity, that creates the conditions for the spread of HIV. But the DL phenomenon may discourage women from exercising personal autonomy. To the extent that we can point our fingers at someone else, we implicitly excuse ourselves from responsibility.

The *New York Times Magazine* article may help us to understand the dilemma. The introduction to the piece set the tone for the article to follow. "To their wives, they're straight. To the men they have sex with, they're forging an exuberant new identity. To the gay world, they're kidding themselves. To health officials, they're spreading AIDS throughout the black community."

Is it possible that they're all wrong? Maybe some of the wives just don't want to deal with the reality of their husbands' sexuality. Maybe men on the down low don't think they're "forging an exuberant new identity." Maybe some gay men should not be so upset about the down low when they're busy seeking "masculine" or "straight-acting" men. And maybe men on the down low are not primarily responsible for spreading AIDS in the black community.

We cannot allow the media hysteria about the down low to drive our public policy, and we especially cannot allow that hysteria to misdirect public resources in responding to the larger public health crisis in America. The down low story encourages us to focus our attention on a tiny subpopulation of the black community that is not responsible for the vast majority of black AIDS cases. For the black community to do so would mark a tragic abdication of our responsibility to help all those in need, not just the most sympathetic victims.

One of our biggest obstacles to overcome is our unwillingness to talk candidly about sex. When it comes to sex, we've created a culture of lies. Men on the down low lie about having sex with men. Men who are infected sometimes lie about their HIV status. Some gay and bisexual men lie about their sexual interests. And some women lie to themselves when they know or suspect their men are cheating. What makes us think people are going to suddenly start telling the truth when we start calling them dirty names?

The truth is, we can't deal with the down low until we learn to deal with our hang-ups about sex. Unfortunately, that's not going to happen right away. That's why we have to accept personal responsibility for our behavior. We all know the drill by now. If you have unprotected sexual intercourse without knowing your partner's HIV status, you're putting yourself at risk. Period.

It doesn't matter that your man is "fine." It doesn't matter that he's good in bed. It doesn't matter that he looks like a "real man." Unprotected sex is still risky behavior. If we want to fight the spread of AIDS, we need to understand what we can do to stop it. Men blaming women and women blaming men will not stop the AIDS epidemic. Changing the way we conduct our relationships, on the other hand, can stop the spread of AIDS.

That also means we have to move beyond some of the conspiracy theories. Some of us have speculated that HIV is a biological warfare agent developed in secret laboratories in the 1950s. Others have suggested that AIDS was introduced as a population control measure in the developing world. A few have argued that HIV was specifically designed to wipe out blacks and gays. Those theories may be appropriate for researchers and activists to explore, but they do not change the reality of the AIDS epidemic today. As the activist Tony Wafford told the *Los Angeles Times,* "Too many people are still talking about 'AIDS comes from the white man, AIDS is a gay disease,'" he says. But "the white man ain't in the room with you telling you not to put the condom on," he adds.

Therein lies the challenge. For some reason, we in the black community just can't seem to stay focused about AIDS. First, we denied it affected us. Then, we ignored it because we thought it only affected a few of us. Next, we preached morality because we thought it only affected the ones we didn't like. Then, we tried to figure out which secret laboratory developed it. And, finally, we dramatized it by creating a self-destructive story line about victims and villains. At what point do we just deal with it? That point is now.

No matter how good it makes us feel to lash out at the men on the down low, that is not the answer. Demonizing men on the down low as "villains" will not make them straight, and stereotyping women as "victims" will not keep them safe. AIDS is a huge problem in our community. It doesn't matter how we got here. We're here. It doesn't matter how anyone got it. They have it. It doesn't matter who's to blame. It matters how we respond to it. The biggest lie of the down low is not just the lie that men tell their women. The biggest lie is the lie we tell ourselves about AIDS—that it's somebody else's responsibility.

CHAPTER 8

Seven Deadly Lies and Other Myths

THE FORMER SURGEON General Joycelyn Elders once said that 90 percent of American men report that they masturbate on a regular basis, and 70 percent of American women report that they masturbate regularly. The rest, she said, lie.

Elders was joking, of course, but the truth about sex is no joke. People lie about sex every day. We lie about who we have it with, who we want to have it with, and how often we have it. Some of us lie to our spouses, our lovers, our friends, and even our doctors about sex. Lying about sex is to be expected in a culture where many of us have been conditioned to believe that sex is dirty and wrong. But lying about sex can still have harmful consequences, and believing the lies can be just as dangerous.

When it comes to lies, the down low is second to none in the number it generates. First, there is the lie that men and women on the down low tell themselves about who they are. Then, there is the lie they tell their partners about who they are. But that is not where the lying ends. There is also the lie we use to convince ourselves that we are not at risk. There is the lie that enables us to deny our own complicity in our risk. And there is the lie that precludes us from accepting personal responsibility for our behavior. The down low is filled with lies, myths, and contradictions, but it is not just the usual suspects who do the lying. Yes, the men and women on the down low are lying, but many of the rest of us are lying as well.

With that in mind, I have put together a list of the seven deadly lies about the down low and thirteen myths that follow. The research is still fluid and not always conclusive, but it does allow us to dispel some of the common myths and lies we've been told about the down low.

Seven Deadly Lies

1. *We all agree on what the down low means.* Not true. The down low means different things to different people. Since its debut in 2001, it has never been universally defined. Some say it refers to men who have sex with men but do not identify as gay, while others say the men must be bisexual and involved with women. On the other hand, some self-acknowledged gay men call themselves "down low" because they perceive it as a stamp of masculinity.

2. *The down low is new.* No. The down low is definitely not new. It's been around since the beginning of time. The only thing that's new is the name we call it. We can find examples in the Bible, in literature, and in popular culture to show that men have been secretly having sex with men for centuries.

3. *The down low is about bisexual men.* Wrong. The down low is about cheating. It doesn't matter if you're straight, gay, bisexual, male, or female. People of all races, genders, and backgrounds cheat. That's what the down low is really about. Bisexual men have become the recent focus of the down low, but the actual term in black popular culture

seems to have originated in the 1990s in reference to black men and women cheating on each other in heterosexual relationships.

4. *The down low is primarily black.* Not by a long shot. When New Jersey's Governor Jim McGreevey came out in August 2004, he laid to rest the lie that black men are the only ones on the down low. White, Hispanic, Latino, Asian-American, Native American, and other men and women have all dabbled on the down low.

5. *The concern about the down low is because of AIDS.* Not exactly. The down low was around long before AIDS and will continue on long after it. Contrary to popular belief, AIDS is not spread by the down low. AIDS is caused by a virus, and those without it can't spread it. Some men on the down low do have AIDS, but so do some heterosexual men who have never been on the down low. Those who are concerned about HIV should be concerned about their own behavior, and not about their partner's identity. Despite the widespread media hype, the down low is not responsible for the AIDS epidemic in the black community.

6. *You can tell if someone is on the down low.* Wrong again. This one seems obvious. If you could tell that someone was on the down low, they wouldn't be very down low. But many of us have invested considerable time and energy in this type of amateur sleuthing. Don't waste your time. There are no signs to tell if someone is on the down low, and don't believe anyone who tells you there are.

7. *Demonizing men on the down low will help solve the problem.* That's not likely. Those who have been lied to by men on the down low have the right to be upset. But demonizing men on the down low as "villains" will not make them

straight, and stereotyping women as "victims" will not make them safe. Vilifying men as demons may actually push them further into denial, and stereotyping women as victims may discourage them from exercising personal responsibility to protect themselves.

Those are the seven big lies about the down low, but there is a lot more to be said. Here are the other little lies that also need to be challenged.

8. *Blacks don't know as much about AIDS as whites do.* Not true. A study conducted by the Kaiser Family Foundation and reported in August 2004 found that blacks may actually know more than whites about HIV prevention. For example, 93 percent of blacks and only 91 percent of whites knew that HIV could be transmitted from unprotected oral sex. Blacks were also more likely than whites to know that a pregnant woman with HIV can take drugs to reduce the risk of her baby becoming infected (48 percent to 42 percent), that one in three people with HIV don't know they're infected (89 percent to 83 percent), and that having another sexually transmitted disease increases a person's risk of getting HIV (54 percent to 36 percent). In addition, almost all black adults (99 percent) knew that HIV could be transmitted by unprotected intercourse or from sharing an IV needle. These statistics contradict the widespread assumption that black HIV infection rates result from lack of education about AIDS.

9. *Blacks are less likely to be tested for HIV.* Not so. Blacks are much more likely than whites to report that they have been tested, according to the August 2004 Kaiser Family

Foundation study. Two-thirds of blacks (67 percent) reported that they had been tested for HIV but less than half of whites (44 percent) reported the same. In fact, blacks were twice as likely as whites to report that they had been tested recently. Only 15 percent of whites reported that they had been tested in the previous 12 months, but 36 percent of blacks reported that they had been tested during the same time period.

10. *More black women are getting AIDS than ever before.* We have to be very careful with this one. In 1991, the CDC reported 11,156 black female AIDS cases. In 2001, the CDC reported just 7,023 such cases. While the percentage of women with AIDS who are black has increased steadily, the percentage of blacks with AIDS who are women has not increased as dramatically. Because of HIV education and the introduction of powerful new drugs in 1996, overall AIDS incidence has decreased significantly since the late 1990s. The problem is that the rates decreased much less significantly for blacks than for whites. Thus, black women make up an increasing share of overall female AIDS cases because the number of white females with AIDS has dropped sharply.

11. *Black women make up two-thirds of all new AIDS cases.* Not true. This figure has gotten a lot of play since the publication of J. L. King's book, *On The Down Low.* Fortunately for black women, it's not true. Black women actually make up 18 percent of all new AIDS cases, not 68 percent. The confusion comes when people misinterpret CDC data. Black women are grossly overrepresented among *female* AIDS cases, but they have never been even close to a majority of *all* AIDS cases. Nor are black women the

majority of *black* AIDS cases. In 2001, for example, there were almost twice as many black men diagnosed with AIDS as black women.

12. *Black women are the fastest growing group for HIV.* Not according to the CDC. Commentators often claim that black women are the fastest growing risk group for HIV, but the CDC has never made that claim. In fact, the information available during the down low media crazy seemed to contradict that claim. In November 2003, the CDC reported that "the number of new HIV diagnoses did not change significantly during 1999–2002 among females." Nor did it change among African Americans. "No significant changes were observed for non-Hispanic blacks" during this time period, the CDC reported. That was exactly the time period involved in the down low media hype, but there was no significant change in HIV infections for blacks or for women.

13. *Black women who become infected tend to be in mongamous relationships.* Not necessarily. A February 2001 study of 441 blacks in North Carolina found high levels of "concurrent sexual partnerships" among blacks, and especially among those who were HIV positive. The term "concurrent sexual partnership" refers to sexual activity outside of a relationship. Involvement in concurrent partnerships was "particularly high among those with recently reported heterosexually transmitted HIV." In addition, a December 2003 study of 5,156 HIV-positive MSM found only 12 percent of bisexuals in the group reported having one female partner and multiple male partners. More than half of bisexuals with multiple male partners also had multiple female partners. According to the researchers, "This

finding contradicts the common belief that bisexual men often are in a committed relationship with a woman and have many male sex partners that she doesn't know about."

14. *Most women don't know their men are cheating on them.* This may be true, but it requires some background information. A 2002 study published by *Psychology Press* looked at sex differences in response to partners' infidelity and found that women sometimes stay with their men even when they know or suspect the men are cheating. One of the dirty little secrets about the down low is not just that men don't tell their female partners about their clandestine affairs. Another secret is that some of the female partners already know *or suspect* the affairs in the first place. In a culture where so-called good men are considered hard to find and keep, some women have been conditioned to take whatever they can get, leaving some men with little incentive to change.

15. *Black men on the down low are more likely to be HIV positive.* Actually, we don't know for sure, but some of the evidence from the CDC seems to contradict this assumption. The reason we don't know for sure is because no research has been published about men on the down low. The closest we have is research about bisexual men or bisexual men who do not disclose their sexual orientation. A 2003 study of 5,589 MSM found that black MSM who do not disclose their sexual orientation were actually more likely to be safe in some of their sexual practices and more likely to be HIV negative than other black MSM. For example, 72 percent of black disclosers reported five or more lifetime partners but only 56 percent of black nondisclosers

reported the same number of sexual partners. Similarly, 41 percent of black disclosers reported unprotected anal intercourse while only 32 percent of black nondisclosers reported the same. But once again, we have to be careful not to draw conclusions either way about men on the DL because the men in the study were not necessarily on the down low.

16. *Black men with AIDS are usually on the down low.* That is definitely not the case. At the end of 2002, the CDC reported that 48 percent of the 111,000 black men living with AIDS were infected by injection drug use or heterosexual contact. Fifty percent of black men with AIDS reported male-to-male sexual contact, and 8 percent of them were also drug users. In the end, only 42 percent of black men with AIDS were exposed solely by male-to-male sexual contact. But even that figure does not tell us the whole story. No doubt, some of those men openly identify their sexual orientation. Others are not involved with women. And of those who are involved with women, given the disproportionate incarceration rates of black men, we can expect that some of them contracted the virus in prison, not on the down low. The truth is that most black men with AIDS are probably not on the down low.

17. *Bisexuals are more likely to engage in unsafe behavior than gay men.* Not necessarily. A 2000 study of 3,492 men who have sex with men (MSM) conducted by Dr. Linda Valleroy of the CDC found that bisexual men were actually less likely than their gay counterparts to have unprotected receptive anal sex. Another study of 2,500 bisexual men conducted by the San Francisco Department of

Health also found that bisexual men may have fewer risk behaviors than exclusively homosexual men. In other words, bisexuals may be less likely to engage in unsafe behavior.

18. *Black bisexuals are more likely than white bisexuals to lie about their bisexuality.* Yes and no. A December 2003 study published in *AIDS CARE* looked at 5,156 men and found that black bisexuals were actually more likely than their white or Hispanic counterparts to identify themselves to researchers as bisexual. However, they did tend to be less honest than others in dealing with their intimate partners.

19. *Black gay and bisexual men don't practice safe sex.* Not true. Despite the widespread belief that black gay and bisexual men are not using condoms, a December 2001 study by Dr. John Peterson indicated that black MSM were actually less likely than other minority MSM to engage in unprotected anal intercourse. Another study in February 2003 confirmed this report and found that black MSM in Los Angeles engaged in less risky behavior than white MSM. That raises a difficult question. If black men are actually safer than their counterparts, why are they more likely to be HIV infected?

The answer may lie in the social networks of black MSM, suggests Dr. John Peterson. Imagine two groups of men and two swimming pools. Now imagine that a certain percentage of men in both groups use an antibacterial agent to prevent them from becoming infected from pool germs. Even if a greater percentage of black men use the protection, black men as a group could be more likely to become infected if the black pool is not as clean from the beginning. Since black MSM tend to socialize with one another in a fairly closed population, this could allow HIV to be spread efficiently within that network. Another possible factor is that young black MSM tend to socialize with older partners, according to the Los Angeles study, and older partners may be more likely to have HIV.

20. *Men on the down low are responsible for the black AIDS epidemic.* We see this claim everywhere. "The Centers for Disease Control and Prevention connected black men on the down low with the rise of HIV infection rates among black women," the *Chicago Sun-Times* reported. But there's one problem. It's not true. The CDC has never made any connection about men on the down low and HIV infections among black women because no research has ever been reported about men on the down low. Once again, it is hard to figure out how to define the men in this group, and it is even harder to find them. Even the widely quoted Young Men's Survey (YMS) did not blame men on the DL for the black AIDS epidemic. That was the study that first launched the down low media frenzy back in February 2001. Three years later, the lead researcher for that study, Dr. Linda Valleroy, told the Fifteenth International AIDS Conference in Bangkok that the YMS study was not about men on the down low. As Dr. David Malebranche has said, "The majority of public health and behavioral research doesn't support the theory of 'Down Low' black men as the 'bridge' of HIV to the general black community."

Those are the facts. They don't answer all the questions but they do raise new questions about what we've been told before. So much of the information we've been told about the AIDS epidemic in the black community is just not accurate. And so much of our hysteria about the down low has been rooted in this misinformation. Now that we know the truth behind the facts and the statistics, it's time to think about the issues that led us here in the first place. It's time to think about sexism, racism, homophobia, and classism. It's time to think about the role of the government, the media, the church, and the family in shaping our values. It's time to deconstruct our perception of morality, masculinity, sex, and relationships.

It's time to move beyond the down low.

CHAPTER 9

Never Underestimate the Power
of a Woman

A FEW YEARS ago, I was invited to speak at the University of California at Santa Cruz. The crowd seemed stiff the night of my speech so I started with a joke. A man goes to a doctor and discovers that he is ill but the doctor cannot figure out the problem, so he recommends a specialist. A few days later, the man and his wife go to the specialist's office. The specialist notices their interaction in the waiting room and summons the couple to talk to him. "I know exactly what the problem is," he announces. "Let me speak to your wife for a minute and I'll be right back," he tells the man. In his office, the doctor tells the wife the secret. "Your husband has a rare case of Affection Deficit Disorder. To save him, you have to attend to his every need for the next year, or he will die. Do you understand what you have to do?" The shocked woman nods, and then returns to the waiting room. The anxious husband runs up to her: "What did the doctor say?" he asks. The woman looks at her husband straight in his eye and says, "You're gonna die."

A few members of the audience laughed at the joke while one or two others chuckled or smiled. But most of the audience reacted with stony silence. I tried to explain the point of the joke. It's always a bad sign if you have to explain the point of your joke. Anyway, I told the audience, "The point is this. Knowing the right thing to do is not the same as doing it. In this case, even knowing the right thing to do, the wife was unable to help her husband. And similarly," I said, "knowing the right thing to do is not the same as doing it when we talk about public policy."

I thought the joke was a lighthearted but clever segue to discuss more serious issues, but I completely misread the audience. Before I could even finish my speech, a woman's hand shot up from the crowd. "Are you saying that a woman's job is just to attend to her husband's needs?" she asked. "No, not at all. I was just trying to tell a joke to get the crowd warmed up." Silence.

I continued cautiously. "Regardless of whether it's the husband or the wife, if you assume that a spouse's role is to take care of a partner in sickness or health, then knowing that and doing that are two different things," I said. More silence. I thought about how to dig my way out of the hole but decided to give up instead. Knowing the right thing to do is not the same as doing it.

Despite the criticism that day, I considered telling the joke again a few months later at another speech. This time, it was World AIDS Day, and the stakes were higher. World AIDS Day takes place every year on December 1 to remind us of the millions of lives lost to the disease and to encourage us to continue the struggle. I did not want to minimize the real-life disease that is AIDS with the fictitious "disorder" I had created for my joke, so I knew to tread carefully. An offensive speech would have alienated the audience on what was supposed to be a special day, but a dry speech about statistics would have bored the audience and motivated no one. There had to be a balance, but it was going to be a difficult decision. A high school teacher once told me, "When in doubt, do without." That seemed like a wise strategy for the occasion, but another teacher once told me that "nothing worthwhile is accomplished without risk." I weighed the options. If it worked, the speech would be a hit, and the audience would be energized. If it failed, I would never be asked to speak there again.

The host started the program by introducing two speakers who were living with AIDS and one speaker who had lost a family member to AIDS. Then, it was my turn to deliver the keynote address. With the familiar red AIDS ribbon fastened to the lapel of my suit jacket, I walked confidently to the podium and thanked the host for inviting me. I was still not sure if I should tell the joke, so I spent a few moments praising the institution for holding the event. With no more time to stall, I finally started the speech. "A man goes to a doctor," I said. And from there, it was too late to stop. The audience looked perplexed. Was this a serious story or a warm-up joke for the speech? A few eyeballs darted back and forth to gauge the reaction from the other audience members, and then a smile broke out in the middle of the story. By the time I reached the scene with the husband and the wife, the audience members were eagerly waiting for the funny part. I plunged forward with the punchline. "You're gonna die," I said. And almost everyone in the crowd seemed to get it.

It was an unusual joke to tell in the middle of an epidemic, but there seemed to be a collective sense of relief and enjoyment in the audience. Some of them might have experienced survivors' guilt after burying their loved ones. Others certainly knew the physical, emotional, and mental challenge involved in taking care of someone who had once been independent. And a few may have wondered how they would have responded if posed with the challenge of a year's worth of intense commitment to a partner. But almost everyone seemed to get the point of the story before I could even explain it. "Knowing the right thing to do is not the same as doing it," I said.

The health professionals in the audience knew the statistics better than I did. They knew that blacks were 12 percent of the U.S. population but made up more than half of all new AIDS cases. They knew that two-thirds of the international AIDS cases were in sub-Saharan Africa. And they knew that many of us had stopped paying attention to AIDS when the new drug treatments were introduced in the late 1990s. Many of the AIDS activists in the room also believed that we needed to develop more "culturally relevant" prevention messages specifically targeted to the communities at greatest risk. But there was another, more controversial question I wanted to raise that day. Were we fighting the wrong battle?

I knew it was politically and statistically incorrect to suggest that the battle against AIDS was over, and that was not my point at all. The fight against AIDS was actually a war, not a battle, I said, and the AIDS community had achieved two major victories in the first twenty years. The first was the development of the highly active anti-retroviral therapy (HAART) in 1996. Those powerful new drugs cut the mortality rate in half. In 1995, there were more than 52,000 U.S. deaths related to AIDS, but two years later the number dropped to 22,000 and continued to drop for several years afterward.

The second victory was in the battle for education. By 2001, almost everyone in America knew the basics about HIV and AIDS. Blacks were no exception to this rule. A Kaiser Foundation study released that year showed that 99 percent of African-American adults knew that a person could become infected with HIV by having unprotected intercourse or sharing an IV needle. Ninety-nine percent! The public was already educated. But if everyone knew how to prevent the spread of HIV, why were 40,000 new infections occurring every year? That brings me back to the joke I told at the beginning. The answer to the question was in that joke. *Knowing the right thing to do is not the same as doing it.*

Almost everybody already knew the right thing to do. What they did not know was how to do it. It was not enough to teach people to use condoms. They already knew that. We had to teach people how to talk about condoms. And it was not enough to teach people about clean needles. They knew that too. Instead, we would have to provide those needles and then change our policy to encourage treatment instead of incarceration for drug users. That would require a dramatic shift in thinking, but there was no other choice. We could not moralize our way out of the epidemic. We had to take a radically different approach to the problem.

Like it or not, we have reached a turning point in the battle against AIDS. We can continue along the current path with mostly stable levels of HIV infection that are increasingly concentrated in people of color. Or we can take a different route and expand our approach to the war on AIDS. Either way, we cannot win the war with the equipment that has been provided to us. We need new resources for new challenges. We cannot limit our concern to the surface issues that lead to HIV infection. We—the government, the church, the community, the family—have to deal with the deeper socioeconomic conditions that lead people to engage in risky behavior in the first place. We will not stop the AIDS epidemic by AIDS education alone. Instead, we have to deal with jobs, health care, education, homelessness, poverty, drugs, and the disproportionate incarceration of minorities. We have to deal with racism, sexism, classism, misogyny, homophobia, heterosexism, and cultural imperialism.

We have a new battle to fight. The purpose of this battle is to empower people who have been disenfranchised so that they can begin to protect themselves. Who has time to think about AIDS when you don't have a roof over your head, or food on your table, or diapers for your baby? It's hard to make the right decisions when you don't know where your next check is coming from or don't know how you're going to pay your light bill. Before we can expect people to make healthy decisions, they have to have jobs, health care, education, and homes. They have to be invested in their own future. They have to be convinced that their lives are worth saving. Men who have sex with men need to be empowered to protect themselves in a world that seems to despise them. Poor people need to be empowered in a society that neglects them. Drug users need to be empowered in a culture that criminalizes them. And women need to be empowered in a climate that reduces and objectifies them.

That is the real challenge. It is one thing to know to use a condom, but it is quite another to negotiate the use of a condom in the passion of intimacy. What do you say to your partner? When do you bring it up? Will it ruin the moment? Could it turn off your partner? Those are some of the real questions that women want to know. The Kaiser study that found nearly universal knowledge about the way HIV is spread also found widespread hunger for other information. More than half of African Americans said they needed more information on how to talk to children about AIDS, nearly four in ten wanted to know how to talk to their partner about AIDS and 34 percent wanted more information on how to talk to a doctor about AIDS. Learning to talk about AIDS without fear or embarrassment is the next challenge.

We cannot simply tell women to make sure their male sexual partners wear a condom. We also have to understand women's relationships with their men. Women who are economically dependent on men might make different choices from women who are financially independent. Women in abusive relationships might feel pressured to engage in unprotected intercourse while other women might have more leverage to be able to influence their partners. And women involved with drug users or ex-convicts might make entirely different decisions from the others.

There's another reality that we sometimes gloss over in our discussion about black woman with HIV. Many of the women becoming infected with HIV are poor, and unfortunately, many of them are not practicing safe sex. A study by Professor Ellen Yancey at the Morehouse School of Medicine found that nearly half of low-income African-American women surveyed in Atlanta did not use a condom during any sexual encounter in the previous two months and 60 percent did not know their partner's HIV status. Those are troubling numbers that should lead us to face the larger reality. For many poor black women, HIV is far from their minds. In an interview with the *New York Times,* Hamza Brimah, a physician in Mississippi who specializes in HIV, explained the challenge. "There are issues of looking after children, trying to get insurance, the lack of a father in the home, alcohol [and] drugs. They have so much going on," he said. Many of his patients already knew that HIV could be spread from unprotected heterosexual sex, but many of them placed themselves at risk nonetheless, Dr. Brimah told the *Times.* That seems consistent with the research from the Kaiser Foundation showing that almost all African Americans know how HIV is spread. *But knowing the right thing to do is not the same as doing it.* We cannot fight the AIDS epidemic among black women if we do not deal with the attendant issues of poverty, homelessness, substance abuse, unemployment, access to health care, and lack of education.

A small study published in 2004 by Lisa Bowleg, a psychology professor at the University of Rhode Island, found that young black women expressed a range of different reasons for using and not using condoms. The results, published in the *Psychology of Women Quarterly,* found that issues other than HIV prevention affected women's decisions about using condoms. Infidelity was one such issue. At least one woman said she used condoms as punishment, mostly on days when she thought her man was with another woman. Some women simply did not like the feeling of condoms during sex. Even some of the women at high risk for HIV did not like to use condoms. Some stopped using condoms after they got tested for HIV, while some wanted to use condoms at the beginning of the relationship but not throughout. The results of the study seem to contradict the assumption that all women want to use condoms until their men persuade them not to do so. Yes, that often happens, but it's not always the case, and our approach to HIV prevention has to go beyond the stereotype that men alone reject condoms and understand that many women do not like condoms either.

The study also noted that African-American women often deal with something other researchers called "psychological androgyny." According to Merriam Webster's Collegiate Dictionary, things that are androgynous are "neither specifically feminine nor masculine," and that definition may also apply to the psychological condition of many African-American women. Long before white women started to enter the work force in droves in the 1970s and 1980s, black women were already working outside their homes to support their families. But black women were also expected to maintain traditional gender roles at home, and this division of labor created added stress in black relationships. In addition, because society limits the options available to black men, African-American women often compensate for racism by building up the men in their community and in their relationships.

I had never heard the term "psychological androgyny" before, but it seemed to make sense to me. I remember thinking about a similar idea during the Clarence Thomas confirmation hearings in October 1991. I was upset that President George H. W. Bush had nominated a conservative black opponent of affirmative action to replace Thurgood Marshall on the U.S. Supreme Court. I was also disappointed with some of the black leaders in the country who chose to remain silent instead of criticizing another African American. As I watched the hearings with my friends from law school, I thought it was obvious that Thomas was lying through his teeth. In my judgment, he had already perjured himself once in his official hearings a month earlier when he denied that he had ever thought about the famous 1973 abortion case *Roe v. Wade* while he was in law school. Here was a man who wanted to sit on the highest court in America, and he had no opinion on the most controversial Supreme Court decision to come down since *Brown v. Board of Education* outlawed racial segregation in schools in 1954. Thomas was at Yale Law School when *Roe* was decided, and he expected us to believe that none of his friends or professors even mentioned what some consider the most divisive case ever to be decided by the U.S. Supreme Court. That had to be a lie, and I felt that if he lied about what he did in law school, he was just as likely to lie about everything else.

When Anita Hill, a law professor and former colleague of Thomas's, came forward to testify in the hearings a month later, she was immediately attacked by the right-wing propaganda machine. They impugned her character, questioned her sexuality, and argued that she had a political axe to grind. And it was not just the Republicans. Mississippi's Democratic Senator Howell Heflin turned to Professor Hill with his thickest southern drawl and asked, "Are you a scorned woman?" Even the question, however innocently intended, was offensive. The attack on Hill seemed patently unfair. Why would she lie about Clarence Thomas? She had little to gain from her testimony and much to lose by speaking out against an influential judge who was likely to become a member of the

Supreme Court. And her testimony was so vivid and detailed that it was hard to imagine how or why she would have fabricated such a startling tale about Thomas. The pubic hair, the Coke can, the porn videos, and all the other elements of sexual harassment she detailed seemed quite real, and Hill seemed extremely credible and almost reluctant to raise the issues. She had not sought the limelight; it was brought to her.

The anti-Hill forces did their best to portray Professor Hill as the perpetrator and Thomas as the victim. In denying Professor Hill's allegations, Thomas even called the hearings "a high-tech lynching for uppity blacks who in any way deign to think for themselves." The same man who said we should move beyond race was suddenly willing to play the race card when it suited his personal interests. It sickened me, and I thought it was an obvious ploy, even though it would probably work to pacify guilty whites who were too afraid to challenge a black Republican on his own racial hypocrisy. But in black America, I thought Thomas's ploy would backfire. Apparently, I thought wrong.

A few days after Anita Hill testified, I took a trip to St. Louis to visit my grandmother. Exhausted from class, I sat in the den and watched television for much of the time I was in her house. My grandmother walked in one afternoon just as I flipped to a news channel that was covering the Thomas hearings. She glanced at the screen, shook her head at the image of Anita Hill, and then shocked me with her statement. "I wish that woman would stop lying on that man," she said.

Before I could even register what she had said, she walked off to another room. I followed her to continue the conversation. My grandmother had never been old-fashioned. She was active in Democratic Party politics and had run for local office once herself. She was a strong woman who spent her life working for the federal government and always had a job, even after she retired. Outside of politics, she kept herself busy as an member of the local and national Daughters of Isis and Delta Sigma Theta sorority and was an active member of her church. My grandmother had always been outspoken and independent, so I was shocked to hear her comments about Anita Hill. But as I listened to her explain, I definitely understood the dual role that strong black women play in black families all the time. The black woman, especially in my grandmother's generation, was expected to be a co-provider, but she was always taught that the black man is the cornerstone of the family and the community. When a strong black man gets a good job, a black woman was not supposed to tear him down. She was supposed to support him. That was my grandmother's way of thinking, and it made perfect sense for her and her generation.

But it did not stop with my grandmother's generation. It continues even today. My mother is another strong, outspoken black woman, and she too spent her life working for the federal government. A talented singer and gifted pianist, she was told that a woman's role is to find a husband, not to nurture her own interests. Like many of the women in my family, she was taught to balance a work role outside the house with a traditional gender role at home. But that experience seems common today. Women of all colors develop their careers and simultaneously help run their families. The feminist movement and the women's liberation movement opened up opportunities for millions of women to join the workforce. Naturally, then, white women and other women should experience the same conflict of emotions.

What's different about black women is that their husbands (usually black men) have been disempowered by the racial prejudice in society, while white women have husbands (usually white men) who have been the greatest beneficiaries of America's prejudice. Thus, black women often feel the need to build up their black men who have already been beaten down by the world. In a culture that attempts to emasculate black men in so many ways, the black woman can provide a sanctuary where the male figure can be the man of the house. Professor Bowleg speculates that some black women may "allow men to control some aspects of relationships as a way to compensate" for other things the men may not be able to bring to the table.

Of course, not all black women think this way, but we still have to understand the connection between our cultural norms and our sexual choices. Our understanding of what is romantic may complicate the problem. Traditional images of male-female romance envision a passive woman, and a strong man who sweeps her off her feet. But according to some researchers, this Prince Charming idea of romance may actually discourage women from playing an active role in generating a dialogue about safe sex. If you believe that the man should be the one to initiate sex, you may also believe that the man should be the one to initiate *safe sex,* making it less likely that the woman will raise the issue of condoms. When you add the concerns of many black women about the lack of suitable black male partners, you can understand why some women may be reluctant to give up on a good man. One woman in the Bowleg study put it this way: "If I want a serious relationship and he is a professional and I would like to be with a professional . . . well there are certain things that I'm going to have to actually be a little more lenient about." Another woman described her man as "completely crazy," but at the same time she admitted "no matter what he did I found a way to deal with it and put it into perspective."

The most troubling aspect of the Bowleg research was that many women described infidelity as the norm in male-female relationships. Several women in the study were willing to tolerate infidelity, and some seemed to think that cheating was to be expected by both partners in a relationship. More than half of the women in the focus group suspected their partners had other sexual partners. But the women were not just victims sitting at home waiting for their men. More than half of the women themselves also reported having other sexual partners.

Yes it's true. Sometimes women cheat on their partners too. We spend a lot of time analyzing male infidelity but we often neglect the fact that women sometimes do the same thing. In fact, a survey of 8,000 women in the October 2004 issue of *Ebony* magazine found that 48 percent of women were "very concerned" about "brothers on the down low," but almost the same percentage of women (44 percent) admitted they too had cheated on their partners. And those are just the ones who admitted it. It seems that both male and female infidelity are far more common in our relationships than we like to acknowledge.

Perhaps that explains why women sometimes continue in relationships where they suspect or know their partner is cheating. It is difficult to question someone else's behavior when you are doing the same thing. Professor Bowleg reported that not one of the women in her focus group said she had ended a relationship with a cheating partner. That observation seems consistent with other research that shows women of all races often stay with men who they know are cheating on them. For example, in a study published in 2002 called "Forgiveness or breakup," Professor Todd Shackelford of Florida Atlantic University and two other researchers found that women tend to be more upset about "emotional infidelity" than about "sexual infidelity." Similarly, women were much less likely than men to end a relationship because of "sexual infidelity."

Remember the Salt-N-Pepa song "Whatta Man" from 1993? The female rap artist seems ready to apologize for her man's infidelity in

that familiar verse about the down low: "Although most men are hos /
He flows on the down low / Cuz I never heard about him with another
girl." Truth be told, many of us—male and female, regardless of sexual
orientation—have a "don't ask, don't tell" policy about dating and
relationships. What we don't know can't hurt us, many of us think,
but that assumption is not necessarily true. A woman in the Bowleg
study provides an example of the risk. She said she suspected her
partner of eight years was having unprotected sex with men and
women, but she was willing to tolerate it "as long as he just don't flaunt
it in my face [and] . . . don't give me no sexual diseases or anything."
That's a dangerous perspective to take. If you wait until your man
brings home a sexually transmitted disease before you question his
infidelity, you may be putting your health at risk.

With all the recent hype about the down low, some black women
may even be thrilled to find a man who cheats with a woman
instead of a man. That's a big mistake. HIV is not spread by identity, it's spread by behavior. A completely straight man can give you
HIV, but a down low man who has sex with men may not. It all
depends on which one has HIV, not on the man's identity.

There's another reason for concern. If your man cheats on you
with women, he may also cheat on you with men. We have this perception that men on the down low tend to have one steady female
partner and multiple male sex partners. There's no evidence to support that perception, and some evidence actually contradicts it. For
example, a December 2003 study in Michigan by the researcher J.
P. Montgomery looked at 3,000 women and more than 5,000 men
who have sex with men. The study found more than half of bisexual
men with multiple male partners also had multiple female partners.
Only 12 percent of bisexual men reported having one female
partner and multiple male partners. What does this mean? To put it
more bluntly, the men who cheat with other men may also be

cheating with other women. A cheater is a cheater, and a ladies' man may also be a man's man. While many women have been taught not to confront a man or end a relationship because of a man's infidelity with another woman, that lesson may be a big problem. If you don't pay attention when your man is cheating with women, don't be surprised to find your man is cheating with men. And even if your man is only cheating with women, don't be surprised if he brings home HIV or some other STD from other women.

Let's be honest. Some women enter into relationships where they know their partner is sleeping with other women. That is a choice for women to make, but if you make that choice and also choose to have unprotected sex with your partner, you are putting yourself in danger. You cannot blame your partner for a risk you knowingly accept. And you cannot and should not assume that it is safe to have unprotected sex with your man just because you know, or think you know, that he is heterosexual. Women need to be educated, empowered, and encouraged to stand up for themselves. Pointing fingers at men on the down low is an easy way to take the finger of responsibility away from ourselves, but it does not change that fact that we are individually responsible for our own health and safety.

Unfortunately, a lot of the dialogue we have heard about the down low is based on misinformation and fear. That path will not lead toward a solution. Our solutions have to be based on real facts and information, even if that information challenges our stereotypical assumptions about gender.

Fortunately, there are some constructive steps we can take to move beyond the sensationalism of the down low and deal with the real issues. Our solutions to the AIDS epidemic among black women have to be understood in a comprehensive context, says Professor Bowleg. "Comprehensive interventions that address a variety of aspects of African American women's lives (e.g., employment, relationships, education, etc.) may prove more effective than those that focus solely on HIV, particularly when other life realities supersede concerns about HIV," she writes. That means we have to change the way we sometimes structure our relationships. We have to encourage black women to exercise personal responsibility to protect themselves. We need to communicate a new message. It is okay to trust your partner, but your partner should also trust you. If you want to use protection or want to be tested, a good man, a "real" good man will want you to do so, too.

We also have to change the culture of finding partners. Many black women have been conditioned to settle for a halfway decent man instead of waiting for a good man. Many are simply tired of waiting. AIDS organizations, women's groups, sororities, churches, and other organizations need to provide safe sex counseling, support groups, and role-playing models to teach women how to have these difficult conversations.

One of the most important things we need to do is to destigmatize homosexuality in our families and our communities. I've heard scores of black women complain about the no-good, low-down, two-timing knucklehead "bisexual" men who can't make up their minds and end up ruining the lives of black women. That's a fair complaint, but let's understand how to address the matter. Many of these men have been pressured into heterosexual relationships that they know are not sincere. Where does that pressure come from? From us. They get pressure from their parents, their aunts, their uncles, their godparents, their siblings, their friends, and their peers. They get this same message from their churches, their schools, the movies they see and the television shows they watch. Even the comedians on BET's *Comic View* have an impact. We all know the comedians who tell the funny little fag jokes that we laugh about. But while we're laughing, the man in the third row who is struggling with his sexuality decides that he cannot be accepted even among his own people, the same people he expected to be there for him in a world full of racial hatred.

We may wonder where these men get off by endangering the lives of women, but we should also stop to think about the ways in which we contribute to our own oppression by participating in a culture that drives these men underground. If we do not want so many men to be on the down low, then we need to stop helping to push them there in the first place. We need to challenge the homophobia in our own lives, in our families, in our churches, and in our social settings. If we participate in this homophobia or fail to challenge it, we are part of the very problem we supposedly seek to end.

At least some comedians seem to understand this problem. Interviewed by *POZ* magazine, an AIDS-themed publication, the comedian Mo'Nique was wise enough to explain why down low men exist in the first place. "They're on the down low because nobody's talking to them," she said. "We can't deal with the honesty. We want to be lied to."

Destigmatizing homosexuality and changing cultural norms about relationships will not happen overnight, but fortunately there are little things that women can do that can protect their lives and make a huge difference about AIDS and the down low. But we also have to understand that AIDS is a disease of opportunity. HIV is a virus that is spread by behavior, not by lifestyle. The most common and dangerous behavior for the spread of HIV is unprotected intercourse. So here are five things you can begin to do right now.

First, talk to your partner about safe sex. Let your partner know that protection is important to you. This is usually easier to do at the beginning of a relationship than after a pattern of unprotected intimacy has already been established. But even after the relationship has begun, you still have power. Don't give it away if you don't want to, and don't be manipulated by a partner who tries to use your suggestion against you.

Second, go to the drugstore and buy condoms. Many AIDS organizations and community groups supply condoms for free, so you don't even have to spend the money if you don't have it. Once you have condoms, carry a couple with you at all times. Put them in a secure part of your purse if you need to, but always keep them on you. One of the main reasons men and women don't use condoms is because they don't have them at the point of intimacy. You can eliminate that excuse by carrying your own.

Third, use the condoms. Don't use them only when you think a man might be HIV positive or might be on the down low. You have no way of knowing that, and your life is too important to risk on a gamble. One rule of thumb is to assume that everyone you sleep with is HIV positive and act accordingly. It might seem overly cautious, but the rule actually does make some sense. If you ask your partner about his HIV status, how many men do you think are really going to tell you that they are HIV positive? Some may, while others won't. But why should you have to ask? If they're willing to have unprotected sex with you without volunteering that information, that's a bad sign.

There is also another reason to use this rule of thumb. Many men simply don't know their HIV status. A 2001 study of young men who have sex with men found that only 29 percent of those who were HIV positive knew they were infected. If you rely on your partner's word, you're taking a risk. Your partner may tell you what he thinks is the truth, but your partner may not know the real truth. That doesn't mean your partner lied to you. It means he just did not know. But which is most threatening—an honest partner who infects you without knowing it or a dishonest partner who does not infect you because you use protection?

Every time you have sex with someone without a condom and you don't know his HIV status, you put your life at risk. Every time! It doesn't matter what your partner looks like, how healthy he appears, or what his sexual orientation may be. Your man may be straight as an arrow, but he could still carry HIV, or your man may be on the down low and he may not have HIV. We have to let go of the down low thing. It is not the answer.

Phill Wilson of the Black AIDS Institute gives us a simple reminder. It takes two people to spread HIV, he says, but it only takes one person to stop it.

Fourth, get tested with your partner before you have unprotected intercourse. Using a condom is an effective strategy for single women who do not want to become pregnant, but married women often face a different set of challenges. Once you get to the point where you are ready to have unprotected sex, then both of you should go get tested together. If you both test negative, you can feel some sense of safety before you begin unprotected intercourse, but you should know that HIV tests do not always detect recent infections, so you may want to wait awhile and get tested again to be sure that nothing has changed.

Fifth, get tested regularly. Remember, it takes less than a minute to become HIV infected. Although you may begin your relationship with both partners testing negative, one partner could easily acquire HIV later in the relationship. An HIV test only measures one point in time. It does not give you or your partner lifetime immunity against future infection. So get tested again. Make an annual event out of HIV testing. You might even pick a date and get tested every year on that date with your partner. Regular testing is important to detect the virus before it progresses to an advanced stage. HIV is more likely to be treatable if it is detected early. It is also important to be tested if you become pregnant. Even if you and your partner test positive, you can still take drugs that can significantly reduce the risk of infecting your baby.

Fortunately, many black women are already taking a stand. They are moving beyond the fear and moving toward positive solutions in their own lives. Many of them have found good men by refusing to accept the behavior of the men who do not meet their standards. In Professor Bowleg's research, all the women who refused to tolerate infidelity in their relationships were also involved in relationships with "emotionally invested partners." That can make a big difference.

All women have a right to expect the men in their lives to treat them with respect, and women have the responsibility to make sure that they set the standards for their relationships. One woman in Professor Bowleg's study told her partner that she would leave him if she caught him cheating. Both partners knew the expectations of the relationship. Another woman told herself what she would do in that situation. "I know that I'm a strong person and I love myself," she said. "So I know that if anything came up that would compromise the relationship as far as breaking up, I don't mind being alone because I've been alone."

That message reminds me of the lyrics from an old Whitney Houston song. "I'd rather be alone than unhappy," Houston sang, but most of us would rather we didn't have to make that choice. That is why we search to find a way to balance our desire for love and intimacy with our need to maintain respect for ourselves and our integrity. Writing in *Ebony* magazine in April 1996, Nicole Walker, then a junior at Northwestern University, warned black women not to lock themselves in what she called "emotional prisons." In a commentary on the 1995 film *Waiting to Exhale,* Walker encouraged women to reject the "Prince Charming fallacy" and instead find true peace and happiness inside themselves. "We are ready to stop giving men the burden of making our lives complete," she wrote. "We are ready to be the authors of our own joy and serenity. We are ready to live our lives for ourselves. We are ready to exhale."

CHAPTER 10

Black Men: Married, in Jail, or Gay?

THEY SAY A good black man is hard to find. "All the black men are either married, in jail, or gay," I've been told. Many of us who are black men have heard this complaint over and over. We've heard it so many times that we have begun to believe it and repeat it. But is it true?

From a casual observer's perspective, it certainly looks like the odds are not good for black women hoping to find a black male partner. It seems a new report is issued every month that confirms the plight of the black man. We've all heard the bad news.

From the criminal justice system, a study by the Justice Policy Institute showed there were more black men incarcerated than in college. A different study from the American Sociological Association found more young black men have done time than have served in the military or earned a college degree. And a Justice Department study found more than 12 percent of black men in their twenties and early thirties were in prison or jail in 2002.

In terms of the economy, nearly half of all black men in New York City between the ages of sixteen and sixty-four were not working in 2002, according to an organization called the Community Service Society. Another study found that one of every four black men in the United States was idle all year long in 2002, twice the rate for white and Hispanic males.

On the health care front, AIDS is the leading cause of death for black men between the ages of 25 and 44. Black men born in 1999 have a life expectancy of just 67.8 years, while black women and white men born the same year can expect to live about 75 years.

The statistics around education are no brighter. More black women than black men have earned a bachelor's degree, according to the Census Bureau. The college graduation rate of black men is lower than that of any other group. Only 35 percent of black men who entered college in 1996 graduated within six years, compared with 59 percent of white men and 45 percent of black women. Even in college enrollment, only 37 percent of eligible black men are enrolled, compared with 42 percent of black women.

To hear the barrage of statistics, it seems as though we've created a culture that robs black women of equal partners for relationships just at the time when more black women are going to college and becoming professionals. And for those without a college background, the disparity seems even worse. The employment rate for young black men with a high school education or less has dropped from 62 percent in 1982 to 52 percent in 2002, according to a study from the Georgetown Public Policy Institute. In contrast, the employment rate for young black women with the same background rose from 37 to 53 percent in the 1990s.

Is the situation really that grim for black men? It certainly seems that way to the media, and also to some black women.

You can read about it on the Internet. A woman on SistaPower.com writes: "I find it very hard to find a good black man who is a professional, down to earth, loving and kind, exciting, who secretly gets my engines going. I am an attractive black woman in my 40's and I am smart, [I have a] good job, my own car and place, nice shape and lovely personality. But when I do meet a professional black man he just wants to have fun and kick it. (Sex) No type of meaningful relationship, and I am not having it. I am tired of games, and drama. The other men are drug addicts, jailbirds, or down low brothers. Now I know there has to be the other good ones out there, right? I am not giving up on men."

We see a similar story in the newspapers, on the radio, and on television. In addition to all the negative statistics, we also hear a few names over and over. O. J. Simpson, Michael Jackson, R. Kelly, Kobe Bryant, John Lee Malvo, John Allen Muhammad, and Jayson Blair have practically moved into our living rooms for the evening news. It seems like the only time black men make the news these days is when we're accused of violence or deception.

So let's look at the question. Are most black men really married, in jail, or gay?

Let's start with marriage. The percentage of black men age fifteen and older who are married dropped from 64 percent in 1950 to 42.8 percent in 2000, according to the Joint Center for Political and Economic Studies. That is a dramatic reduction in the number of married black men, but that is exactly the point. For better or worse, the rumor that the "good black men" are already taken may not be true. If less than half of black men are married, that means more than half of black men are still available. The Census Bureau confirms this conclusion. In 2001, 5.1 million black men over 18 were married, leaving 5.7 million black men who were still available.

Are black men in jail? In 2002, there were 819,000 black men in jail or prison, and 73 percent of them were in their twenties and thirties, the prime age for dating and marriage. That's an extraordinarily high number. Twelve percent of black males in their twenties or early thirties were in jail. But as shocking as that number is, we have to remember that 88 percent of young black men were not in jail. So when we subtract the 819,000 incarcerated black men from the 5.7 million left after marriage, we still have about 4.9 million black men available.

Well, are they gay? There's no way to answer this question for sure, but it does seem unlikely that most of the black men who are not married or in jail would be gay. The U.S. Census Bureau does not measure the number of black gay men. Nor does the CDC. Even if they tried, it's unlikely that they could identify and record the thousands of black gay and bisexual men who may not want to identify their sexual orientation to the U.S. government. We do know there were 10.8 million adult black men listed in the the 2002 U.S. Census data. If we use the widely quoted (but just as widely discredited) assumption that 10 percent of the male population is homosexual, that would give us a little more than 1 million black gay and bisexual men. And when we subtract the 1 million black gay and bisexual men from the number left after incarceration, we still have more than 3.8 million straight black men who are available.

Perhaps those straight men are involved with white women. After all, the number of black men with white wives more than doubled from 1980 to 2002. In 1980, there were 122,000 such couples, but by 2002 there were 279,000. That is a huge increase, but it only accounts for 2.6 percent of the 11 million adult black men in the United States. And since the men who are married to white women are already included in the overall number of black men who are married, there's nothing left to subtract here. That means there were 3.8 million single, potentially eligible African-American men in 2002.

But here's the problem. There were 13.5 million African-American women over the age of 18 in 2002. That's a huge disparity with the 10.8 million black men in that age range. Before we consider who is married, incarcerated, or gay, we have to remember that there were 2.7 million more black women in the population than black men. That is a big part of the problem. Even if every black man in America was single, straight, and not in jail, there would still not be enough for all the black women in the population.

Of the 13.5 million adult black women in America, 5.2 million were married in 2002. Another 3.1 million were widowed or divorced. That leaves more than 5 million black women who have never been married. Some of these women may not want to be married, some may be interested in men of other races, and some may even be homosexual or bisexual. But if you assume that most of these women want to marry black men, then the odds are not good. But again here's the point. The problem is not that black men are married, in jail, or gay. The problem is that there are not enough black men to go around in the first place. The incarceration rates exacerbate the problem more than any other factor, but they are not the cause of the problem itself. Nor should we place the blame on those who are married or gay. If the objective is to encourage black men to be married, we should be grateful for the 5 million black men who are married. And if the objective is to encourage black marriages to endure, we should not try to pressure the black men who might be gay or bisexual into a heterosexual marriage that may not last.

If there are not enough black men for the black women in America, are the available black men really as bad as America seems to think they are? The truth about black men is much more complicated than the statistics we hear all the time on the news. In many ways, black men are in crisis today, but it is precisely because of that crisis that we should recognize the black men who are surviving and succeeding in a world that seems out to get them.

Let's not forget about the black men who have run major companies such as American Express, Fannie Mae, Merrill Lynch, and

AOL Time Warner. And don't neglect to mention the ordinary black men who work hard and stay out of trouble. Everyday, millions of black men go to work, support their families, and obey the law, but don't expect to see that on the news anytime soon. That's why we may need a new standard to measure the performance of black men. Considering all that black men have to overcome, it's actually amazing that we're doing as well as we are.

Black men still have to deal with racism. More than half of all black men report that they have been the victims of racial profiling by police, according to a study conducted in 2001. Given that profiling, it's no wonder that the Justice Department estimates that 30 percent of young black men will end up in jail at some point in their lives. And we're still the most likely *victims* of crime, not just the perpetrators. Young black men ages twelve to nineteen were 25 percent more likely to be victims of crime than whites of the same age group, according to a 1992 study. Considering all that black men go through, maybe we're not doing so badly after all. But when researchers look at our condition, they tend not to look at the unique situation of black men in America. Instead, they often compare black men to black women. That is a fair comparison, but it needs some context. First, as I mentioned earlier, there are far more black women than black men. Second, men and women are different in all races. The vast majority of the people in prison, for example, are men. Even among whites, the white male prison population dwarfs the white female prison population. Men of all races, including whites, have a lower life expectancy than women of the same race. And the population of women of all races outnumbers men of all races. White women also face a shortage of men. In 2002, there were 78 million adult white women and only 73 million adult white men.

But there is another reason for caution with the comparison

between black men and black women. It seems part of the assumption behind the comparison is that black men are falling behind and unable to be the leaders of their families and their communities that they are expected to be. That seems to be a reasonable argument, but it also appears to be based on the paternalistic assumption that men should be better off than women because women cannot take care of themselves. If that assumption is the foundation of our comparison, then we are simply replicating antiquated notions of patriarchy from the majority community and imposing those ideas on the African-American community. To change that pattern, we should not expect black men to do better than black women. Nor should we expect them to do worse. Instead, we should expect both black men and black women to do well.

In some ways, black men are doing relatively well as compared to black women. For example, there seems to be an assumption in the dialogue that black men are not making as much money as our female counterparts. But the truth is that black men still make considerably more money than black women, according to the National Committee on Pay Equity. That is not good news for black women, but it does challenge the notion that black men are falling behind economically. In fact, there has been no dramatic change in the black male-female wage gap in thirty years. But even if black men earn more, they might not have as many job opportunities as black women, so we might expect the unemployment rate to be higher. But the numbers do not support that argument either. From 1980 to 2003, unemployment for black men was not dramatically different from unemployment for black women, according to the U.S. Labor Department. In August 2003, for example, the unemployment rate for black men was 10 percent and the unemployment rate for black women was 10.1 percent.

Black men are doing okay in education too. Black male college enrollment has increased steadily in recent decades. In 1980, less than 8 percent of black men over 25 had completed college, but by 2000 the figure had doubled to more than 16 percent. This is about the same increase for black women (from 8.1 percent to 16.8 percent). And black men have actually done better than black women in high school graduation. In 1980, a slightly larger percentage of black women (51.5) than black men (51.2) graduated from high school, but by 2000 the roles had reversed, as 79.1 percent of black men graduated from high school compared to 78.7 percent of black women.

Even in the criminal justice system, the overwhelming majority of black men will never see the inside of a jail or prison. Remember the study mentioned earlier that said there were more black men in prison than in college? Well, that was very misleading. The reason that imbalance exists is because the authors of the study looked at the black male prison population of all ages instead of the college-aged prison population. In other words, there were more black men in prison because there were more black men in the sampled population, but if you just look at black men between the ages of eighteen and twenty-four, there are actually twice as many black men in college than there are in prison and jail. In 2002, there were 195,500 black men ages 18–24 in prison or jail. However, there were 469,000 black men in this age group who were enrolled in college in 2000.

But for every statistic showing that black men are doing well, someone else can produce another statistic that appears to show the opposite. And some African Americans fear that positive statistics about blacks may be used against us by giving white America an excuse to ignore the continuing racial imbalances in society. That is not my intention. However we choose to measure the success or failure of black men, we have to consider the unique circumstances of being a black man in America. It's the same sentiment reflected in Lorraine Hansberry's classic play *A Raisin in the Sun* when the family matriarch, Lena Younger, admonishes her daughter for criticizing her brother. "When you starts measuring somebody," she says, "measure him right, child, measure him right. Make sure you done taken into account what hills and valleys he come through before he got to wherever he is."

So how do you measure a good black man? Despite some of the imagery in popular culture, black manhood is more than just muscles, guns, sex, sports, and rap. Being a black man has nothing to do with being on the down low, but the down low story is so popular because it confirms our one-dimensional image of black men. The truth, of course, is more complicated. No doubt, we have plenty of issues to deal with as black men. The news media portray us as criminals and thugs, and then our own culture reinforces that image as a legitimate expression of black masculinity. But even if we are not in the dire predicament the media say we are, we are also not where we should be or could be. We still have much more work to do as black men. So here are some constructive steps that we can take to move beyond the down low.

First, we should examine our outdated concepts of masculinity and rethink what is masculine. The down low promoter J. L. King helps us understand the problem. "Some little, dainty-looking guy who is five feet five, weighing a buck twenty-five, can be packing a nine-inch penis. That's power," says King. No it's not. With all due respect to King, our power is not in the size of our dicks, or how well we use them, or how many kids we've made with them. If we see our penis as the sole source of our power, then we should not be surprised by society's attempts to reduce us to one-dimensional hypersexual creatures.

Nor should we judge our masculinity by our physical stature.

King's notion that a man who is five-five and 125 pounds is not masculine without a big dick is itself problematic. The brain, not the dick, is the most powerful organ in our bodies, and we as black men must emphasize mental strength as much as we highlight physical prowess. Perhaps in a premodern era before computers and technology, physical strength was an important measurement of masculinity. And in many neighborhoods today, a boy's physical ability is still the symbol of his maturity. But black men will not succeed in the modern business-oriented world on the basis of our physical power alone.

In fact, popular culture, in quiet complicity with African Americans, has been very successful at perpetuating an idea of physically dominant black men, and that image has traveled all across the globe. I experienced the effect of the stereotype when I visited a souvenir shop in St. Thomas in the Virgin Islands. While my partner Nathan and I were looking for magnets to take back home, we overheard an older white customer in a very loud and long conversation with an Indian store employee. I thought to myself, that poor sales clerk probably wants to do his job but the old guy won't stop talking. But I was wrong.

When we finally picked out our magnets, we took them to the counter to purchase, and the old guy finally stopped talking and walked away. Then the sales clerk asked us if we were basketball players. No, we told him. "Well, you look like ball players," he said. But we're not, we said again.

We had already gotten the basketball player look a few times on the trip. I'm six feet tall, and Nathan is six feet three inches. We were two black guys traveling together in the Caribbean, so we had to be basketball players or brothers. Never mind the fact that we don't look alike and we're not as tall as most professional basketball players. In the eyes of many in the Caribbean, we were athletes.

"Why is it that black American men are so athletic?" the store clerk asked.

I guess he thought he was praising our race, but I had my doubts. I know the secret code that black men are not supposed to challenge the racial stereotypes that confirm our physical superiority and sexual prowess, but I just could not see how that code would help us in this situation.

"Not all black men are athletic," I corrected him, thinking that would do the trick. But again I was wrong.

"Did you see the man who just left?" he asked. Nathan and I nodded. "He used to play basketball with Oscar Robertson, and he said that black men have something in their legs that makes them stronger, faster, and jump higher."

"That's not true," we said.

"But he said it is. He said he's played with several blacks, and that's why you're such good athletes."

"But I'm telling you it's not true," I told him.

"Why would he say that if it's not true? He seems to know what he's talking about."

"But he's wrong," we said. "Are you going to believe him or us? We're black. We know. Jimmy the Greek said the same thing a few years ago and got in trouble for making that remark."

"Then why are so many black athletes dominating sports? Whites can't compete. Indians can't compete. You guys are built differently."

"No, we're not built any differently," I said. "I've studied the issue of race for years, and most scientific evidence shows there are more differences within a race than between the races."

"But he . . ."

"He doesn't know what he's talking about."

"Then why are there so many black kids who go into sports?"

"Many of these kids come from backgrounds where sports are seen as the only way out of the community," Nathan said.

"It's a stereotype," I added. "It's just like the stereotypes about Indians, whatever that is."

"That we're all computer programmers," he said.

"Right, and you're not a computer programmer are you?"

"I am," he said.

I guess you don't have to be a logical thinker to program a computer, I thought to myself. He seemed incapable or unwilling to hear what we were saying.

"We all own businesses," he said. "In fact, most of the businesses on this strip are owned by Indians."

"And that's partly because of economic opportunity," I said. "Many African Americans don't necessarily have the same access to resources that people in your community may have."

"Sports is really a way out for many of the kids in the black community," Nathan said. "That's why they excel at it, because they're driven."

"It's very interesting," he said. "I hadn't thought about that before. Now I have something to think about." He finished the conversation and rang up our orders. "Enjoy St. Thomas," he said as we left the store. But somehow we knew the dialogue was not over. My guess is that the store clerk was not likely to believe us until our words were confirmed to him by an "objective" white source. In his estimation, we were just a couple of black athletes. What did we know?

The widespread perception of black physical and sexual prowess may make us proud as black men, but it does very little to advance a more realistic image of who we are. Now it's time for us to redefine what manhood is all about.

When I was in college, I won an award at the end of my freshman year as the outstanding freshman man in the class. The award was called the William S. Churchill Prize, and I actually thought it was a mistake when I first heard about it. I had done reasonably well my first year but a dismal grade in spring semester Spanish ruined my GPA. I figured the school would take back the award once the Spanish professor reported the final grade, but they never took it back. Instead, I got a cash prize to buy whatever books I wanted through the library. Every book was inscribed with a plaque that defined the purpose of the award. It read very simply. *"Honesty with oneself, fairness toward others, sensitivity to duty and courage in its performance: these qualities make manhood, and on manhood rests the structure of society."*

I was eighteen years old when I first read that inscription, and ever since that time I have used those words to define manhood. The definition applies to men of all races, but black men would do well to adopt that philosophy as our own. If each of us could just apply the four principles in the definition, we would eliminate the down low right away. If we could be honest with ourselves, fair toward others, sensitive to our duties, and courageous in performing those duties, we would have no reason to be on the down low in the first place. We can respond to the down low by creating an environment of honesty among ourselves as black men.

But far beyond the down low, we should remember that honesty, fairness, duty, and courage are important principles for men in any situation. That is what manhood is all about. It's not about how many women we've fucked or how much money we've earned. It's not about how much weight we can bench press or how many free throws we can sink. Manhood is much simpler than that, and much more difficult. It is honesty with ourselves, fairness toward others, sensitivity to duty, and courage in its performance.

Second, we have to practice safe sex. Many of the same rules that apply to women apply to men as well. Talk to your partner about safe sex, get condoms, use them, and get tested regularly. But as men, we have a greater responsibility not to mislead our partners about our sexual orientation or about our HIV status. In male-female relationships, women often look to us to set the tone of the relationship, and men often have more power to determine the nature of the relationship. What will our relationship be like? Will we talk about safe sex or not? Will we use condoms or not? Many women will go along with us if we integrate safe sex as a part of our sexual practice. The study by Professor Lisa Bowleg confirms that "when men initiated condom use at first sex, women readily accepted the use of condoms." One participant in the study described at as "just a thing he does." Even after first sex, "men also controlled current condom use in terms of initiating or refusing condoms, regardless of whether women wanted to use condoms," according to the study.

Every time you have sex with someone without a condom and you don't know their HIV status, you put your life at risk. It doesn't matter if you're having sex with a man or a woman or if you're a top or a bottom, and it doesn't matter what your own HIV status may be. A negative HIV test is not a license to practice unsafe sex. As men, we have great power to make a positive influence on our relationships. But with great power comes great responsibility.

Third, we have to deal with our hangups around homosexuality. In his book *Who's Gonna Take The Weight,* Kevin Powell talks to black men about homophobia. But Powell, a straight black man, explains how he overcame his own biases when he rented an apartment from a landlord who was a middle-aged black gay man. The experience taught him that his homophobia was a misplaced expression of his own weakness as a man. "And this man," Powell writes, "this gay Black man, taught me more lessons about manhood than one would think possible: that one could be a man, be responsible, be kind, be loving, show love, give love, without compromising one's self-worth and dignity."

That's what being a man is all about. It's about responsibility, kindness, love, principle, and dignity. We don't dignify ourselves when we demean others because of their sexual orientation. Those who are comfortable with their own sexuality have no reason to make light of anyone else's sexuality. But those who are uncomfortable with their own sexuality are sometimes the most vocal critics of homosexuality and bisexuality.

The burden to challenge homophobia falls on the shoulders of all black men, regardless of their sexual orientation. Unfortunately, black gay and bisexual men and black men on the down low can be just as homophobic as their heterosexual counterparts. Many of us have sat quietly through homophobic sermons, antigay comedy routines, vicious music lyrics, and offensive conversations with our friends. Many of us are concerned about being typecast as gay if we simply speak in defense of the rights of those who are. Those fears are understandable, but they must be overcome. Being a man is about standing up for what is right, even when you are sometimes afraid to do so. It will not get any easier to stand up until we simply stand up. Society will not change on its own until we begin to change it.

I have been through the experience of overcoming my own fears many times, and I know how difficult it can be, but I also know how empowering it can be. One of those experiences took place in the fall of 1995 when I had just started a job as the executive director of a national black gay organization based in Los Angeles. I asked the men in the office where to get a haircut and they recommended two places in the 'hood. The first, they told me, was closer to the office. The barbers were older and pleasant, but they were not as skilled as the younger barbers at other shops. The second location was a barbershop in South Central that was much more popular but also homophobic, they told me. In the interest of vanity, I decided on the second shop. A good haircut was more important than a good conversation.

I walked into the barbershop and waited patiently while thumbing through some old magazines and watching television. When my turn came about an hour later, I finally sat in the barber's chair. Most of the conversation in the shop that day was about sports, and none of it was homophobic. Except for the long wait at the beginning, the experience at the barbershop was fine, and the haircut was great. The guys must have been mistaken, I thought to myself. To show my appreciation for the barber and to keep me from waiting on my next visit, I gave him a big tip, and he told me to look for him when I returned.

More than a month later, I returned to the same barbershop and sat in the same barber's chair. The barber asked me where I had been, and I told him that I was out of town. I explained that I worked in Los Angeles but I actually lived in Washington, D.C. He seemed interested in my bicoastal living arrangements so he kept talking. "Where do you work?" he asked. For some reason, I wasn't expecting that question. When most people get that question, they can usually answer without telling too much about themselves. For me, it was a little different. My job was a part of my identity, and I was still learning how to talk about that in awkward situations like this one. I decided to simply tell him the truth.

"I work for the National Black Gay and Lesbian Leadership Forum," I said. The barber paused and pulled back his clippers for a moment. I could almost feel the wheels processing in his brain as he prepared his next question. "The National Black what?" he asked. I told him once more. "The National Black Gay and Lesbian Leadership Forum." He turned off the clippers and continued with the questions. "So how did you get that job?" he asked. I took a second to question my decision to return to the same barbershop with the reputation for homophobia, but I mustered up the courage to keep speaking. "I applied for the job, and I got selected," I said, but clearly he was not satisfied with my response. He wanted to know more. He knew that I knew what he wanted, and I knew that he knew that I knew what he wanted. We both danced around the issue for a few moments, and then he finally blurted it out. "So are you gay?"

I know the TV was still on, and the conversations around me were still taking place, but for a brief moment when he asked that question and I prepared to respond, it felt as if the entire barbershop was staring at me and waiting for my reply. Why did I come here? The guys at the office already warned me about this place, and now the barber is standing behind me waiting for my answer. I took a quick breath, and I told him. "Yes, I am."

The barber stopped for a split second, then turned the clippers back on. "That's cool," he said. And he continued cutting my hair. There was no big incident. No drama. No angry confrontation. No preaching. Just a barber and his client having a conversation about the client's job. When he finished the hair cut, I gave him another tip and promised I would come back on my next visit a month later. And I returned as promised. For two years, I continued to patronize the same barber at the same barbershop that everyone had warned me to avoid. And for two years I never heard a homophobic word out of anyone in the shop.

I learned from that experience the importance of standing up for who we are and what we believe. It doesn't matter what your sexual orientation may be. It doesn't matter what people think about you. It matters what you think about yourself. If we expect people to treat us badly, they will. If we expect our communities to forsake us, they will. If we walk around in shame with a chip on our shoulders, someone will try to knock it off. But when we have the courage to be open and honest about who we are, people in our community not only accept us, they respect us more.

One of the main reasons men are on the down low is because many of them do not believe that they can be who they are in a culture where homophobia and heterosexism are widespread. Homophobia exists not just in black America, it's in all of America, but the feeling of hurt can be much more profound when it comes from your own people. Most black men grow up in a world where we are feared, despised, and distrusted. We respond to that environment by creating a safe space of our own, but for those men who are not heterosexual, their sexual orientation can become an obstacle to their full acceptance in their own community. Since they already face prejudice as black men, they are reluctant to acknowledge their sexual orientation and take on even more prejudice because of whom they love.

If we truly hope to break the cycle of the down low, we have to create an environment where men can be free to be who they are, and not just who we expect them to be. Being a black man has nothing to do with your sexual orientation. It has everything to do with your sense of honesty, fairness, duty, and courage. And many of the greatest black men who personify that courage were gay or bisexual themselves.

Civil rights activists, like Bayard Rustin, who organized Dr. King's historic 1963 march on Washington, have helped to motivate us. Soldiers, like Perry Watkins, have defended us. Authors like James Baldwin, Countee Cullen, Alain Locke, Samuel R. Delany, Essex Hemphill, E. Lynn Harris, and James Earl Hardy, have educated and enlightened us. Performers, like Johnny Mathis, Billy Strayhorn, and Alvin Ailey, have inspired and entertained us. Filmmakers, like Paris Barclay, Isaac Julien, and Lee Daniels, have told our stories. Playwrights, like George C. Wolfe, have dramatized us. Athletes, like the baseball player Glenn Burke, the bodybuilder Chris Dickerson, and the soccer player Justin Fashanu, have excited us. Politicians, like Ron Oden and Ken Reeves, have led our cities. And ministers, like the Reverend James Cleveland and the Reverend Peter Gomes, have led our congregations.

Black men come in all different shapes, sizes, colors, and backgrounds. We are straight, gay, bisexual, same-gender-loving, questioning, and on the down low. All of us have something to contribute, and we cannot expect to advance as black men if we create a culture that deprives us of the talents, skills, and contributions of some of our very own.

Fourth, let's take control of our image. The playwright and director George C. Wolfe once said, "Anytime anyone comes up with a definition of who you are, it has absolutely nothing to do with who you are. It has to do with how they can process in a way that they can feel in command of whatever impact you're having."

So let's tell the truth about who we really are as black men. Most black men are not in jail and not on the down low. Millions of black men are hard-working, law-abiding, tax-paying citizens. We are not all saints, but we are certainly not all criminals either. The mass media have constructed an image of us that reduces black manhood to a cultural commodity to be bought and sold in the marketplace. But we are more than XXXL T-shirts, oversized jeans, and basketball jerseys. That is a part of who we are, but it is not all of who we are. And we are more than just rappers and ballplayers too. That is also a part of who we are, but it is not all of who we are.

The problem with many discussions about our image is that we often end up trading one stereotype for another. Some of those who reject the image of black men as pimps and thugs would like to replace it with a sanitized image of black men as lawyers and doctors.

But we don't need censorship to make our point. We need reality. Some black men are doing very well, but too many of us are not. Too many of us are in jail or prison or out of work, but we have to figure out a balanced way to say that without feeding into the stereotype that *all* black men are in jail or prison or out of work.

To do all that will require a delicate balancing act. We cannot ignore the suffering in our community, but we cannot be defined by it either. We must find a way to challenge America's persistent racial barriers without allowing those barriers to paralyze us into inaction. We have to fight against our one-dimensional media identity without fighting against the black men who embrace that identity. We have to create a culture that discourages the dishonesty of the down low without shaming men on the down low into more denial.

It will not be easy work, but we have faced many difficult challenges before. Ten years before I wrote this book, I took part in a defining event that helped to shape the collective sense of possibility for black men. It was the Million Man March. Many of us worried about the exclusionary message in producing an all-male event, and many of us also worried about the exclusion of gay and bisexual men from the podium. But on October 16, 1995, more than a million black men took a leap of faith and came together. We stood on the mall in the nation's capital in all of our beautiful diversity. We were young and old, rich and poor, straight and gay, standing side by side. Men with college degrees marched alongside men without high school diplomas. Black men from the south joined hands with black men from the north, east, and west. It was a day that began with a chilly morning and ended with a balmy afternoon. The police and the media expected violence, but there was none. A million black men came to the nation's capital peacefully to show our unity as a people and to commit ourselves to heal and rebuild and grow. No one had ever seen anything like it, and almost all of us left with a sense of awe and wonder in the possibilities for the future. If we could get a million black men to come together in Washington, we thought, we could do almost anything. We could empty the jails, educate our children, eliminate diseases, inspire our families, rebuild our communities, lead our churches, change our diets, write our own books, produce our own films, create our own music, buy our own homes, and start our own businesses. The opportunities were endless.

Those of us who were there that day promised to go back to our communities and our families and be better men. Some of us did not survive, while others made great strides toward that goal. But all of us knew the challenge would last throughout our lifetimes. As black men, we have always known that we have much more work to do. And we know that we must do it.

That is what being a man is all about.

CHAPTER 11

Homothugs, Helmets & Hip Hop

LIKE MANY YOUNG men, I was pushed to play sports at a very early age. From the time I entered grade school to the time I graduated from college, I was almost always on a team. In grade school, it was Little League baseball. In high school, it was football, wrestling, cross country, and track. In college, it was track once again. From my experience, I can think of no place in America that is as homophobic and as homoerotic as the sports team locker room.

The sport I know best is track and field. Track has always seemed a very homoerotic sport. Men prance around the track with hip-hugging tights and tiny tank tops that tuck into their tiny shorts. Even as a teenage runner, it seemed to me there were quite a few gay men in the track world, and one of them was on my high school team. If Steve was in any way trying to hide his sexual orientation, I could not tell. It was an open secret on the track team that he was gay. But he had one quality that made him acceptable even to his most homophobic teammates: He was fast. He could outrun anyone on the team, and he helped us win track meets when no one else could. But a few years after high school, a classmate called me with bad news. Steve had passed away. He died of AIDS.

Over the years, I had almost forgotten about Steve and forgotten about the idea of gay athletes. When I ran track in college, there were no openly gay members of our team. A year after I graduated, however, I got a call from a friend that one of our teammates who was still on the team had come out of the closet. That was a bold move. Gay men were not exactly welcome in the locker room of most sports teams at the time. And that was in the late 1980s. Then things started to change. Pushed forward by the impact of the AIDS epidemic, gay men began to play a much more visible role in society in the 1990s. Instead of ignoring the existence of homosexuality, America found itself speculating about gays in the miltary, gay marriage, gays in sports, and gays in hip hop.

By the end of the twentieth century, homosexual and bisexual men seemed to be visible almost everywhere, and yet there were still a few bastions of masculinity that were reluctant to acknowledge the presence of gay men in their midst. Professional sports was one of those places. In a 1998 speech to the Wisconsin legislature, the Green Bay Packers defensive end Reggie White said gay men were "malicious and backstabbing," equated them with "liars" and "cheaters," and blamed homosexuality for the decline of Western civilization. So when the track star Derrick Peterson appeared in the pages of a gay magazine in the summer of 2002, it seemed a breakthrough for gay and bisexual athletes. Peterson, an American champion 800-meter runner, was hailed as the first active black professional athlete to come out of the locker room closet.

Genre magazine, the gay publication that interviewed Peterson, said that his willingness to announce his sexuality would "make an enormous impact on the issue of gays in sports." Outsports.com, a gay Web site, called Peterson a "rare" and "courageous" individual.

The *Daily Pennsylvanian* newspaper described Peterson's "revolutionary" actions as a "lesson in heroism."

When the Peterson story broke, only a handful of black college or professional athletes had come out to the public, and almost all of them suffered through tragedy or controversy. Glenn Burke, the first black professional athlete to come out, was eventually run out of the Los Angeles Dodgers team in 1979. A dozen years later, he was reported to be living on the streets and drug addicted until he died of AIDS in 1995. The British soccer star Justin Fashanu was described as "erratic" after he came out of the closet. He claimed and then retracted a statement that he had had sex with two British cabinet ministers. Accused of sexually assaulting a teenager in Maryland, Fashanu took his own life in 1998. The former New York Giants guard Roy Simmons came out on the *Phil Donahue Show* in 1992 but then disappeared from the public, and had not been heard until he appeared on an ESPN show in 2004. The Stanford football player Dwight Slater came out to his coach and teammates after hearing homophobic conversations that left him feeling depressed. Slater soon quit the team altogether.

Until Peterson's announcement, Chris Dickerson and Kisha Snow provided the only positive examples of coming out experiences for black athletes. But Dickerson, the first black bodybuilder to win the title "Mr. America," came out years after his career had ended, and Snow, the top-ranked female heavyweight boxing contender, later announced that she was engaged to be married to a man.

The negative experiences of black gay and bisexual athletes who did come out made Peterson's disclosure all the more significant. But the story was not the breakthrough it appeared to be. Even in the *Genre* interview, Peterson was very careful about what he said. "One thing I will say for sure [is that] I'm definitely not heterosexual," the magazine quoted him. But Peterson never said he was homosexual or bisexual either. Was Peterson on the down low? It's hard to be on the down low when you're interviewed in a national gay magazine.

When I interviewed Peterson for a magazine article, he denied that he was gay or bisexual and declined to define his sexual orientation. "I don't want to be called something or labeled something that I am not," he said. His comments echoed earlier remarks reported in *Genre,* in which he said, "I hate labels. I don't really care what people think of my sexual orientation. I like men and women."

Irritated by the press, Peterson reserved much of his outrage for the media coverage of his sexuality. Although a friend of Peterson's wrote the *Genre* article, Peterson said he was "very very appalled and upset at being labeled as a gay person in the article." When asked if he was upset at the writer, he acknowledged, "I wasn't so much upset with him, with what he did, I think I was more upset with what people were saying or doing on websites." But Peterson also seemed a bit naïve about the media. "I honestly thought it was just going to be another story . . . that had nothing to do with my sexuality," he said, adding that he expected the story to focus on his "athletic prowess." But why announce your sexual orientation in a story about athletics? "I like to see everyone represented equally," he replied, describing himself as an activist concerned about the underrepresentation of African Americans in the gay media. The comments about his sexuality, he said, were "fabricated by myself."

Derrick Peterson's coming out reversal is complicated and unusual, but in some ways it mirrors the larger problem for black gay and bisexual athletes. Many of these athletes are "following the script that was given to them," according to the author Randy Boyd. "You're black, you're an athlete, you're a Man with a capital M, and this is what you do," he said, describing the script.

Sports plays a unique role in the black community. It provides a social ladder that motivates thousands of young black men, undaunted by the slim odds of professional success, to pick up basketballs and footballs with dreams of future glory. It is a counterweight to racism and white supremacy that instills a sense of pride in many African Americans, as when Jesse Owens won four gold medals at the 1936 Olympics in Hitler's Germany, or when Jackie Robinson passed through baseball's color barrier in 1947, or when Tommie Smith and John Carlos gave the defiant black power salute at the 1968 Mexico City Olympics. In a world where black men are beaten down every day, sports enables black men to establish masculinity. When the all-black men's 4 x 100 meter relay team stripped off their shirts and posed with flexed muscles after winning at the 2000 Olympics, or when the legendary basketball player Wilt Chamberlain boasted that he had slept with 20,000 women in his career, they were demonstrating not their athletic prowess but their perception of their masculinity. In few other public arenas are black men afforded the luxury of creativity and individuality or excused for the excesses of bravado. We see this freedom in the colorful pranks of the Harlem Globetrotters, the artful dancing of the boxer Muhammad Ali, or the fancy footwork of the football player "Neon" Deion Sanders.

Although a few white athletes have revealed their sexual orientation to the public, very few black athletes have taken the same step, leaving many to speculate that it is more difficult for black athletes to come out than it is for whites. If so, black hypermasculinity and homophobia may be to blame. The openly gay track coach Eric Anderson cites the "cool pose," adopted by African-American men as an indication of a "hypermasculine" image that may be "partially based on homophobia" or "hyperheterosexuality."

Despite social changes in recent decades, coming out of the closet is difficult for athletes of all colors. If the issue affected only black athletes, then more white athletes would be out of the closet too. But only a handful of major white athletes have come out, and their stories are not all positive. Greg Louganis only came out after winning the Olympic gold medal in diving. But the openly gay football player Dave Kopay and the baseball player Billy Bean both emphasized how difficult it is for any gay or bisexual athlete to come out in their footsteps. And the tennis players Billie Jean King and Martina Navratilova both lost some support and endorsements after they came out.

But coming out may not be necessary for African-American sports figures. Black athletes have long brought a flamboyant presence to their game. With a name, a style, or a flair, they teased audiences and moved athletics to the edge of acceptable sexual expression. In the 1960s, the pro wrestler Sweet Daddy Siki dyed his hair blond, wore dark sunglasses, and carried a mirror with him into the ring. Georgia Tech's offensive guard Roy Simmons won the nickname "Sugar Bear" a dozen years before he came out of the closet. The Olympic gold medalist Carl Lewis teased his fans in a pair of red stilettos in a famous picture for the photographer Annie Leibovitz in a Pirelli tire ad. "Power is nothing without control," the ad said. The basketball player Dennis Rodman once showed up in a wedding dress as a publicity stunt. And the NFL running back Ricky Williams posed on the cover of a popular sports magazine in a wedding gown as well.

Athletes can get away with some things that other black men, perhaps, cannot do. Magic Johnson of the Los Angeles Lakers and Isaiah Thomas of the Detroit Pistons made history in 1988 when they began kissing each other before their basketball games. When Mark Aguirre was traded from the Dallas Mavericks to the Pistons, he too joined in the kissing game, but virtually no one suggested that any of the three black athletes might be same-gender-loving. On the other hand, Dennis Rodman of the Chicago Bulls acknowledged "many homosexual aspects of sports" in his 1996 memoir, *Bad as I Wanna Be*. "Watch any football game. What's the first thing guys do when they win a big game? They hug each other. What does a baseball manager do when he takes his pitcher out? He takes the ball and pats him on the ass . . . Man hugs man. Man pats man on ass. Man whispers in man's ear and kisses him on the cheek. This is classic homosexual or bisexual behavior," Rodman says.

Rodman became the first active black professional athlete to acknowledge a same-sex attraction in a 1995 *Sports Illustrated* article, where he said he "fantasized" about being with another man. Although he parties at gay clubs, paints his fingernails, colors his hair, and sometimes wears women's clothes, Rodman says he is not homosexual. "I'm not gay," he said in his book. "I would tell you if I was. If I go to a gay bar, that doesn't mean that I want another man to put his tongue down my throat—no. It means I want to be a whole individual." Rodman added, "Mentally, I probably am bisexual."

Even when athletes do engage in homosexual behavior, it does not necessarily mean that they are homosexual. Homosexuality and homoeroticism have played a secret role in sports for decades, but is it not always labeled gay. Phil Petrie was a college athlete at Tennessee State University in the 1950s, and he recalls that "it was common for athletes to, in effect, sell themselves . . . to have sex for men." Petrie, who is married with children, remembered football players who talked about receiving oral sex or "packing shit," but the athletes at the time did not consider their actions to be homosexual. Instead, it was a business transaction between cash-strapped players and men who wanted to have them. "If you have a group of people who are considered desirable, and you live in a capitalistic society, can you get them with money?" Petrie asked. "And the answer is you can get some." It took a kind of cognitive dissonance for some of the straight athletes to engage in homosexual sex without acknowledging what they were actually doing. But it was not uncommon.

In some ways, the pro sports world has been more receptive toward out black athletes than what society expects. Blacks are actually well represented among the relatively few out gay athletes in the top sports. As of 2004, a third of the pro football players (one out of three), half of the pro baseball players (one out of two), and the only pro basketball player to acknowledge a same-sex attraction (Dennis Rodman) were all black. But for every out black athlete, there are two or three examples of athletes who have denied that they are homosexual or bisexual. When the boxer Hasim Rahman accused Lennox Lewis of "gay moves," Lewis, who was thirty-six and still single at the time, responded firmly to London's *Daily Telegraph:* "I am definitely, definitely not gay and never have been." He said, "I love women."

When rumors spread about the Pittsburgh Steelers quarterback Kordell Stewart in 1999, Stewart confronted the rumors in a private locker room session with his teammates. Using graphic descriptions of heterosexual acts he said he enjoyed, Stewart told his teammates, "You'd better not leave your girlfriends around me, because I'm out to prove a point." Three years later, when asked to comment on a rumor about another player, Stewart replied: "I'm a man . . . 110 percent man. . . . My daddy did a wonderful job of raising a man, period, hands down, no more, no less."

When Magic Johnson made his stunning annoucement about his HIV status in 1991, a few eyebrows were raised about his sexual behavior as well. To stop the speculation, Johnson quickly arranged an appearance on the *Arsenio Hall Show* the next day and told Hall and the audience exactly what they wanted to hear. "I'm far from being homosexual," he said. "But that's the whole thing. [People] think it can only happen to gay people, and that's so wrong. Even I was naïve to think, 'well it can't happen to me.' Well that's wrong. [For] heterosexuals it's coming fast and we all have to practice safe sex."

Johnson was right about one thing. We all do have to practice safe sex, but at the time there was little evidence that the HIV epidemic was "coming fast" in the heterosexual community, at least not for straight black men. In fact, in the year that Johnson tested positive, only 7 percent of all black male AIDS cases resulted from heterosexual contact. When you exclude sex with injection drug users and with members of other risk groups, the percentage shrinks to less than one-tenth of one percent. Only 383 of the 47,000 black men diagnosed with AIDS in 1991 contracted the virus exclusively from heterosexual sex with no other risk factors. When you consider the likelihood that some of these 383 men lied in reporting their behavior, it makes you realize that AIDS was not a disease that seriously threatened drug-free straight black men in 1991. But Johnson dutifully stayed on message.

Johnson's confirmation of his sexual orientation reminded me of the energy some people spent in proving that the ABC News anchor Max Robinson was straight after he died from AIDS in 1988. After Robinson's death, the author Haki Madhubuti made it clear that Robinson was not gay. "It was [Max's] wish to let people know he died of AIDS and that he did not contract it through the *assumed avenues* of drug use or homosexual activity," Madhubuti wrote. "Max was a woman's man to the bone," he explained. Of course that explanation was possible but highly unlikely. Of the nearly 18,000 black male AIDS cases the CDC reported in 1988, only 40 of them (not 40 percent, but 40) resulted from heterosexual sex with a woman who was not a drug user or a member of some other obvious risk group. Yes, that is not a misprint. Only 40 out of 18,000 cases. That is just two-tenths of 1 percent of all black male

AIDS cases. And again that number is probably inflated because some of the 40 men may have lied about how they contracted the virus. In other words, Max Robinson would have been *extremely* unlucky to have been infected from heterosexual sex with a woman who was not a drug user. It's not impossible, just highly unlikely. But AIDS was still a dirty word in the 1980s and 1990s, and the black community was heavily invested in protecting the reputation of its heroes like Robinson and Johnson. The last thing we needed was another reason to "beat down" a good black man.

If Magic Johnson were gay, it would be his own business. And the sports reporters who know the truth would never reveal his secret, according to some observers who see a conspiracy of silence among reporters, athletes, and teammates. Although the public does not realize that many professional athletes are gay or bisexual, some of those closest to the athletes do know. As with the military, the policy seems to be "don't ask, don't tell." For example, at the 2002 National Basketball Association draft, when Charles Barkley was asked by a television crew if there were any gay players in the NBA, he replied: "I don't kiss and tell."

The truth is that many high-level athletes live in glass closets visible to those around them. The sports columnist Wallace Matthews wrote in *Newsweek* that "it is a common practice among ballplayers who suspect a teammate is gay to confide to friendly reporters, 'He's a little funny,' with a roll of the eyes." Some black professional athletes even take their boyfriends to sporting events, according to the author Randy Boyd. "There are reporters who know this and they don't report about it," he said, in part because they "don't want to breach trust and be thrown out of the inner circle." Boyd likens the situation to the media's relationship with the 1960s Kennedy White House, where some reporters knew of the president's alleged extramarital affairs but never reported on them.

Another sports author told me a "sad story" of a black college basketball player whose boyfriend would sit and watch the games in the stands but could never be recognized. "Everybody knew who the girlfriends were, but nobody knew about the boyfriend," he said. When the games were over, the player would join his teammates and their girlfriends to celebrate, while his own boyfriend would be left to himself. "Teams can deal when a guy has a drug problem or an alcohol problem," says Dennis Rodman, "but not when they find out someone's doing something they don't like in the privacy of their own bedroom. It doesn't make sense."

The same double standards apply to the hypermasculine world of hip hop. Privately, everyone in the industry knows there are gay and bisexual men in the hip hop world, but publicly the industry seems unwilling to admit the presence of homosexuality, except in stereotypical expressions. Several of the most powerful men in hip hop are gay or bisexual. Some have arranged marriages. Some date women and sleep with men. Some have never really tried to hide. And some just don't talk about it. Almost everybody on the inside knows the deal, but they don't talk about it on the outside.

They don't talk about it because they know the public has its own double standard about homosexuality. If a rapper gets arrested, goes to jail, or spends time in prison, we not only forgive him, we anoint him with praise and street credibility. If he's a drug addict, an alcoholic or a womanizer, the public will barely bat an eyebrow. But if there's even a hint of a rumor that someone is gay, then the public is up in arms. That is a classic double standard. The rap artist 50 Cent becomes a legend for being shot nine times as a drug dealer. The rapper Shyne goes to prison on gun charges and ends up with a record deal behind bars. And R. Kelly's album sales soar after he is busted for allegedly videotaping himself having sex with a minor. We can forgive all that, but we can't forgive an artist for being gay?

But don't think the public isn't interested. No, the public is fascinated by the idea of homosexuality in hip hop. Just ask New York's most popular urban radio and television personality, Wendy Williams. Her audience was once riveted by tales of a gay rapper on the down low. Many of us pretend we don't want to know, but deep down we do. I've seen the interest at events I've attended all across the country.

A few years ago, I walked into a crowded room on the campus of the University of Pennsylvania for a panel discussion. The audience members had taken all the chairs and occupied all the wall space, so my fellow panelists and I stood near the doorway as the organizers rushed in new chairs to accommodate the overflow. I had no idea the audience would be so large, but the topic was hot—"Hip Hop and Homosexuality."

I began by speaking about hip hop artists who have recorded homophobic music. My list included Brand Nubian, Canibus, Common, Cypress Hill, DMX, Eazy E, Eminem, Goodie Mob, Allen Iverson, Ice Cube, Ja Rule, Jay Z, Mase, Mobb Deep, Public Enemy, Snoop Dogg, T.O.K., and 50 Cent.

Then I moved to hip hop artists who have challenged homophobia, and here the list was much shorter. I cited Queen Pen, Queen Latifah, Common (who reformed after dating Erykah Badu), Meshell Ndegeocello, and Will Smith (who played a gay man in the film *Six Degrees of Separation*). The moderator also reminded me of the Disposable Heroes of Hiphoprisy, a hip hop group who recorded an underground CD back in 1992 but hadn't surfaced since.

I was also intrigued by P. Diddy and LL Cool J, both of whom are popular hip hop artists who have rarely, if ever, used antigay lyrics in their music. And I mentioned some openly gay hip hop artists, including Caushun, DeepDickCollective, Dutchboy, Tori Fixx, and Rainbow Flava.

But before you can understand hip hop's role in homophobia, you have to understand hip hop's role in black culture. I am left to wonder if hip hop is still as revolutionary as it once was. The answer depends on how you define hip hop. Hip hop is not all about music, and it is not all about rap music, and even then, not all rap music is homophobic. Gay activists tend to focus on the most offensive artists who record music with homophobic lyrics and neglect to mention the scores of other hip hop artists without homophobic lyrics. Some hip hop is still on the cutting edge, while other hip hop music has become so commercialized that it seems to have lost its soul. It seems that a lot of the radio-friendly hip hop has become more evolutionary than revolutionary as it has evolved deeper and deeper into mainstream culture. Rather than communicate progressive messages that challenge the status quo, too much of mainstream hip hop seems willing to generate materialistic videos, overproduced music, and watered-down messages. How can performers complain about rundown projects in the ghettoes when they're driving their Hummers and their Bentleys and drinking expensive bottles of Cristal?

With jobs disappearing and the country at war, the political side of hip hop re-emerged in 2004. The entertainment mogul Russell Simmons and Dr. Benjamin Chavis at the Hip Hop Summit Action Network have persuaded hip hop artists to encourage young people to vote, and P. Diddy's Citizen Change organization sparked a revolution of politics through fashion with his "Vote or Die" campaign. But I imagine the artists can only go so far. In today's consumer-driven hip hop music culture, it seems the public may not want to hear the most controversial messages, and the most successful artists may not be the right messengers. Meanwhile, a few popular artists record increasingly political music, like Public Enemy's "Son of a Bush," Wyclef Jean's "President," and Eminem's "Mosh."

Maybe we should expect nothing at all from hip hop artists. After all, hip hop music is a business. It's a business that often uses black talent to generate hundreds of millions of dollars for nonblack record companies. And many of the hip hop artists are themselves businesspeople. No matter what they say, you cannot be a practicing gangsta and a successful hip hop artist at the same time.

So who am I to expect more from hip hop than I expect from the rest of the community? It's just entertainment, after all. Snoop Dogg once said he can't knock nobody's hustle, and he was right. It is, after all, a hustle. But it's a hustle that has extremely important consequences on the larger society and on the black community.

Hip hop creates and reinforces exaggerated images of black masculinity and then uses its market power to regulate and restrict our perceptions of black authenticity. Thus, hip hop enables the commercialization and commodification of black culture for nonblack business interests. Those who don't fit the newly popular pimp and thug image can be easily discredited by their own communities, creating a vicious cultural cycle that values style over substance, money over mission, and ignorance over education.

But maybe I was wrong. During the discussion at the University of Pennsylvania, a gay rapper named Caushun said that he did not feel the hip hop music industry is particularly homophobic. He cited his own positive experiences with various industry leaders as an indication that the business may not be what it appears to be from the outside. I don't have the direct experience he does as an artist, but I do think it's important to distinguish between an artist's personal relationships and an executive's institutional obligation. Personally, the music executives may be very friendly, but I think we should demand more than a polite smile and a pat on the back to get new music and new talent released.

Given the trends in our culture, perhaps it is not surprising to find gay artists, producers, musicians, stylists, and song writers in hip hop. But few of these people are out publicly, and many sit by silently while their artists seemingly promote intolerance of gays and lesbians. Although Caushun said that he was not offended by homophobic music lyrics, I was not so sanguine about it. Caushun suggested that we give too much power to words sometimes, and perhaps he was right. Words can only hurt us if we allow them to do so, but that philosophy works best for well-adjusted adults who are secure in their identity. I am not convinced that young people struggling with their identity have the same capacity to dismiss the significance of homophobic lyrics from the mouths of the artists they and their peers most admire. The thirteen-year-old boy or the fifteen-year-old girl who internalizes the animus in the words "fag" or "dyke" may not react as positively as adults do.

Strangely enough, many black adults who are gay or bisexual seem to have made peace with homophobic music. Only a few minutes after watching the drag queen Harmonica Sunbeam host her popular Sunday night variety show at Escuelita's nightclub in New York, black and Latino men were dancing with each other to the familiar melody of Tok's "Chi Chi Man," a reggae song that appears to encourage the burning and killing of gay ("chi chi") men.

From dem a par inna chi chi man car
Blaze di fire mek we bun dem!!!! (Bun dem!!!!)

At a party in Washington a few year ago, black gay men were tapping their feet to the beat of Jay-Z's *Blueprint* CD, in which the artist uses some variation of the word "fag" three times on different songs. And in the same year, black gay men across the country were buying DMX's new *Great Depression* CD, which criticizes "faggots" in the song "Bloodline Anthem."

What once seemed unimaginable has now become reality. Mainstream black gay male identity now embraces a popular music and culture that often seems inconsistent with homosexuality. Many of these men have constructed themselves as homothugs, every bit the image of the hard-edged thugs in the rap music videos, indistinguishable from the Tims-wearing men in the 'hood. In fact, many of them have been living the thug life for as long as they have being dealing with men. The two images are perfectly consistent, particularly if you do not identify with the term "gay" or with the popular representation of gayness.

The marriage of hip hop and homosexuality has created a divide in the black community with surprising new fault lines. The new divide is not so much between black homosexuals and heterosexuals as it is among black homosexuals themselves, split along generational, political, and social boundaries. The divide appears more clearly in the music. In the 1980s and early 1990s, house music reigned supreme in black gay nightlife, but by the year 2000 it seemed an ancient religion, practiced primarily by "oldheads" in tight-fitting spandex muscle shirts. Aided by the hypermasculinity of hip hop culture, black homosexual identity in the nineties evolved away from house music and other gay-identified representations of self and instead created the homothug and the down low. Some would argue that black gay and bisexual men were adopting this new thug drag even before their straight counterparts had embraced it.

As a result of the changing norms, many black men have been left to reconcile their sexuality with their newly exaggerated sense of masculinity. At a town meeting of black same-gender-loving men in Washington, one man explained that the homophobic lyrics in some rap songs did not refer to him. Another explained that the lyrics did not offend him. No matter what the explanation, increasing numbers of black same-gender-loving men are making peace with a music and culture that sometimes appears to be anti-homosexual and antibisexual.

Older black gay men sometimes do not understand the younger hip hoppers who adopt the new culture, and yet the embrace of hip hop among black gay youth seems strikingly similar to the embrace of black church culture among many older black gay men who socialize in gay settings on Saturdays and then attend homophobic churches on Sundays. In different times, we find different ways to identify with our communities.

For years, I have struggled to understand how and why same-gender-loving men and women can embrace homophobia in their midst, but I have come to realize the difficulty in separating one's self from the dominant cultural paradigm. Hip hop is the dominant popular culture for millions of Americans. Most of society has embraced hip hop at some level. Everything from soda pop to pop music is being promoted by and influenced by hip hop, and young people from the suburbs to Serbia shake their booties to hip hop beats. If music is truly the universal language, then hip hop is the hot new slang.

I realized just how much the world had changed one day while I was looking for a pair of shorts to wear to the gym. I walked into an Urban Outfitters store where they were playing "Rapper's Delight" on the sound system. Afterward, I walked a few blocks to an Old Navy, where the speakers were blaring the sounds of "Five Minutes of Funk." The white people strolling through the store seemed just as comfortable as I did singing the lyrics of the songs. The cutting-edge music of the 1980s and 1990s had become the commercially marketable sounds of the new generation.

But even the newer, harder music is becoming more widely accepted. I remember, for example, an experience on the campus of Oberlin College in Ohio. I was visiting for a speech and staying at the Oberlin Inn, a quaint little place in a liberal-arts-college town. When I walked down to Main Street for a bite to eat, I heard the familiar thumping of a bass line pumping out hard rap music into the street. It was a sound I had heard many times walking in Harlem and Brooklyn, but I had never expected it in a rural white college town. Still, Oberlin had a small but active black community, so I was not entirely surprised. I heard the word "nigga" punctuated throughout the music from the car speakers, but even that was old news to me by then. It was only when the car drove by and I looked inside that I really understood what was going on. Much to my surprise, the three young men in the car were all white.

That took place years ago, and since that time almost everyone has heard that young white men are the primary consumers of rap music. The bold black masculinity of the early rap artists is no longer as threatening to white America as it was in the 1980s and early 1990s. Even black rage has become a commodity to be bought and sold, played on the latest CD, or worn with the latest urban designer wear. Young white men in the suburbs seem to identify with the culture of rebellion as much as, if not more than, the black and Latino youth in the inner city. No longer subjected to the legacy of derision left by Vanilla Ice, white rap artists like Eminem have become more widely accepted. And so black men have won. The cultural dominance of black manhood has been acknowledged and commercialized. But what exactly have we won?

With whiteness comes privilege in America, and young white men are still afforded the luxury of experimentation rarely granted to African-American youth. The white kid arrested for selling marijuana to his suburban classmates calls his parents, who hire a lawyer to negotiate a deal that spares a conviction, while the black kid could go to prison simply for smoking weed. The young white guy who tries and fails to succeed as an athlete falls back on other opportunities made available to him, while the young black guy falls back onto the streets. And the white youth who spend their college days listening to the hardest of the hard rap artists can still graduate and assimilate into the white elite network, while the young black fans of rap may not find those opportunities.

The problem here is not with hip hop, helmets, or homothugs. The problem is the lack of options available to too many young black men. Black youth in the cities deserve the same opportunities made available to white youth in the suburbs. They deserve the right to make minor mistakes as juveniles that do not jeopardize their future as adults. They deserve the right to receive a quality education that gives them the opportunity to make choices about academics and athletics. They deserve the right to listen to the music of their choice and still find good jobs to support themselves. And they deserve the right to express their manhood and their sexuality with all the diversity of options available to other men in society.

It is unfair to complain about the choices that many young black men make without understanding the limited options that we make available to them. We need to communicate positive messages to them to make healthy choices, but they need to be encouraged to make their own choices, not just the choices that we would make. Even if they never listen to hip hop, pick up a ball, or sleep with a woman, they can still be strong black men. And if they do love hip hop, love to play ball, and love to make love to women, that's not a problem either. Black males do not have to be stereotypes, caricatures, or clones. They do not have to dress a certain way, talk a certain way, or act a certain way. It doesn't matter if they are straight, gay, bisexual, questioning, or something else. We need all kinds of black men in our community—football players as well as construction workers, rappers as well as businessmen, doctors as well as actors. We need them all.

CHAPTER 12

Let's Talk About Sex

LET'S TALK ABOUT sex. Ever since Salt-N-Pepa released their 1992 hit single with that name, people have been using the song title to underscore the need to talk about sex. But for many of us, it's easier to talk about the need to talk about sex than to actually talk about sex. That's why I like to acknowledge and applaud the courageous people who do get us to talk about sex. One of those people is Dr. Joycelyn Elders.

Hers was one of the first names I learned to spell when I worked in the White House. She started her job some time after I started mine, but I knew who she was from the beginning. Her name was pronounced "Jocelyn" but for some reason it was spelled "Joycelyn," and it took me awhile to remember to add the extra "y" in the first syllable. She was the Arkansas state health director that President Clinton had appointed to be the United States Surgeon General, and she was one of a few powerful black women in the Clinton Administration.

To be honest, I had little or no reason to deal with Dr. Elders in my position as White House director of specialty media. I was working with the press, while she was dealing with health policy. But I respected her outspokenness and candor, and I wanted to know more about her. There were only a few African Americans who ran things in the U.S. government. There was Alexis Herman, the White House director of public liaison who later became secretary of labor. There was Rodney Slater, the secretary of transportation, and Mike Espy, the secretary of agriculture. And of course there was Ron Brown, the influential secretary of commerce who was killed in a plane accident. In the first year of the Clinton administration, there was also Colin Powell, a Bush appointee who remained on to serve as the chairman of the Joint Chiefs of Staff.

I had met all of them before, and I had worked closely with Alexis Herman in the White House. They were all dedicated public servants who had risen to the top of their fields. But Dr. Elders was different. She was not just a public servant. She was a lightning rod for attention. Unlike so many people in government, she spoke her mind publicly, and that pissed off a lot of people in both parties. She talked about sex education, AIDS, teen pregnancy, condoms in schools, and other issues that health care professionals should be able to discuss openly and candidly.

In one speech in which she compared high school drivers' education with sex education, Dr. Elders said that we have taught teenagers what to do in the front seat of cars, so now we have to teach them what to do in the back seat. In other remarks, she said that girls who go to the high school prom should carry condoms in their purses. That was honest advice, but as a reward for her candor, the right wing labeled her a "condom queen" and vowed to stop her at all costs. Even then, she refused to back down. "If I could get every teenager engaged in sex to use a condom, I'd gladly wear a crown of condoms on my head," she wrote in her memoir.

Confirmed after a divisive Senate debate in the summer of 1993,

Joycelyn Elders refused to hold her tongue, even after she was appointed. That made her a star in my book, and I tried to think of any excuse I could to meet her. You meet a lot of famous people when you work in the White House. Almost everybody who is well known comes through the West Wing at some point. World leaders, senators, governors, cabinet secretaries, business executives, five-star generals, movie stars, musicians, professional athletes, and television news anchors have all walked through the hallways of the Executive Mansion. I had seen everyone from Nelson Mandela to Yasser Arafat, but there were few people I wanted to meet more than Joycelyn Elders.

After the first few months of working in the White House, I was starting to get a little restless. Then I made an important discovery. I realized that working in the White House was just like working in any other job. There were good moments and bad moments. The good moments were unlike any experience you could have at any other job. But the bad moments were much worse than anything at any other job. And there were times when it seemed that everything was falling apart and that the administration was unraveling at the seams. There was also office politics and personality conflicts and all the other work-related drama you would find in any other office in America. After a few months, going to work was just like going to work.

I was unhappy with my job, so I quickly involved myself in a number of other issues that went well beyond my job description. Although I was paid to work in media affairs, I made time to work on civil rights issues, gay and lesbian issues, and AIDS issues as well. It was in that capacity that I finally arranged to meet with Dr. Elders. I joined a White House colleague on a trip to her office, and we sat down with Dr. Elders for a wide-ranging discussion about administration policy. Her office was surprisingly unimpressive. There were no big flags and formality and such. It looked just like any other government office. Dr. Elders explained that she spent a lot of time on the road, so I assumed there was no reason to get attached to an office. My impression was that the office fit her personality. She was down-to-earth and honest, and I was impressed that she was willing to sit and spend a few minutes in her busy day talking to us.

Meanwhile, back at the White House, the Clinton administration started to change dramatically in 1994. Reporters were writing stories that the staff was too young and undisciplined and the president needed to do something about it, so he did. The president appointed Leon Panetta as his chief of staff, and he was given the task of imposing order. I resisted some of the discipline that came from above. The new deputy chief of staff made a number of changes in the way our department operated, and I resented the sense of micromanagement that was being imposed. We were told to take shorter lunch breaks and to return reporters' phone calls within the same news cycle, and we were given other basic instructions that I thought were insulting. From my vantage point, we were all professionals and should be treated as such, and I did not want someone in the West Wing telling me when to use the bathroom.

At the same time, I was frustrated by the conservative shift in White House policy. We were still recovering from the defeat of the president's policy on gays in the military, and no one wanted the president's health care plan to be defeated as well. Health care was supposed to be the defining legacy of the Clinton administration, while the issue of gays in the military was merely a diversion for the White House. I had worked on the military issue from the beginning, and I knew what a distraction it was for the president. Still, I expected he would keep his promise and lift the ban, but I was wrong.

A few weeks before the president announced his final decision, I got a call from my boss, George Stephanopoulos, on Air Force One. It was almost six o'clock in the morning, and I was still in bed. George asked me to write a memo to the president listing the public statements Bill Clinton had made about the issue of gays in the military. I quickly prepared a memo that I thought might influence the president's thinking, but I was wrong again. Two weeks later, the president finally announced his policy. It was called "don't ask, don't tell, don't pursue." Instead of banning gays from the military, the government would simply stop asking recruits about their sexual orientation as long as gays and lesbians in the services stopped talking about it. It was a horrible policy, and it seemed to undermine the sense of duty, honor, and integrity expected from members of the armed forces. How could the military expect to uphold a sense of honesty if soldiers were essentially encouraged to be dishonest? With the wave of a magical presidential wand, the military would begin to implement a policy of winks and nods.

It was supposed to be a compromise, but instead it was a disaster. The liberals were upset because the president did not lift the ban, and the conservatives were upset because he tried to change the ban. Nobody was happy about the outcome. As a result of the debacle, the White House staff became gun-shy about all things gay. "Don't ask, don't tell" became the unofficial policy of the Clinton administration in acknowledging its own positions. When Deval Patrick, the assistant attorney general for civil rights, wanted to testify at the congressional hearings on the Employment Non-Discrimination Act (ENDA), the White House told him not to do it. The bill would have outlawed workplace discrimination based on sexual orientation. In most states in the country, it was still legal to fire gay and lesbian employees because of their sexuality. President Clinton wanted to change that. He had endorsed ENDA long before he was elected. But that was before the gays in the military failure.

In the long conference table in the Roosevelt Room of the West Wing, Deval Patrick and I argued the issue for more than an hour. There was no federal law that prohibited sexual orientation discrimination in the workplace. Most states did not prohibit this discrimination. The president had already endorsed the legislation. What could be the issue? The issue was the president's ability to govern. Influential senior staff members felt that the White House had already taken a big hit with the gays in the military debacle, and they did not want to risk expending any political capital when the president needed all his energy to push for health care reform. That made sense, but this was not a controversial position. This was not the military. Most Americans agreed that job discrimination was wrong, and I felt the public would respect the president more if he stood up for his beliefs. And to be honest, most Americans were not going to pay attention to the testimony of an assistant attorney general. I argued more passionately that day than I had argued with anyone about anything in the White House. But at the end of the discussion, we lost that debate almost unanimously. Even the top liberals in the White House disagreed with us. In the end, we worked out a compromise for Deval Patrick to send written testimony instead of appearing in person.

After that experience, I began to question what I was accomplishing by working in the White House, and I started thinking about an exit strategy. There was one good option I had dismissed earlier, but maybe it was time to reconsider. I had received a phone call from a writer named E. Lynn Harris who had self-published a novel called *Invisible Life.* Lynn had since signed with Doubleday, and his editor told him about an essay I wrote for a book that was never published. When we talked on the phone, I felt a breath of fresh air just thinking about other opportunities outside of politics. Lynn was the one who suggested that I develop my essay into a book. That was a new direction for me. I had never seriously thought about writing a book, but with Lynn's encouragement, I contacted an agent and created a book proposal. The agent sent the proposal directly to Doubleday, and I waited for a response.

I had almost forgotten about the book proposal when an intern came into my office on a Friday afternoon in December and told me that Joycelyn Elders had just resigned from her job. "No way," I said. I knew there had been controversy swirling around her, but I had no idea it had escalated to this. I called around to some of the other White House staff members until I found someone who could tell me what happened. Apparently, Dr. Elders had been forced to resign because of some controversial comments she made during a World AIDS Day appearance at the United Nations. One of the people in the audience at the event asked Dr. Elders a question about a sensitive but important topic. "What do you think are the prospects for a discussion and promotion of masturbation?" Dr. Elders's only mistake that day was her honesty. She did not try to sugarcoat her answer or develop a politically correct response. She simply told the truth.

"In regard to masturbation, I think that is part of human sexuality, and perhaps it should be taught," Dr. Elders responded. That was it. No one in the room was alarmed. None of the reporters even asked a followup question about it. All she said was that masturbation should be discussed in the context of sex education. She had not advocated that schools should teach kids *how* to masturbate, but that was how her comments would be reported later. Eight days after the speech, the transcript of that exchange made its way to Donna Shalala, the secretary of health and human services (HHS). Although the surgeon general is appointed by the president, she works under the HHS secretary. Shalala was apparently concerned about the remarks and spoke to White House Chief of Staff Leon Panetta. Panetta then called Elders and asked for her resignation. Dr. Elders said she refused to resign unless the president personally asked her to do so. That was a bold move, but it did not work. By the time I left the office that night for the weekend, Elders was already history. She was another casualty of the policy of "don't ask, don't tell."

I returned to work dispirited the following Monday. Dr. Elders had been forced to resign, the Republicans had just won control of the Congress for the first time since Franklin Roosevelt was elected president, and I was no longer happy working in the White House. Then came an important phone call. Later that day, I received good news from my agent in New York. Doubleday had agreed to publish my book. To accept the offer would require me to give up my job working in the White House and spend six months writing the book. It took me less than a minute to decide what to do. After I hung up the phone, I walked into my boss's office and announced that I was resigning from my job. It was the easiest decision I ever made, and I never looked back.

Two years after I left the White House, I met with Dr. Elders once again. This time I introduced her at a conference where she was speaking in Long Beach, California. When she recounted the experience of being fired, she simply explained that she was a doctor, not a politician. I understood exactly what she meant. Politicians are afraid to talk about sex. They are not afraid to have it, of course, but they are afraid to talk about it approvingly. The rest of us, on the other hand, would be wise not to follow the example of politicians in how we conduct our sex lives.

That means it's time to talk about sex. We need to talk about it openly, honestly, candidly, even passionately. We need to talk about it with our partners. We need to talk about it with our families. We need to talk about it with our friends. And we definitely need to talk about it with our children.

Far too often, we avoid discussions about sex because we are uncomfortable with the dialogue. We are ashamed to talk to our friends and family about our sexual behavior, or we are afraid that the conversations may turn off our partners. But we have to have those discussions in order to save our lives. There are at least five different conversations we need to have about sex.

First, parents should talk to their children about sex, sexual orientation, pregnancy, and sexually transmitted diseases before they become sexually active. My parents never talked to me about sex when I was growing up. Maybe they were afraid. Maybe they didn't think I was having sex. Maybe they thought I would learn on my own. I don't know. But I grew up with lots of misinformation and misconceptions about sex and sexuality. My life would have been a lot easier if my parents had talked to me about sexuality, homosexuality, and bisexuality when I was younger. I might not have deceived myself for ten years about my own sexual orientation. I might have come to terms with my identity when I was in high school or college instead of when I was twenty-five years old. I'm just fortunate that I didn't do anything that jeopardized my life when I was young and dumb and impressionable. In any case, I would not want my children to grow up with the same misinformation I had.

Second, middle schools and high schools should provide regular sex education sessions with accurate information. I went to middle school in St. Louis and high school in Clearwater, Florida. Aside from a passing reference in a health education course, I don't recall a single instance when a teacher, a nurse, a counselor, or a school official even acknowledged the fact that we were sexual beings as adolescents. The policy there was "don't ask, don't tell," and the assumption seemed to be that students would not have sex if the schools just didn't talk about it. That assumption was way off base. Almost everyone I knew was having sex in high school, and many of us were getting our information about sex from the same unreliable sources—each other. I know that some parents do not want their kids to learn about sex from a school teacher, but too many parents just don't talk about sex with their children, and the schools have a responsibility to teach. If the parents don't like what the schools teach, they should teach their kids in their own way, but they should not deprive the overwhelming majority of students of the vital information they need to protect themselves against pregnancy, HIV, and other sexually transmitted diseases.

Third, families, friends, and community institutions need to talk about sex. Too many people are isolated in their sexual lives, and developing a healthy dialogue about sex can help to break the isolation. Let's talk about masturbation. How often do we really do it? Let's talk about intercourse. How many different ways do we explore it? And let's talk about safe sex. How do we get our partners to try it, and how do we make it exciting?

Over the years, I've been conducting an unofficial and unscientific experiment with friends, acquaintances, and strangers. From time to time at parties and dinner tables, I'll wait for the right moment and then strike up a spicy conversation that has something to do with sex. "Have you ever cheated on a partner? How many times a month do you have sex? When was the last time you masturbated?" Those are the types of questions I like to ask. And you would be surprised how receptive most people are to answering those questions. Even the ones I don't expect to participate in the discussion will often become very engaged. Although I cannot draw any scientific conclusions from my experiments, I do think they confirm my belief that we are nation in denial about our sexual desires. I think people respond to these conversations because they have pent-up sexual energy and they don't have as many outlets as they would like to have where they can talk about sex. At some level, they want their own sex lives to be validated by the experiences of others, even strangers, and they want to know that it's okay to be who they are and to do what they do.

The fourth conversation we need to have is even more public. That's the conversation the media needs to initiate with us. Media outlets should develop story lines that show couples negotiating safe sex issues in the context of intimacy. It's not a big stretch. You can hardly turn on the television these days without seeing a couple in bed, making out on a sofa, or simulating intimacy. But for all the sexuality in the media, images of safe sex are not nearly as frequent. Sitcoms and drama series went through a stage in the 1990s when they started talking about safe sex more often, but that conversation needs to continue on today. Most adults already know about safe sex. They already know to use condoms to protect themselves from pregnancy and HIV. But they don't know how to talk to their partners about it. The media can show us how to do it by providing useful examples of couples who talk about safe sex in the heat of the moment. Almost everyone acknowledges the difficulty of initiating those conversations, so why not use our popular television shows and movies to give us some ideas on how to do it?

That leads us to the fifth and final conversation. Sexual partners need to be able to talk to one another without shame or judgment. Of course, that is much easier said than done, but we still have to find a way to talk to our sexual partners about our deepest fears and desires. That level of dialogue seems pretty basic in a relationship, but the research suggests that a lot of couples are just not having those conversations. So we should not be surprised to see more HIV infections and more STDs until we begin to talk about safe sex to our partners. As one AIDS activist told me, if you can't have a conversation with your partner about safe sex, should you really be having sex with that person in the first place?

But once we do start talking, what should we talk about? Should those who are HIV positive reveal their status? Should men on the down low admit their preferences? Should women who practice infidelity disclose their behavior patterns? The simple and politically correct answer is yes to all these questions. But the truth is not always simple and politically correct. The truth is that people lie. For various reasons, some more noble than others, a lot of people tend to lie about their sex lives. If that's the case, how do we know whom to trust? The answer may disappoint you. We don't. Instead, we make judgments that are sometimes irrational about the level of risk involved in having sex with various people. Yes, we know he just got out of prison, but he looks so hard that we can't believe he would let a man inside of him. Yes, we know he said he's bisexual, but he will surely give up on men once he falls in love with the right woman. Yes, we know he's a drug user, but he looks clean to me. Or even worse, no, we don't know anything about him, but what we don't know can't hurt us. Ignorance is bliss, we tell ourselves. But ignorance is no excuse for blindness.

Over the years, I've dated several men who told me they were HIV positive. I respected them for their honesty, and we always practiced safe sex. But I did not assume that everyone else was HIV negative because they didn't tell me otherwise. Instead, in all my years of dating, I have never asked anyone, male or female, about his or her HIV status. I have told my partners that I am HIV negative, but I have never insisted that they tell me about their own status. It's not because I'm afraid to ask. Instead, it is because I want to be safe with everyone. So I assume that everyone I have sex with is HIV positive, and I act accordingly.

I believe the recent trend toward demonizing those who are HIV positive for failure to disclose their HIV status sends the wrong signal. It stems from our need to blame other people for our own failures, and it is based in an unhelpful concept of victim-based morality that takes away our personal responsibility and assigns all the blame and puts all the responsibility on those who are HIV positive. Blaming someone else for our own actions will not change our actions, nor will it change the past. By the time you get to the point of blame, you have already passed the point of responsibility.

Some people lie about their HIV status. That doesn't mean we have to become distrustful cynics, but it does mean we are on notice. The best way to protect yourself is to protect yourself, not to let someone else do it for you. Another truth is that many people do not know their HIV status. Far too many people have never been tested, and many others have only been tested once or twice. Those who think they are negative may actually be positive. We can't blame them for their ignorance and then fail to take precautions on our own. The only way to be sure is to be tested, and even that is not the end of the process. When a person is infected with HIV, the body's immune system produces antibodies to fight off the virus. HIV tests measure the presence of these antibodies, but it often takes up to two months before the antibodies are detected, and in some rare cases it can take considerably more time to detect the antibodies. Therefore, some people may get negative test results after the body has been exposed to the virus but before the antibodies are detectable. That's why health officials encourage follow-up tests and regular testing for those who engage in risky behavior. And that's why using protection is much safer than trusting your partner's word.

One of the biggest mistakes we can make in dealing with our sexual partners is falling into the trap that using protection means we don't trust them or we don't love them. Nothing could be further from the truth. In fact, using protection is the ultimate form of love because it reflects a desire to protect both partners from harm.

Once we start having an open dialogue about sex, we can finally dismiss some of the misinformation that's already out there. For example, no matter what you may have heard to the contrary, AIDS is not a curse on homosexuals. In fact, most of the people in the world with AIDS are not gay. Moralistic misinformation in the 1980s and early 1990s led to collective neglect of the AIDS pandemic because too many of us thought it was somebody else's problem until we woke up one day and realized it was our own.

In addition, AIDS is not a curse on the promiscuous. Promiscuity does not cause AIDS. HIV does. Many people wrongly believe they are not at risk for HIV because they are monogamous or because they practice serial monogamy. But AIDS doesn't care if you are the biggest slut on the street or a virgin on a first date. It only takes one time to be infected. You can sleep with a different person every night of the year and never get infected, or you can sleep with only one person one time in your life and be infected the same day.

The truth is that AIDS is entirely preventable. From this day forward, there's no reason why anyone in the world has to be infected with HIV. We may not have a cure, but we do know how to stop it. HIV is spread by behavior and ignorance, so let's talk honestly about changing our behavior and ending our ignorance.

The most effective way to prevent the spread of HIV is by abstinence. HIV cannot be spread by casual contact such as kissing or sharing water glasses, so as long as you refrain from sexual activity, then you're not likely to be exposed to the virus. Of course, HIV can also be spread by infected blood, but unless you're a health care worker or an injection drug user, you're not likely to come in contact with such blood on a regular basis.

Human beings are sexual creatures, so the idea of abstinence is not practicable for most adults. Therefore, we have to come up with other mechanisms to protect ourselves from the virus. Maybe Joycelyn Elders was right about masturbation. You cannot get HIV by having sex with yourself. But the morality police are so hell-bent on controlling our sexuality that they want us to hate ourselves for it. There's nothing wrong with masturbation, and those who want the enjoyment of sexual pleasure without the risk of sexual intercourse should be encouraged to do it.

If abstinence and masturbation aren't enough, then safe sex is the best option to prevent the spread of HIV. That means using a new condom every time with every partner, not just for the partners who you think might be HIV positive. Some argue that we should limit the number of our sexual partners. That may or may not be a good idea, but it will not necessarily limit our risk of getting HIV. That argument has more to do with morality than reality. HIV is not spread by sex, and it does not matter how frequently you have it. HIV is spread by sex with someone who is infected. That is the only way to get the virus from sexual contact.

Sexual intercourse without a condom is inherently risky. There is no way around it. Even married heterosexual couples should seriously consider the risks of condomless sex. The best way to protect yourself in this situation is for both partners to get tested before unprotected intercourse and to continue doing so on a regular basis. By exercising simple caution and using basic common sense, you can protect yourself even in this situation.

Unfortunately, all the talk about sexually transmitted diseases has convinced some of us that sex is something to fear instead of something to embrace. But we need not fear these discussions. Knowledge is power, and knowledge about sex can give us the power to save our lives and enjoy our sexual experiences. Sex is a wonderfully healthy form of human expression, and we would be wise to learn to talk about it. We would be wiser still to protect ourselves.

CHAPTER 13

Can I Get a Witness?

IN MY TWO and a half years as executive director of the National Black Lesbian and Gay Leadership Forum, I had three distinctly memorable experiences. The first was in 1995 when I joined more than two hundred black gay and bisexual men in a controversial contingent in the Million Man March. The second was in the summer of 1997 when I traveled to Zimbabwe on a presidential delegation with Coretta Scott King and the Reverend Jesse Jackson. The third was in October 1997 when I appeared with Angie and Debbie Winans on *BET Tonight* hosted by Tavis Smiley.

In some ways, the Million Man March and the trip to Zimbabwe prepared me for the BET appearance. Some of us had expected condemnation from the Nation of Islam for joining in the Million Man March, but there was hardly a whisper of criticism as we marched along that day. The crowd of men on the mall split like the parting of the Red Sea as we marched and chanted, and most of those who had any reaction at all simply clapped. Similarly, I was not sure what to expect from the homophobic leadership of the government of Zimbabwe when I arrived in Harare. President Robert Mugabe had announced a crackdown to arrest gays and lesbians and had made incredibly offensive remarks about homosexuality. But when I got to Zimbabwe, I met with the president and with members of his cabinet, and I traveled on my own to meet with the leaders of the national gay and lesbian organization. The experience was empowering and productive with no drama or confrontation.

Perhaps those experiences softened me. If I could participate as an openly gay man in the Million Man March and travel as an openly gay man to Zimbabwe, then I had no reason to be concerned about appearing on BET. I had been on BET several times before. I had appeared on the *Bev Smith Show* years earlier, and I had appeared on Tavis Smiley's show to promote my first book, *One More River to Cross*. Those experiences were mostly enjoyable, but the issue of religion always managed to surface whenever I appeared.

I had no plans to make any new appearances on BET until I received a couple of phone calls on Friday, October 24. The first was from a friend who told me that two gospel recording artists, Angie and Debbie Winans, had recorded a new song called "Not Natural." The song was a direct attack on homosexuality, and more specifically on the comedian Ellen DeGeneres, who had recently come out of the closet. We quickly put out an alert to our e-mail network and asked our members to call the record company about the song. The second call was from BET. They wanted me to appear on a show with Angie and Debbie Winans the following Tuesday. I accepted the invitation without thinking of the possible controversy surrounding my appearance.

The day before the appearance, I got a second phone call from BET. This time, the news was not good. I had been disinvited. Angie and Debbie Winans would not appear on the show if I was also a guest. I could not believe it. I tried to persuade the producers to change their opinion, but they would not budge. In all my years working with the media, I had never been so outraged. A few hours later, we issued the strongest press release we had ever put out. Not only did we take on Angie and Debbie Winans, we also took on BET "for providing a biased, one-sided forum for the Winans to promote their homophobia." That was just the beginning.

"BET has stooped to a new low of cowardice by caving in to the homophobic demands of two anti-gay performers," I wrote. "To allow controversial guests to dictate the content of a news show reflects a complete and total lack of journalistic integrity by BET-TV," I added. Mindful that we had less than a day to turn things around, we threatened a boycott and a protest. "When we go to BET headquarters Tuesday afternoon, we're going to show BET and the Winans once and for all that we will not be the whipping boy for the black church," the press release said. "The black church and the gospel music industry are filled with black gays and lesbians, and it's time to open the closet doors and show the world who's who," it said.

Within a few hours of issuing the press release, we were getting inundated with phone calls from people who had called BET to protest their decision and from reporters who wanted to know what was going on. We were even more outraged when we learned that Angie and Debbie Winans were also scheduled to appear on another BET show, *Teen Summit,* which was directed at African-American youth. But that was not the big shocker. The big surprise was when I heard that the publicist for Angie and Debbie Winans who had started the controversy was a black gay man. When I found out, I publicly accused him of "serving as a mercenary in the Winans' battle to denigrate his very own community." That may have been a low blow, but I was fed up with the hypocrisy of self-hating homosexuals who were profiting from religious homophobia.

Although they came from a prominent family in gospel music—

the Detroit-based family had been recording albums since 1981—nobody had ever heard of Angie and Debbie Winans before that controversy, and some of my colleagues felt the whole incident had been manufactured by the publicist to sell records. Cathy Renna, a spokesperson for the Gay and Lesbian Alliance Against Defamation (GLAAD) told the *Washington Post* that the first time her organization heard of the controversy was from a press release issued by the publicist, which seemed to be promoting a controversy that did not yet exist.

His press release launched a back-and-forth media war about the Bible and homosexuality. Quoted in the *Washington Times*, Angie and Debbie Winans said, "What we're saying is not what we think but what Jesus thinks." Our organization quickly put out a press release to remind the public that Jesus never mentions homosexuality in the Bible. "Not only is their music mediocre, but so is their knowledge of the Bible," the press release said. "For that matter, the Bible says that women should 'adorn themselves with modest apparel' and 'not with gold or costly array' (I Timothy 2:9), but that doesn't stop the Winans sisters from sporting gold necklaces and diamond earrings in their promotional photos. If they really believe in every word of the Bible, then they can't have it both ways."

We were harsh, quick, and effective. I had learned the lesson from my experience in the 1992 Clinton campaign when we ousted the incumbent, George H. W. Bush, from office, and the strategy worked. Under pressure, BET finally backed down and re-invited me. Tavis called me himself to apologize for the controversy and told me he was not responsible for disinviting me. I have always respected Tavis so I had hoped he would come through for us.

When the show finally appeared, I sat in the BET studio in Washington with Bishop Noel Jones of Los Angeles, while Angie and Debbie Winans joined us via satellite. The Reverend James

Forbes from Riverside Church in Harlem also joined us by satellite. And for one hour, we had a wide-ranging debate about the Bible and homosexuality. Bishop Jones and the Winans sisters were against homosexuality, while the Reverend Forbes and I argued on behalf of love and equality. I have never been convinced that these biblical debates are as useful as we like to think they are. Most of the observers tend to have preformed opinions about the issue, so it is difficult to really change anybody's thinking. One side quotes a biblical passage to make its case, and then the other side quotes its own. At the end of the debate, it all comes down to which side you agreed with in the beginning. In addition, these debates rarely delve into the related issues about the role of religion in society. For example, in the unlikely event that we could develop a consensus about what the Bible says, should we use the Bible to dictate our public policy? How do we reconcile the use of biblical beliefs to guide our laws with the separation of church and state?

Despite my misgivings about these types of debates, I thought it was important to be on the show. If the discussion helped to save the life of one kid who was struggling with his sexuality, then it would be worth all the effort. And even if the discussion failed to change a single mind, it would at least present a debate instead of a one-sided diatribe against homosexuality. The viewers would at least get to see the split in opinion about what the Bible really does and does not say. That had to be better than an unfiltered hour of Angie and Debbie condemning homosexuality.

The dialogue was heated and passionate but mostly respectful. The Winans sisters explained why they recorded the song. I explained my concerns that the song would adversely influence young people. And the two ministers debated the biblical implications. We each had our role on the show, but when Angie and Debbie ventured away from their role and started talking about

Jesus, I interjected. Jesus says nothing about homosexuality any-where in the Bible, I said. "I beg to differ," Angie said, shaking her head in disagreement. "I have a stack of Bibles at home that say otherwise." Bishop Jones also joined in on the attack, accusing me of distorting the Bible. But to this day, years after that appearance, no one has ever produced a single scripture where Jesus mentions homosexuality. They haven't produced such a scripture because none exist. Jesus never mentions homosexuality anywhere in the Bible.

Maybe I was misunderstood. Maybe they thought I was saying that homosexuality is never discussed by anyone in the Bible. But that was not my point and not what I said. I was talking specifically about Jesus. Based on the previous comments that the Winans sisters made in the media, I think they honestly thought that Jesus had discussed the issue. But they were wrong.

For some reason, a lot of Christians who use religion to justify their dislike of homosexuality seem to think that no one else has read the Bible, or that everyone else who has read it has reached the same conclusions that they have. Religious scholars who have studied the Bible in its original languages have reached different conclusions about what it says, and doesn't say, about homosexuality. Instead of taking my word for it, I usually try to direct critics to a few other books that discuss the issue. The first, *What the Bible Really Says About Homosexuality*, was written by the Reverend Daniel Helminiak, and it goes through each one of the biblical passages that has any connection to homosexuality. The second text, *The Good Book: Reading the Bible with Heart and Mind*, was written by the Reverend Peter Gomes, and it provides understanding of how the Bible has been used and misused by various groups over time.

Over the years, I have found a lot of misinformation and mis-representation about the Bible and homosexuality. I used to argue with people toe to toe when they questioned my sexual orientation, but I realized that many of them had never really studied the biblical passages related to homosexuality. Many of them were too busy quoting bumper stickers to quote the Bible itself. "God made Adam and Eve, not Adam and Steve," they would say. If I had a nickel for every time I heard that, I would be a rich man. The argument is based on an overly simplistic reading of the creation story in the book of Genesis of the Bible. Since the creation story mentions Adam and Eve, a few people would like to interpret that to mean that God did not also create Steve. But the creation story fails to mention a lot of things in the world that we now believe to exist. Chief among these is race. The story never mentions blacks or whites, but no one would argue that the absence of race from the story means that God did not create black people.

Religion has been misused by many well-intentioned believers to justify their dislike for others. The Bible was used for centuries to justify the slavery and oppression of blacks ("slaves be obedient to your masters," Ephesians 6:5–9), and we, of all people, should know not to use the Bible to justify the oppression of others. But instead we practice the same prejudice practiced against us, and with the same hypocrisy used by our oppressors in selecting which parts of the Bible to accept and reject. Religious critics of homosexuality often quote the passage from Leviticus 18 that man should not lie with man, but they conveniently overlook the passages in Leviticus 19 that prohibit haircuts, tattoos, and shaving a beard. Leviticus 19 even prohibits wearing mingled fabrics such as wool and linen together, but we rarely condemn people to Hell for wearing polyester-cotton blends. Other passages outlaw the eating of pork and seafood (Leviticus 11), but we seldom follow those rules either. That's because the prohibitions in Leviticus were developed to separate the Jews from the Gentiles of the time and bear little relevance to modern-day life. Leviticus cannot be taken seriously as a guide to twenty-first-century living. But when it comes to homosexuality and bisexuality, many of us do not operate out of logic. We operate out of fear and bias. That is true for people of all races, but the religious hypocrisy is particularly disappointing among African Americans.

I was out on tour for my first book when I sat down for an interview at a black radio station in Chicago. I never discussed religion on my own, but almost every caller wanted to debate with me about the Bible. When one self-described Christian caller told me that Jesus condemned homosexuality, I corrected him. "Actually, Jesus never discussed the issue," I said. He questioned my information, so I challenged him to find a passage where Jesus mentions it. He thought about it for a moment, admitted he could not think of a passage, and then decided to take another route. "What Jesus says is irrelevant," he told me. I did not even bother to point out the inconsistency in using Jesus to justify an argument and then denying the importance of Jesus once the argument failed.

After a speech to a conference of college student leaders meeting on diversity in Seattle, two students stood up and argued with me about the Bible. When I responded with my own knowledge of the Bible, they retreated. But they ended the confrontation with a promise to pray for me. Anyone who had a different opinion from the one they had been taught was wrong. Then, shortly after the Massachusetts Supreme Court struck down the state's discriminatory marriage law in 2004, a black minister in Chicago was so outraged that he told the *New York Times* that he would march with the Ku Klux Klan against gays and lesbians. On a television show in Washington, another minister told me that God doesn't like my "lifestyle." And in an interview for my first book, a different minister told me that homosexuality is the worst possible sin. That's a lot of criticism for anyone to take.

Given all the religion-based venom spewed out against homosexuality and bisexuality, it is no wonder that so many same-gender-loving men have difficulty accepting their sexual orientation. Who would want to acknowledge their real identity in a world that teaches them they are immoral just for being who they are? We cannot expect most men on the down low to come to terms with their sexuality when the rest of society has not yet come to terms with it either. And when the people who claim to be following the teachings of Jesus communicate hatred and fear instead, we are only fooling ourselves if we think we have created a climate for openness. In fact, if you want one explanation as to why men are on the down low, look no further than our local churches.

The church is the arbiter of moral decency in the black community. Whether or not we attend church, we learn most of our values and our sense of right and wrong from what the church teaches us. Even as we breach the rules expected of us, many of us have a sense that the rules laid down are right. And the church, for the most part, has told us that homosexuality is wrong. In fact, many of our churches have invented special ministries and campaigns simply to convert the homosexual men in their midst. They are not interested in talking about it or learning about it. They are more interested in preaching against it. And that attitude is exactly the cause of the problem.

I am not on the down low and have never been on the down low, but I have met enough men who are to understand why they exist. We create them. Yes, you and I create them. We create them with our condemnation of homosexuality. We create them with our insulting stereotypes. And we certainly create them with the offensive words we use in our families, our communities, and our churches. And every single time we complain about men on the down low without acknowledging the ways in which we create the conditions that make them exist, we become the hypocrites.

Over the past few years, I have heard dozens of women who want to know why men on the down low just don't "come out" and stop living a lie. That is a valid concern—in fact, many in the gay community have asked the same question—but it is often not a very deep one. If we want the men on the down low to be honest with us, then we first have to be honest with ourselves. The problem is not just that the men are on the down low. The problem is that they feel *the need* to be on the down low. And that is where we as a community come in.

Unfortunately, too many black churches have become active co-conspirators in the silencing of black men on the down low. More than almost any other institution in our community, our churches have perfected the policy and practice of "don't ask, don't tell." As a result, the black church has developed a paradoxical reputation as the most homophobic institution in the black community and also the most homo-tolerant. When ministers deliver the company line fire-and-brimstone sermon, the church is at its most homophobic. But when you look behind the minister at the members of the choir, the choir director, the music director, the organist, and the deacons, the church is often homotolerant. In few other places in the community do black gay and bisexual men play such a visible leadership role. Anyone who has been to black churches knows that our churches are filled with gay and bisexual men, and yet many of these churches rarely acknowledge the odd reality that these men support and fund the very institutions that beat them down. Many of our churches are still in denial about homosexuality in their own congregations.

Fortunately, there are some ministers and churches that are beginning to change that pattern. The Reverend Jeremiah Wright of Trinity United Church of Christ in Chicago, the Reverend Cecil Murray of First AME Church in Los Angeles, the Reverend James Forbes at Riverside Church in Harlem, and the Reverend Cecil

Williams at Glide Memorial Church in San Francisco have led the way to develop open and welcoming congregations. These churches are coming to grips with sexuality and opening up a dialogue with heterosexuals, homosexuals, and bisexuals in the pews. Other churches have begun to re-examine biblical texts with new eyes. And a few new churches have opened with affirming ministries. Some churches actually started to deal with sexuality back in the 1980s and 1990s at the height of the AIDS epidemic when many of them learned that many of those who died were homosexual or bisexual. They also have help from organizations like Balm In Gilead, a New York–based nonprofit that helps churches across the nation to develop their own AIDS ministries.

Then there are churches that cater to the needs of the black LGBT community. The biggest of these is the Unity Fellowship Church, which has opened up churches in cities across America. But there is also the Breath of Life Fellowship Community Church, which welcomes black gays and lesbians in Tampa, and the Church of the Open Door, which has been serving the black LGBT community in Chicago for years.

If the bad news is that we have much more work to do in our churches, the good news is that many churches are already setting an example of what can be done. There will be plenty of resistance to change, but it needs to happen. What exactly can churches do? In an ideal world, we would get our churches to initiate a long-overdue dialogue about sexuality and to stop preaching against homosexuality. In reality, that will take time. In the meantime, we still have an epidemic to fight, and there are things that churches can do to save lives without compromising on their own positions.

Most important, churches should develop active AIDS ministries. The church leadership should help set a positive tone for the ministry, but members of the congregation—male, female, straight, gay, and bisexual—should be encouraged to become active participants. There are several major components that could be included in these ministries.

First, provide safe sex education to the members. This information can be in the form of a pamphlet inserted in the program or flyers given out at the end of the service. Just make sure the information is accurate and up to date. Consult with an established AIDS organization to develop the literature or to prepare your own.

Second, provide free HIV testing in the church. It could happen once or twice a year, or once a month, depending on the needs and size of the church. Again, churches can work with local agencies to administer the program, and with the development of new oral fluids rapid testing, this can be conducted without drawing blood or other invasive procedures. The oral tests simply swipe a sample from inside the mouth and test that sample for the HIV antibodies.

Third, provide free condoms to church members. We know that one of the factors that contributes to unprotected sex is the absence of a condom. If women and men can pick up these condoms at church instead of buying them at a drug store, we may be able to increase the number of sexually active people who use protection. In addition, when churches provide condoms, they can also provide instruction booklets to teach people how to use them, and they can provide educational materials to advise members how to prevent pregnancy, HIV, and sexually transmitted diseases. They can even use the condom distribution materials to encourage abstinence.

Fourth, develop peer support groups. Too many people living with HIV feel isolated and alone. To avoid prejudice and judgment, some of them may not want to identify themselves to members of the church. Support groups made up of other members of the church may provide a mechanism to deal with the isolation. Churches might even develop two different types of support groups—one for anyone who is concerned about HIV and AIDS, and another, confidential group exclusively for those who are living with HIV.

Fifth, offer financial assistance to low-income members with HIV needs. Drug therapy for HIV can be very expensive, and many African Americans with HIV cannot afford the treatment. Some government programs, such as the AIDS Drug Assistance Program (ADAP), help to fund access to prescription drugs for those with HIV. Churches can help members prepare the paperwork for the ADAP application and for other government assistance programs. Churches can also incorporate people with HIV and AIDS into their sick and shut-in programs. In addition to prayer, church members can provide free meals, temporary housing, grocery shopping assistance, and other necessities to low-income members with HIV or AIDS who may need these services.

Sixth, provide nonjudgmental counseling. Far too often, our approach to sexuality and AIDS is shaped by our prejudice. Many of us have been taught to "love the sinner but hate the sin." That's a clever little bumper sticker, but like the "Adam and Steve" refrain, it's not in the Bible. If we approach people with AIDS as sinners instead of children of God, we communicate a message of condemnation. That is not our role. Let God decide on judgment. Our role is to comfort those in need. If we truly want to encourage people with HIV or AIDS to come forward in the church, the best way to do that may be to open our arms and welcome them, listen to them, and help them where they need help. Not everyone with HIV or AIDS wants or needs counseling, and they certainly don't all need the same counseling. Our counseling approach should fit the individual, not the stereotype, and the only way to determine people's individual needs is to listen to their concerns in an environment that encourages them to be open and honest.

Religion plays an important role in the lives of many African

Americans. Whether we go to church or not, we are influenced by the church. Whether we are Christian or not, we have been exposed to Christian teachings. In our darkest hours, many of us turn to faith for hope and salvation. Religion has long been used for good in our community, to fight against slavery and segregation, to challenge society, and to comfort those in need. That is the proud tradition of the African-American church. We know that religion should be used as a tool for love, not as a weapon of hate.

CHAPTER 14

Sick and Tired of Being
Sick and Tired

NIKKO BRITERAMOS STARTED college in South Dakota in the fall of 2001. Even as a freshman, he was tall, attractive, muscular, and athletic. He had a 3.6 grade point average, was one of the leading scorers on the school's basketball team, and he never had a problem with the law. As an African-American city kid from Chicago in an overwhelmingly white rural community, he stood out, both literally and figuratively.

From the outside, Briteramos was a great kid with a world of opportunity before him, but on the inside he was having a rough first year in school. In the spring of 2002, the eighteen-year-old Briteramos tried to do his part to help out the local community by donating blood. Not long afterward, the health officials who screened the blood discovered that it was infected with HIV. They could not accept the donation, and they told Briteramos that he was HIV positive. It is not clear whether Briteramos fully understood the consequences of his HIV status or if he was still in denial about it, but a few weeks after he learned of the test results, he was arrested in his dorm room for having intimate relations with his girlfriend.

Although his girlfriend was not infected with the virus, he was charged with violating the state's tough new HIV transmission law, which prohibits any persons with HIV from having unprotected sex without disclosing their status to their partners.

In a matter of days, Briteramos went from star college athlete to public enemy number one. Before the trial even began, the governor of South Dakota—the one public official with the power to grant clemency—publicly accused Briteramos of attempted murder. Not surprisingly, Briteramos was later tried, convicted, and imprisoned for his crime.

South Dakota passed its HIV transmission law after another AIDS scare involving another African American in a different state. In 1996 and 1997, NuShawn Williams, a twenty-year-old black man, was accused of spreading HIV to at least ten women in upstate New York, which is mostly white. Without an HIV transmission law to use, the state of New York had to prosecute Williams on a related charge of statutory rape since one of his sexual partners was under age. Following the uproar, dozens of states rushed to pass their own legislation to criminalize HIV transmission, and South Dakota passed its law in 2000. Until Nikko Briteramos was arrested in 2002, no one in the state of South Dakota had ever been charged under the law.

To many observers, the HIV transmission laws appear to be reasonable measures to discourage those with sexually transmitted diseases from passing them on to unsuspecting partners. But these new laws will not reduce the spread of HIV. Instead, they will make it worse. The best way to stop the spread of HIV is to encourage testing and protection, but the HIV transmission laws accomplish neither goal. By punishing those who fail to disclose their HIV status, the laws actually discourage those in need from being tested. If a man thinks he may be HIV positive but knows he will have to reveal his HIV status to all of his partners if he is, the requirement to disclose his status may stop him from being tested. Why find out the truth if you can't be blamed for your ignorance? If you penalize someone with HIV for *knowingly* having unprotected sex, then you simply discourage people from knowing, because as long as you don't get tested you can never go to jail.

The laws could also discourage us from self-protection by providing us with a false sense of security as long as we believe our partners will not behave inappropriately because of the legal consequences of their deception. The problem with these legal approaches is that they fail to recognize our own ability to protect ourselves, and in so doing they actually discourage us from doing so. The governor, the mayor, and the sheriff cannot protect us from HIV. Only we can do that for ourselves.

We all want to reduce the spread of HIV and encourage those with the virus to be open and honest in their sexual relations, but the HIV transmission laws fail to achieve those goals and instead add to one of the biggest problems in our community—the disproportionate incarceration of black men. With staggering HIV rates among African Americans and two black men as the poster boys for bad behavior, the new HIV transmission laws create another opportunity to send more black men to prison. Although I firmly believe that sexual partners should honestly disclose their HIV status to one another, I do not believe the police should put people in jail who fail to do so. The punitive approach fails to solve the problem and instead adds tragedy on top of tragedy.

Sexual activity is a joint responsibility that requires joint accountability. More than two decades after the AIDS epidemic, almost every adult in America knows that HIV can be spread by unprotected sex. That's why both partners should bear the burden of protecting themselves. It is not a good thing that people lie about their HIV status, but it should not be a criminal thing either.

Instead of putting people with HIV in jail, let's provide them with access to valuable services that can save their lives and the lives of others. What Nikko Briteramos needed was counseling and treatment, not incarceration. With our prisons already swelling with minority inmates locked up during the war on drugs, the last thing we need is more black men in jail for a crime that shouldn't be a crime in the first place. Should we lock up men like Mor Rondo Roberts, a thirty-one-year-old black gay man who was convicted in Ohio for failing to tell a sex partner that he was HIV positive? Although Roberts had no criminal record, was active in the gay community, and his female sex partner tested negative for HIV, he was sentenced to four years in prison. "Putting him in prison will kill him," said his attorney, Tom Adgate, who claimed the jail staff would not treat Roberts's HIV infection effectively, leading to the onset of AIDS.

Roberts and Briteramos knew their HIV status, but one of the reasons some people refuse to get tested is because they have no resources to help themselves if they test positive. HIV testing seems pointless without HIV treatment and access to expensive, life-saving medication. Forty-five million Americans lack health insurance, and many of them are young and poor, the groups most vulnerable to HIV. Even if they knew they were HIV positive, some of these people may wonder what they could possibly do about it when they have no health insurance and the drug treatments can cost up to $15,000 a year.

Perhaps the biggest problem with the passage of HIV transmission laws is that they lead our attention down the wrong path. As with the down low, we find ourselves fighting against the people who engage in irresponsible behavior rather than fighting against the socioeconomic conditions that encourage the behavior. The men and women with HIV in America are not the enemy. They are caught up in a larger struggle that we must not ignore. Our society, our nation, and our community are ailing, and we need to remember how we got in this situation.

I remember Fannie Lou Hamer. Born poor and black as the last of her parents' twenty children in segregation-era Mississippi, Hamer suffered from polio in her youth and was left with a lifelong disability. But despite her physical limitations, the defiant share-cropper became legendary for her efforts to register blacks to vote in the 1960s. After being arrested, intimidated, and beaten repeatedly, she continued to fight. "I'm sick and tired of being sick and tired," she said. Rather than allow her circumstances to paralyze her into inaction, she turned her outrage into activism, and we would be wise to follow in her footsteps.

Personal Steps To Take

Those of us who are sick and tired of the down low and concerned about the spread of HIV in our communities need to turn our outrage into activism. We do not have to become statistics in the latest CDC casualty count. Here's what we can do.

First, get tested regularly. If you are sexually active, you owe it to yourself to get tested. Then go back and get tested again. Make it an annual event, and be sure to keep the promise to yourself.

Second, encourage your friends and partners to be tested. One of the best ways to show our love for one another is to express our concern for our mutual health. Tell your friends that you want them to be around to share the memories of the experiences you've had together. And tell your partner too. Encourage your partner to be tested with you. A loving partner should want to protect both of you.

Third, use protection in your sexual encounters. Don't fall into the trap of assuming that you are safe or your partner is safe. Find out for sure by being tested, and until you do, be sure to use a condom.

Fourth, talk about HIV. Let's erase the stigma that closes off conversation about AIDS. Talk about HIV to your children. Tell them how it's spread and how to avoid it. And talk about it to your friends, your family, and your sexual partners.

Fifth, disclose your HIV status to your sexual partners. People with HIV do continue to lead healthy sex lives, and if you have HIV you can do the same. But give your partners a choice to decide whether and how to be intimate with you. When one partner is positive and the other is not, researchers call this "noncordant HIV serostatus." It happens more often than we may think, but it works best when both parties make informed decisions.

Sixth, share your techniques to talk about safe sex. Many of us are dying to know how to bring up the issue of condoms without ruining an intimate moment. Do we just produce the condoms and use them without discussion? Should we raise the issue before we go to bed? Is there a certain way to say it? If you have helpful ideas, please share them with your friends, family, and others who may need some advice.

Seventh, join HIV vaccine clinical trials. Vaccine clinical trials are used to test the efficacy of HIV preventive treatments, but we need people of all races to participate in the trials to determine how potential vaccines work with different populations. In one example in February 2003, a company called Vaxgen released data from a clinical trial for a vaccine called AIDSVAX that seemed to show some distant promise of protecting African-American participants from infection with HIV. Unfortunately, the number of black participants in this trial was too small to draw any conclusions.

In light of the infamous Tuskegee experiments where blacks were knowingly injected with syphilis, many African Americans express understandable skepticism about participating in new testing trials. But this dilemma poses a catch-22. Some of us fear becoming racial

guinea pigs if we participate in the studies, but if we don't participate in the studies, many of us will complain about the absence of
blacks. Somehow, we have to find a way to break down the stigmas
and myths regarding clinical trial participation and continue to educate ourselves about HIV vaccine research efforts. To do so, we have
to work with activists, community leaders, health care workers, scientists, and physicians to build mutual trust.

Eighth, join local HIV community planning boards. Many of the
decisions about the use of federal and state funds are determined by
local planning boards made up of community citizens, activists,
experts, and government officials. If you are concerned about the
way money is spent in your community, you can make a difference
by participating in the local planning board that makes the decisions.

Ninth, support community-based organizations. Many local AIDS
service organizations are struggling to serve the community and stay
afloat financially. Many need your help. You can make a difference
by calling a local AIDS organization and volunteering your time. If
you don't have a lot of time to volunteer in an office, you can make
a financial contribution, donate a computer, or offer your professional services. You can even host an event in your home to raise
funds for a worthy organization.

Public Policy Action to Support

In many ways, the individual steps we can take are much easier than
implementing the policy steps, but changing our government policies
offers the best hope for developing long-term solutions. After years of
conservative political restrictions that limit the most creative and
potentially effective HIV prevention tools, AIDS activists are well
aware of the challenges involved in developing new public policy.
Over the past ten years, I have spent a lot of time asking experts what
should be done about the AIDS crisis in the black community. The

answers vary widely depending on the individual. Many observers believe that more money needs to be dedicated to the domestic AIDS problem, but they also agree that money alone is not enough. An AIDS activist in Chicago said we needed a "multi-faceted approach" that involves "saturation of the message." A community leader in Los Angeles suggested an approach that understands and considers "black history, culture and circumstances." Another Los Angeles activist argued for a "big emphasis on black masculinity." An activist in Ohio pushed for changing the way safe sex messages are marketed. And a New York activist said "we need to demand that those organizations that are funded are accountable." These are all reasonable ideas, but we cannot afford an "either-or" approach to saving our lives. We have to adopt many different approaches for the many different elements in our communities.

Despite all the work that needs to be done, many of our elected officials and political leaders are still not prepared to respond to the epidemic in our community. When Gwen Ifill of PBS moderated the 2004 U.S. Vice Presidential Debate between Dick Cheney and John Edwards, she asked one question that caught both candidates off guard. "I want to talk to you about AIDS," she said. "And not about AIDS in China or Africa, but AIDS right here in this country where black women between the ages of 25 and 44 are 13 times more likely to die of the disease than their counterparts. What should the government's role be in helping to end the growth of this epidemic?"

Vice President Cheney pleaded ignorance. "I had not heard those numbers with respect to African-American women," he said. "I was not aware that it was that severe an epidemic there." Senator Edwards talked about the international AIDS crisis and the lack of universal health care coverage in America. Those were important issues too, but they missed the point of the question. Government can play an important role in preventing the spread of AIDS in the black community. Government cannot do it alone, but it can provide the valuable resources we need to fight the epidemic. Here's what the candidates could have said.

First, we need free, universally accessible, easily administered HIV testing. If we really want to encourage people to be tested, we have to make it easy for them. Many local AIDS organizations and city health clinics already provide free HIV testing. We need to expand the number of facilities that offer these services so that everyone in America has access to free testing.

Testing should also be anonymous or confidential. There has been a big debate for years about anonymous testing versus confidential testing. Anonymous testing allows patients to find out their HIV status without revealing their name or identity. Confidential testing collects their personal information but keeps it away from unauthorized outsiders. Each form of testing has its advantages. Anonymous testing is likely to encourage more people to be tested because they don't have to worry about divulging their identity, but confidential testing enables government researchers to track reliable information about the spread of the epidemic.

In addition, we should also encourage and support noninvasive HIV testing with rapid results. Recently developed oral fluids tests can provide almost immediate HIV results without drawing blood from the patient. This solves two problems, getting patients to come back to the doctor's office to get their results and getting over their fears about needles and blood.

Second, we need to abolish HIV transmission laws. In November 2004, 32-year-old Anthony Whitfield was convicted of exposing 17 women to HIV by having unprotected sex with them in Washington state. Five of the women tested positive and Whitfield faced a minimum sentence of 137 years in prison. Whitfield is black and his victims were white. It's the same scenario with Briteramos and Williams and likely for future high-profile cases of HIV transmission. These laws appear to be innocent and well-meaning in their intent, but in their enforcement they serve as a tool to regulate black sexuality and penalize black male sexual activity with white women. In Washington state, for example, hundreds of homes were leafleted after Whitfield was arrested. Some were given fliers that read "Don't Have Sex With Blacks; Avoid AIDS!"

As I mentioned earlier, these laws discourage testing and self-protection. People with HIV need treatment and counseling, not incarceration. Let's invest our resources in positive and constructive tools to get people into treatment.

Third, we need publicly financed needle exchange programs for drug users. Injection drug use was listed as an exposure category for 40 percent of black men and 36 percent of black women living with AIDS in 2002. In the year 2000, more than half of all AIDS deaths of African Americans aged 25 to 44 were caused by contaminated needles, according to a 2002 report by Dr. Dawn Day. Some lawmakers fear that needle exchange programs will encourage the use of illegal drugs, but studies have shown that such programs do not encourage new drug use and do prevent the spread of HIV. Needle exchanges target people who already inject drugs. Many of them are poor and do not have access to clean needles, but the simple act of providing them with clean needles in exchange for their dirty needles can significantly reduce the spread of HIV in our communities.

Fourth, we need free condom distribution in prisons. Whether or not we like to admit it, men have sex with other men in prison. The confirmed AIDS rate in state and federal prisons was more than three times higher than in the total U.S. population, according to a study of HIV in prisons in 2001. Given the disproportionate incarceration of black men in the U.S. penal system, black men bear an even greater risk than white men of being exposed to HIV while incarcerated and then bringing the virus back to their community upon release. In the federal prison system, 97 percent of inmates will eventually be released back into society. But condoms are banned or unavailable in more than 95 percent of U.S. prisons, according to the *New York Times*. We cannot think of the prison crisis as unrelated to the larger AIDS epidemic. If we want to protect the non-incarcerated population, we must also protect the incarcerated.

Fifth, we need targeted prevention funding to fight AIDS in the hardest hit communities. Almost everyone agrees we need more money to fight AIDS, but everyone also agrees that money alone will not solve the problem. How we spend the money is just as important as how much money we spend. That's why we need to use our resources wisely. Those communities hardest hit by AIDS need the bulk of the funding, and the funding needs to be administered in a way that not only targets the communities but empowers them by building up an infrastructure. We need more community-based organizations that understand both the scientific research and the community needs. We have too few of these organizations in our communities, and some other groups lack the capacity to administer major grant awards from the government. We cannot develop long-term solutions to the problems that contribute to HIV without also developing and supporting community institutions that can address the problems that go beyond the AIDS epidemic.

Sixth, we need to fund resources for low-income people living with AIDS. What we once mistakenly believed to be a disease of well-heeled gay men has now clearly become a disease that affects people of all income levels. One in four blacks lives in poverty, according to the U.S. Census Bureau, and studies have found a link between higher AIDS incidence and lower income. Low-income people with HIV and AIDS are at great risk for developing deadly symptoms, particularly if they do not have adequate housing, meals, medicine, and counseling. Federal, state, and local government programs help provide assistance to people with AIDS, and these programs need our support.

The Housing Opportunities for Persons with HIV/AIDS (HOPWA) program, run by the U.S. Department of Housing and Urban Development, makes grants to local communities, states, and nonprofit organizations for projects that benefit low-income people with HIV/AIDS and their families. The AIDS Drug Assistance Program (ADAP), run by the U.S. Department of Health and Human Services, provides medications for the treatment of HIV and enables eligible clients to purchase health insurance. Many communities and nonprofit organizations have also developed meals on wheels programs that help provide food to those in need.

Seventh, we need more research on AIDS in the black community. In addition to AIDS vaccine trials with black participants, we also need more behavioral research in the black community. We need to understand what factors encourage men and women to engage in risky behavior and determine what interventions are most effective in discouraging unhealthy behavior. We also need to understand that interventions may vary from group to group, age to age, or region to region, even within very narrowly defined subpopulations of the black community. What works for eighteen- and nineteen-year-old black gay and bisexual men hanging out in New York's Greenwich Village may not work for eighteen- and nineteen-year-old black gay and bisexual college students in North Carolina. What works for college-educated professional women in Chicago may not work for low-income women in Atlanta. And what works for self-identified men on the down low may not work for those men who do not even realize that they are on the down low.

In the early days of HIV prevention, "we were employing various strategies from card parties to rap groups, in bars, parks and bathhouses, from Long Island to Long Beach to discuss risk and behaviors," according to George Bellinger, Jr., a leading activist in the AIDS community. He continues, "If you are more concerned about the men's political affiliations than their activities then you may never get to them change their behaviors. And we all know that knowledge alone does not mean behavior change."

Despite the apparent connection between black gay men and white gay men, prevention methods that have largely worked for white gay men do not appear to be as effective among black gay men. And for that matter, we should not expect that prevention models for black people, at large, will be as specifically effective with every subpopulation of the African-American community.

We need to consider unconventional approaches to reach those African-American subpopulations that are most difficult to access. Many of our AIDS service organizations are already targeting churches, social functions, bars, nightclubs, bath houses, fraternal organizations, barbershops, beauty salons, and the Internet. But many of those in the target groups will not be accessible even in these locales. Those who do not self-identify or acknowledge their identity by their sexual behavior may have to be approached in completely different settings.

Although government resources are limited, multifaceted, multipronged black prevention research can prove cost effective if it leads to practical prevention methods that will reduce HIV infection rates, reduce the strain on our public health system, and reduce the costs to our government and our economy.

Eighth, we need to develop creative treatment and discipline options instead of incarceration for nonviolent drug users. According to the U.S. Bureau of Prisons, 54 percent of inmates in federal prisons in 2004 were being held for drug offenses. Back in 1980, before the Reagan Administration initiated the war on drugs, only 25 percent of federal inmates were incarcerated for drug-related crimes. Most of these inmates will eventually return to our communities, and many will be left without employable skills that can keep them productively engaged, away from drugs and out of trouble. Incarcerating nonviolent young people for drug offenses provides a quick fix to the drug problem, but it misses an opportunity to reach those youth and make a significant positive impact in their lives. Creative solutions that provide job training, child care, education, and basic discipline can help those in need and help the communities at the same time.

Ninth, we need realistic safe-sex education in public schools. An abstinence-only approach to secondary-level sex education is optimistic, but not realistic. Abstinence is an admirable objective that we should strongly encourage among youth, but we should not let our political and moral boundaries blind us to the reality that teenagers do have sex. Most young people begin having sex in their mid-to-late teens, according to the Alan Guttmacher Institute, and more than half of seventeen-year-olds have had sexual intercourse.

Tenth, we need health care coverage for the 45 million Americans who are uninsured. More than 19 percent of blacks had no health insurance in 2003, and a 1996 study found that blacks with HIV/AIDS were more likely to be publicly insured or uninsured than their white counterparts. According to the study, 59 percent of blacks with HIV/AIDS relied on Medicaid (medical support for the indigent) compared to 32 percent among whites. Only 14 percent of blacks with HIV/AIDS were privately insured, compared to 44 percent of whites. Given those statistics, it is no wonder that blacks with HIV/AIDS were less likely to receive adequate treatment and more likely to die.

Of all the public policy action items listed here, the only subject the vice-presidential candidates discussed was the issue of health care coverage. But the candidates need to know about all these issues, and we need to put these items on their agenda and demand action. As long as we allow the media to divert our attention from the serious issues to the sensationalized ones, we give the politicians an excuse to neglect our public policy agenda and ignore our concerns.

Much needs to be done, and we need holistic approaches that address the complex issues of race, gender, class, and culture. Rather than approach the litany of work as a cause for confusion, we should consider it an opportunity for discovery, where careful investment of resources can reap enormous dividends for the populations that have previously appeared to be most immune to intervention efforts. In virtually every area, from the prison system to the health care system, we need to do more. We need more clinical, epidemiological, and behavioral research. We need to support successful prevention efforts and reexamine failing strategies. And we need to direct our resources where they can provide the most benefit.

Since the beginning of the epidemic in the early 1980s, we have taken many positive steps forward to reduce the spread of AIDS. Now, it is time to take bold new action. We cannot micromanage the disease into nonexistence. More Americans have died from AIDS than from barrle during all the wars of the twentieth century combined, and so we must respond to the epidemic with the same level of seriousness we give to terrorism, war, and the other important issues facing our country. There is much we can do in our personal lives to prevent the spread of HIV, but our government must provide strong and visionary leadership. Many of us are waiting for our country to take these issues seriously. Like Fannie Lou Hamer, we are sick and tired of being sick and tired, but we soldier on another day.

CHAPTER 15
Love and Fear

IN THE FALL of 1995, I received a very disturbing phone call from an angry colleague. I had just become executive director of the National Black Lesbian and Gay Leadership Forum, and this colleague had heard that the Forum was planning to apply for a federal HIV/AIDS contract. He called to express his concern.

"I want you to know that if you move forward with this," he said, "I will do everything in my power to prevent you from being funded."

I was stunned that a black man leading a major AIDS organization could be so threatened by another black organization that wanted to help fight AIDS. He feared that the Forum would ultimately compete with his organization for the limited federal AIDS dollars targeted at the black community. "What would you do if you were in my shoes?" he asked. I gave him an answer that he did not believe. "I would be relieved to have an ally because I know that no one organization can do it all," I replied.

My colleague was not impressed, and he refused to back down from his threat. Although my competitive instincts told me to fight back, after discussing the issue with some of my associates in the Leadership Forum, I decided to back off rather than fight. We never applied for the grant, and a few years later, his organization and mine both closed down.

In some ways, I guess we were both victims of the politics of fear. Fear paralyzes our productivity by turning our constructive energy into panic and defensiveness. With fear, rather than see the opportunities for growth and learning, we focus attention on the obstacles that could lead to failure. The battle for limited government AIDS dollars is based on fear and scarcity. We do have the resources to fight AIDS in America, but first we have to change our way of thinking.

A number of writers have published books and articles about the personal choice between fear and love. They suggest that fear is a negative emotion and love is a positive emotion. "The spiritual journey is the relinquishment—or unlearning—of fear and the acceptance of love back into our hearts," writes Marianne Williamson. I believe that fear teaches us to think in terms of scarcity, while love encourages us to think in terms of abundance. With scarcity, we imagine the world has limited resources and, therefore, we must be constantly engaged in battle with one another to acquire and protect our own. With abundance, however, we see the world with plentiful resources at our disposal to be used and managed responsibly.

With trillions of dollars in debt, if our government can find the resources to fight a war on terror and a war on drugs, we ought to be able to find the resources to fight and win the war on AIDS. We can find the resources if we work together. We have to stop falling into the trap of pitting organization against organization, men against women, gays against straights, and bisexuals against everybody else. We have to stop blaming one another for the crisis and start focusing on the answers. We have to stop obsessing about the down low and start focusing on the larger issues that contribute to the down low.

After years of watching African Americans fight among ourselves for a small portion of the federal pie, I am encouraged when I see community leaders moving proactively to set the agenda and engage with the government we elect to represent us. I am encouraged when I see organizations working together instead of against one another. And I am encouraged when I see positive solutions that offer constructive ideas instead of sensationalized stereotypes.

The fundamental choice we face comes down to one simple question: Will we live in love or fear? Every challenge, every obstacle, every difficulty comes down to this choice. And the answer is love.

But fear is not easily conquered. I know women who live in fear of men on the down low and men on the down low who live in fear that they will be discovered. Some gay and bisexual men fear that they will be vilified by the down low, while some straight men fear that they will be unfairly blamed by the actions of men on the down low. Too many of us are operating out of fear, and we cannot build healthy relationships with one another, or with ourselves, in a climate of fear.

As with most things in life, overcoming fear is easier said than done. Perhaps that explains why Audre Lorde, the poet and author, teaches us to use fear to our advantage. Lorde explains: "When I dare to be powerful—to use my strength in the service of my vision—then it becomes less and less important whether I am afraid."

What I like about her statement is that she never says she is not afraid. She simply refuses to allow her fear to paralyze her. Some of our Hollywood action heroes seem to define courage as the absence of fear. They walk into a scene with a swagger and a joke, but we see little of their inner emotional turmoil. I define courage differently.

To me, courage is not the absence of fear, but the willingness to act in spite of fear.

Every time we act in defiance of our fears, we diminish the power they have over us. When we allow fear to disable us, we cannot overcome it. But every time we overcome our fear, we implicitly give permission for others to do the same. When ordinary people do extraordinary things, it inspires other ordinary people to believe that they can do it too. I have seen this happen many times in my own life.

When my partner Nathan and I agreed to take part in a reality television series on Showtime in the summer of 2004, we were both a little concerned about putting our lives and our relationship on display to the public. We weighed the advantages and disadvantages, and ultimately we decided to participate in spite of the fear. In the end, we were glad we did, and we received hundreds of e-mails, letters, and phone calls of support. Many of those who contacted us had never seen two black men involved in a relationship. Without even knowing it, we were able to make a positive impact on the lives of those we had never met.

The same is true for Karamo, a young black gay man who appeared on the MTV series *The Real World* in the fall of 2004. I spoke to Karamo a few weeks after the series began, and he seemed excited about the show, but I doubt he had any idea what an impact his presence would have in the black community and beyond. After fourteen seasons of the longest running reality show in America, he would become the first openly gay African-American cast member on the show. A few weeks into the series, when he met and dated another young man named Dorian, America got a chance to see two young black men holding hands and kissing each other on national television. With his do rag and hip hop clothing, Karamo helped to challenge the monolithic image of black homosexuality, while his friend Dorian—a muscle-bound trainer at a Philadelphia gym—also helped to shatter the stereotypes.

The media images did not end there. There were more images of black gay and bisexual men on television and film in 2004 than in any other time I can remember in my life. ABC's 2004 reality series, *The Benefactor,* featured a black gay man named Kevin, and Bravo's 2004 series *Manhunt: the Search for America's Most Gorgeous Male Model,* included a black gay man named Ron. On scripted television, the HBO series *The Wire* and *Six Feet Under* both featured black gay characters. Meanwhile, four new feature-length films about black gay and bisexual men—*Noah's Arc, The Ski Trip, Brother to Brother,* and *The Closet*—were released in the summer of 2004.

The notion that black men choose to be on the down low because they do not see healthy images of themselves in the media is slowly starting to change. New images are being developed and created in the media, and more and more real-life black men and women are talking about issues of sexuality in their own lives with their family, friends, and partners. They are acting out of love instead of fear.

There is a story in the Bible that illustrates the choice between fear and love. In Matthew 22:37, Jesus is approached by the Pharisees, who ask him which is the greatest commandment in the law. Jesus responds, "Thou shalt love the lord thy God with all thy heart, and with all thy soul, and with all thy mind. This is the first and great commandment. And the second is like unto it, Thou shalt love thy neighbor as thyself. On these two commandments hang all the laws and the prophets."

I love that passage for its simplicity and its instructional value. It seems to me, the principle of love applies to all of us, regardless of our faith. Jesus tells us in that story that we cannot love our neighbors if we do not love ourselves first. Many of us are upset about our failed relationships, broken marriages, and poisoned friendships. We are quick to hold others responsible for making our lives miserable, but we also need to take responsibility for making our own lives better. As long as we focus our energy primarily on what someone else has done to us, we limit the energy we have left to do for ourselves. If we turn our attention outside, we lose sight of all that we can do inside. Most important, we have to love ourselves before we can love anyone else. We have to love ourselves enough to forgive ourselves for our mistakes and to learn from them. We have to love ourselves enough to overcome our fears. We have to love ourselves enough to be honest about who we are and to protect ourselves from harm.

As Marianne Williamson has written, "Our deepest fear is not that we are inadequate. Our deepest fear is that we are powerful beyond measure. It is our light, not our darkness, that most frightens us. . . . And as we let our own light shine, we unconsciously give other people permission to do the same. As we're liberated from our own fear, our presence automatically liberates others."

I discovered early in life not to live in fear. When I was wrongly fired from my job at Sears as a teenager, I learned that fear can stop us from taking action. Fear can discourage us from telling the truth. And fear can prevent us from standing up for what we believe.

I believe that facts are important in the world. Perception is not reality. And despite all that has happened, I still hold fast to the belief that truth will prevail eventually. I remain convinced that no lie, no matter how widely repeated, can stand forever. Maybe I am naïve, but deep in my heart I still believe the truth will always emerge.

Acknowledgments

It took six years from the publication of my last book to find the time, courage, and energy to write this book. Over the years, I have written several book proposals and partial manuscripts that I never finished, and I would never have finished this book if it were not for the love, encouragement, and support of my partner, Nathan Williams. More than just a partner and a lover, he has also been my lawyer, campaign manager, motivator, stylist, makeup artist, travel agent, travel companion, soulmate, and best friend. Thank you, Nathan, for believing in me.

I also need to thank my family, and especially my mom, Shirley Parker, for encouraging me to be myself, and supporting me along the way. I also want to thank Bill, Krystal, Doris, Delores, Michael, Rochelle, Cheryl, Jardin, and Cameron.

I get a lot of e-mails from people who want to know how to get published. Part of it is luck, part of it is talent, and part of it is hard work. I have been very lucky to have three wonderful advisers in my corner. First, I can't say enough about my agent, Mondella Jones, who immediately "got it" with this book. Thanks, Mondella, for saving me. Next, I have to thank my editor, Don Weise, who has been extremely patient, supportive and easy to work with. Every author should have an editor as helpful as Don. Finally I must thank E. Lynn Harris, who got me started as a writer years ago when I was still working in politics.

Someone once told me, when you find good friends, you should hold on to them. I have many wonderful friends who have supported me over the years, but some of them went far above and beyond the call of friendship for this book. Maurice Franklin of Bristol-Myers Squibb was there from the beginning to help me remember the events of the past and discuss solutions for the future. Phill Wilson of the Black AIDS Institute answered dozens of my spontaneous phone calls when I just wanted to find one little piece of information that I knew he would have. Justin Smith of Rutgers University was an invaluable research assistant. And John Peterson at Georgia State University kept me on the phone for hours talking about AIDS research in the black community. I also want to thank Frank Roberts and Brian Keith Jackson for inspiring me. Then there were friends like Mike Ramsey and Gordon Chambers, who helped me locate the music I used in the chapter on pop culture.

Much of the information I used in the book I owe to the professionals who provided it to me. Thanks to Greg Millett and Karlie Stanton at the Centers for Disease Control, David Malebranche at Emory University and Lisa Bowleg at the University of Rhode Island. I also thank the wonderful reporters who have set the standard in their coverage of the down low—Linda Villarosa at *Essence* magazine, freelance journalist Kai Wright and Duncan Osborne of *Gay City News*. I also thank the readers of my Web site, keith-boykin.com, who provided great ideas and resources when I announced I was writing this book.

Finally, no writer can launch a book without the help of great bookstores. Independent bookstores and big chains have both supported me, and I particularly want to thank a few. In New York: Hue-Man Books in Harlem and Barnes & Noble in Chelsea. In Washington, D.C.: Lambda Rising, SisterSpace, Vertigo, and Books-A-Million. In Atlanta: Outwrite Books and Shrine of the Black Madonna. In my hometown, St. Louis: Left Bank Books and Afrocentric Expressions. In Los Angeles: Eso Wan and Different Light. And I can't forget Giovanni's Room in Philadelphia, Afrocentric Books in Chicago, Crossroads in Texas, Marcus Books in Oakland, California, and Open Book in Columbus, Ohio. Thank you all for spreading the word.

Index

Y
Yahoo, 142
Yancey, Ellen, 181
"You Make Me Feel (Mighty Real),"
    58
Young, Neil, 70

Z
Zimbabwe, 255-56